Protestant Social Teaching

Protestant Social Teaching

AN INTRODUCTION

EDITED BY
Onsi Aaron Kamel, Jake Meador,
and Joseph Minich

Copyright © 2022 The Davenant Press

All rights reserved.

ISBN: 1-949716-13-9

ISBN-13: 978-1-949716-13-9

Cover image is "Abstract dark blue watercolor gradient paint grunge texture backround," contributed to Shutterstock by Korkeng.

Cover design by Rachel Rosales, Orange Peal Design

Typeset and proofread by Mikael Good

LIST OF CONTRIBUTORS

E. J. Hutchinson is Associate Professor of Classics at Hillsdale College, where he also directs the Collegiate Scholars Program. His research focuses on the intersection of Christianity and classical civilization in late antiquity and early modernity. He is the editor and translator of Niels Hemmingsen, *On the Law of Nature: A Demonstrative Method* (CLP Academic, 2018).

Bradford Littlejohn is President of the Davenant Institute and Fellow in Evangelicals in Civic Life at the Ethics and Public Policy Center. His research interests include Christian ethics, church history, and political theology. He is the author of *The Two Kingdoms: A Guide for the Perplexed* (Davenant Press, 2017), *The Peril and Promise of Christian Liberty: Richard Hooker, the Puritans, and Protestant Political Theology* (Eerdmans, 2017), and *Richard Hooker: A Companion to His Life and Work* (Cascade Books, 2015).

Glenn A. Moots is Professor of Political Science and Philosophy at Northwood University and also serves as a Research Fellow at the McNair Center for the Advancement of Free Enterprise and Entrepreneurship there. He is the author of *Politics Reformed: The Anglo-American Legacy of Covenant Theology* (University of Missouri Press, 2010, 2022 paperback), and he coedited, with Phillip Hamilton, *Justifying Revolution: Law, Virtue, and Violence in the American Revolution* (University of Oklahoma Press, 2018).

Marc LiVecche is the McDonald Foundation Distinguished Scholar in Ethics, War, and Public Life at *Providence: A Journal of Christianity & American Policy*. He also serves as a non-resident research fellow at the U.S. Naval War College. He is the author of *The Good Kill: Just War & Moral Injury* (Oxford University Press, 2021).

Matthew Lee Anderson is an Assistant Research Professor of Ethics and Theology at Baylor University's Institute for Studies of Religion and the Associate Director of Baylor in Washington. He is an Associate Fellow at the McDonald Centre for Theology, Ethics, and Public Life at Oxford University, where he completed a D.Phil in Christian Ethics. He is the author of two books: *Earthen Vessels: Why Our Bodies Matter to Our Faith* (Bethany

House Publishers, 2011) and *The End of Our Exploring* (Moody Publishers, 2013).

Steven Wedgeworth is the rector of Christ Church Anglican in South Bend, Indiana. He has written for Desiring God Ministries, the Gospel Coalition, the Council for Biblical Manhood and Womanhood, and *Mere Orthodoxy*, and served as a founding board member of the Davenant Institute.

Onsi Aaron Kamel is a Ph.D student in religion at Princeton University and Editor-at-Large at *Ad Fontes*. His academic writing has appeared in *The Scottish Journal of Theology*, and his popular writing has appeared in *First Things*, *Mere Orthodoxy*, *Breaking Ground*, and elsewhere. His research interests lie chiefly in systematic theology, historical theology, and philosophy. He lives in Princeton with his wife and two children.

Alastair Roberts works for both the Theopolis Institute and the Davenant Institute. He participates in the *Mere Fidelity* and *Theopolis* podcasts, blogs at *Alastair's Adversaria*, and tweets at @zugzwanged. He is the co-author of *Echoes of Exdous* (Crossway, 2018) with Andrew Wilson.

John Wyatt is Emeritus Professor of Neonatal Paediatrics, Ethics & Perinatology at University College London and a senior researcher at the Faraday Institute for Science and Religion, Cambridge. He is the author of numerous books including *Matters of Life and Death: Human Dilemmas in Light of the Christian Faith* (IVP, 2009), *Right to Die? Euthanasia, Assisted Suicide and End of Life Care* (IVP, 2015), and *Dying Well* (IVP, 2018).

Joseph Minich is an Instructor of Philosophy at Mountain View College. He is the author of *Enduring Divine Absence* (Davenant Press, 2018) and the editor of several books with the Davenant Press. He lives in Garland, Texas, with his wife and four children.

Colin Chan Redemer is Vice-President of the Davenant Institute, Poetry Editor of *Ad Fontes*, Fellow of the Henning Institute on Catholic Social Thought, and Adjunct Associate Professor at St. Mary's College of California where he co-founded the campus chapter of the SEIU Local 1021 and continues to serve as the Chief Steward. He is currently pursuing a Ph.D. at the University of Aberdeen, exploring the philosophy of friendship.

Eric G. Enlow is Vice-President of Handong Global University and Dean and Professor at Handong International Law School. His publications include *The Christian Theology of Law: An Introduction* (Journal of Christian Legal Thought, 2018) and *Mosaic Commands for Legal Theology* (Cambridge Journal of Law and Religion, 2017). He is an active member of the Missouri Bar.

Allen Calhoun is a McDonald Distinguished Fellow at the Center for the Study of Law and Religion at Emory University. After twenty years working as an attorney and a writer and editor in the legal profession, he is currently researching and writing at the intersection of law and theology. His book *Tax Law, Religion and Justice: An Exploration of Theological Reflections on Taxation* was published in 2021 by Routledge.

Jake Meador is the author of *What Are Christians For? Life Together at the End of the World* (InterVarsity Press, 2022) and *In Search of the Common Good: Christian Fidelity in a Fractured World* (InterVarsity Press, 2019). He is the Editor-in-Chief of *Mere Orthodoxy*. His writing has been featured in *First Things*, *Commonweal*, and *National Review* amongst others.

CONTENTS

	Acknowledgments	i
	Introduction *Steven Wedgeworth*	iii

PART ONE: LAW, JUSTICE, AND PUNISHMENT

I	Law and the Christian *E. J. Hutchinson*	1
II	The Civil Magistrate *Bradford Littlejohn*	23
III	Resistance and Rebellion *Glenn Moots*	45
IV	Just War *Marc LiVecche*	63

PART TWO: MARRIAGE, LIFE, AND DEATH

V	Procreation and Children *Matthew Lee Anderson*	91
VI	Sex, Marriage, and Divorce *Onsi Aaron Kamel & Alastair Roberts*	103
VII	Abortion *Steven Wedgeworth*	115
VIII	Death and Dying *John Wyatt*	143

PART THREE: PROPERTY, WEALTH, AND POVERTY

IX	Work and Labor *Joseph Minich & Colin Redemer*	165
X	Private Property *Eric G. Enlow*	187
XI	Taxation and Welfare *Allen Calhoun*	213
XII	Environmental Care *Jake Meador*	237

Acknowledgments

This book first incubated in the mind of Steven Wedgeworth, who saw a need for Protestant intellectuals to address the complicated moral questions of our time from within the distinctive emphases of the their tradition - not for the sake of rigidifying tribes, but rather because the cultural and civilizational heritage of the Reformer remains especially pertinent to all humans in the twenty-first century. But such an idea could not come to fruition without the generous offers of each of this volume's authors, who pooled together their many talents for the sake of this project. Along the path to completion, many editorial hands have been involved. Thanks are especially due to Jake Meador, Mark Hamilton, and Rhys Laverty, who spent enormous efforts bringing the project along. Onsi Kamel and Joseph Minich likewise offered some aid at crucial junctures. Rachel Rosales (once again) lent her tireless efforts to the cover design. The notion of a Protestant Social Teaching has been at the heart of the Davenant project since its inception, and what the reader has in front of them is the harvest of many years of conversation and intellectual cross-pollination. It is our hope that this is only the beginning of a rich process of recovery.

Joseph Minich, Editor-at-Large
October 2022

Introduction

STEVEN WEDGEWORTH

"PROTESTANT Social Teaching," the title of this collection, is guaranteed to invite debate. Is there such a thing? Which voices and positions should be included? Who has the right to decide? These sorts of questions are endemic to Protestantism in the modern world. And while Protestantism will always have an inherent diversity, as its shape is more of a constellation of schools than a singular institution, it once had a remarkable unity on matters of moral theology.

Additionally, many readers will see in the name "Protestant Social Teaching" a sort of imitation of "Catholic Social Teaching."[1] Rhetorically this is true—the title was chosen with that parallel in mind. Catholic Social Teaching has proven to be an incredibly powerful mechanism for offering moral guidance to Roman Catholics and for providing an alternative to the more common offerings in magazines, talk radio, or cable news channels. Importantly, Catholic Social Teaching claims to offer a unified and coherent body of moral discipleship that integrates doctrine and practice. Many Protestants lament their lack of such a unified body of teaching. Indeed, in 2009, Stephen J. Grabill asserted, "Neither magisterial Protestants nor

---

[1] For a scholarly overview of Catholic Social Teaching, see David J. O'Brien and Thomas Anthony Shannon's "Introduction: Roman Catholic Social Teaching" in their *Catholic Social Thought: Encyclicals and Documents from Pope Leo III to Pope Francis*, 3rd ed. (Maryknoll, NY: Orbis Books, 2016), 1–6; for an attempt at a full systematic presentation of Roman Catholic social teaching, see Pontifical Council for Justice and Peace, *Compendium of the Social Doctrine of the Church* (Washington, DC: USCCB Publishing, 2006).

evangelicals have a theologically unified body of social teaching."[2] He then encouraged them to build such a body of thought, though he confessed that it would not be an easy task.

This book is an answer to Professor Grabill's challenge. We do not, however, accept his premise. Indeed, we hope to offer a unified body of social teaching not by way of creation but recovery. The sixteenth through nineteenth centuries featured a coherent collection of moral and social teachings grounded in basic Protestant doctrinal understandings of God, revelation, law, and humanity. This is now largely forgotten. But it is not truly lost. The sources are still there, in so many catechisms, bodies of divinity, systematic theologies, and practical works. New publishing ventures and the continuing improvement of e-books has made the recovery of such works more accessible than ever before. It has been the central mission of the Davenant Institute to bring the fruits of this recovery to the broader public.

The relevant sources are quite literally immense. Richard Baxter's massive *A Christian Directory* is subtitled *A Sum of Practical Theology, and Cases of Conscience*, and it covers both questions of personal piety and matters of social and political concern. All major Protestant catechisms and doctrinal manuals included commentaries on the Ten Commandments with particular applications. The Westminster Larger Catechism is perhaps the most detailed of the major confessional documents, but it was not unique in its approach or philosophy. It was simply one of the later productions. Zacharias Ursinus's *Commentary on the Heidelberg Catechism* contains a detailed explication of the moral law contained in the Decalogue, with forays into the death penalty, warfare, property rights, and more.[3] William Ames's *The Marrow of Theology* devotes half of its space to "observance," which it defines as "the submissive performance of the will of God for the glory of God."[4] Among these latter chapters, Ames discusses distinctions among loves, duties, and justice. Works of this sort were entirely common in the sixteenth and seventeenth centuries. Martin Luther and John Calvin certainly have their catechetical discussions

---

[2] Stephen J. Grabill, "Protestant Social Thought," *Journal of Markets and Morality* 12, no. 1 (Spring 2009): 1.

[3] Zacharias Ursinus, *The Commentary of Dr. Zacharias Ursinus on the Heidelberg Catechism*, trans. G. W. Williard, 2nd ed. (Phillipsburg, NJ: Presbyterian and Reformed Publishing Co., 1852 reprint), 586–87, 596.

[4] William Ames, *The Marrow of Theology*, trans. J. D. Eusden (Grand Rapids, MI: Baker, 1997), 219.

of the law of God, but both also offer fascinating moral discussions in their biblical commentaries. Less obvious sources also provide important moral casuistry. Martin Chemnitz's four volume *Examination of the Council of Trent* begins with basic doctrinal polemics, but moves into a discussion of sexual ethics, particularly virginity, chastity, marriage, and divorce.[5]

As one continues into the eighteenth and nineteenth centuries, in the United Kingdom and its colonies, Protestant moral and political thought influenced the development of the common law. William Blackstone's *Commentaries of the Laws of England* is typically thought of as a sort of "secular work," and not the sort of thing that one would immediately connect with ecclesiastical writers. But the Protestant imagination of the time did not divide up the intellectual world in such neatly opposed categories. When read in conversation with thinkers like Samuel von Pufendorf, John Selden, or Niels Hemmingsen, the basic family resemblance becomes apparent.

This should also help to explain what we mean by "Protestant." It is true that the word means relatively little in the twenty-first century. It is mostly a negation—not Roman Catholic. But this was not its intended meaning. Originating with the "protest" at the Diet of Speyer in 1529, the name Protestant initially applied to Lutherans. Fairly quickly the churches and theologians now known as "Reformed" were also included in this broader grouping. Indeed, Strasbourg was one of the original cities involved in the protestation, and so the term "Protestant" applied to both the Reformed and Lutheran churches.[6] It did not, however, extend to the Anabaptists, who viewed themselves as a refounding rather than reforming movement and who also had unique positions on anthropology and law. This use of "Protestant" for the Lutheran and Reformed churches can be found in the seventeenth century itself.[7] While Lutherans and the Reformed did not see themselves as a united church, and while they had certain important disagreements, they largely did agree on prolegomena (which is to say the role of reason and revelation), the doctrine of God, anthropology, the natural law,

---

[5] Martin Chemnitz, *Examination of the Council of Trent Parts II & III*, trans. F. Kramer (St. Louis, MO: Concordia Publishing House, 2007) Part II, 717–66; Part III, 15–226.

[6] See Diarmaid MacCulloch, *The Reformation: A History* (New York, NY: Penguin Books, 2003), xx, 171–79.

[7] For instance, William Chillingworth, *The Religion of Protestants, A Safe Way to Salvation* (London: Lichfield, 1638).

INTRODUCTION

and most matters of politics. Where disagreements did arise, they could also be found within each community rather than merely as Lutherans against the Reformed or vice-versa.

So, the "Protestant Social Teaching" of this book is a common understanding of the moral law, a shared exegesis of relevant biblical texts, and the continued reception of earlier Christian writers on the part of both Lutheran and Reformed theologians and statesmen. The foundations of this teaching are found in the Reformation era, namely the sixteenth and seventeenth centuries, but its legacy continued on into the nineteenth centuries among select writers and thinkers. Among the most select, it continued even into the twentieth.

This framework also explains the scope of our sources. We have prioritized what is common to the Protestant Reformation. This usually means what is most basic among the thought of its writers and churches. While many of the chapters in this volume do extend their discussion into the twentieth and twenty-first centuries, they do not interact with movements which began in those centuries. Writers who are uniquely bound to contemporary issues are avoided entirely. Political debates limited to the United States or time-bound cultural disputes are deprioritized in favor of more principial and abiding matters. In this sense, our Protestantism is resolutely catholic. We are attempting to uncover and pass along perennial and ecumenical Protestant truths. Later topics and more specific ones, including controversial and divisive ones, are entirely appropriate items for discussion and investigation, but they must wait for future installments. The present study is introductory. But if we succeed in our task, many of the categories needed for such future essays will be uncovered by our work here.

This approach also shows how our understanding of Protestant Social Teaching differs from Catholic Social Teaching. The content will be strikingly similar. It is the form which differs. There is no central institution, no magisterium, which intervenes to resolve moral and social teaching for Protestants. Our churches do not say, as Rome does, that they are "the authentic guardians and interpreters of the whole moral law."[8] Rather, Protestant Social Teaching exists more like a common law, an ongoing but

---

[8] Paul VI, *Humanae Vitae: Encyclical Letter of His Holiness Pope Paul VI, On the Regulation of Births* I.4, Vatican Website 1968, accessed August 31, 2022 https://www.vatican.va/content/paul-vi/en/encyclicals/documents/hf_p-vi_enc_25071968_humanae-vitae.html.

nevertheless ascertainable collection of consensual exegesis of the Scriptures and moral philosophy, a philosophy built upon Protestant principles.

One of these principles is that of the natural law and original righteousness.[9] A basic moral guidance can be discerned in virtue of humanity's rational nature. Sin causes men to repress this morality or misuse it, but it is never fully lost to the human consciousness. The work of Christ, too, is a restoration of the original righteousness possessed by mankind due to his having been created in the image of God. Protestant Social Teaching, then, does not point man beyond a rational morality towards a new and heretofore unknown frontier. Rather it redirects him back to his own rational morality. The Reformers taught that the human conscience can and eventually will grasp God's truth. Or perhaps it would be better to say that the human conscience, as it is renewed, will *be grasped* by God's truth. As a human being grows in a truer and better knowledge of God, he grows in the knowledge of himself, and as he grows in a truer and better knowledge of himself, he grows in the knowledge of God. Thus, rather than retreating to a final ecclesiastical interpreter, Protestants equip men to progress in understanding.

No claim can be made to a "seamless garment," in Protestant Teaching, at least not if that means that there is never moral disagreement between pious and serious Christian thinkers. Indeed, as Aquinas would remind us, "the more we descend to matters of detail, the more frequently we encounter defects."[10] Where a matter is closer to the basic principle, greater clarity and agreement should be expected. As a moral question becomes more specific and dependent upon circumstance, greater diversity of judgment should be expected and greater liberty allowed. And so we do not look to a final ecclesiastical interpreter who intervenes to put a stop to difficult questions. The boundaries of Protestant Social Teaching are not so much institutional as they are categorical. The authority derives from recognizing the truth of the moral argument itself.

It is because of this framework that it should go without saying that the various contributors to this volume do not pretend total agreement with one another. Indeed, some authors register their own disagreement with certain

---

[9] See the discussion of mankind's original righteousness and its implication on ethics in Herman Bavinck, *Reformed Dogmatics, Vol. 2: God and Creation*, trans. J. Vriend (Grand Rapids, MI: Baker Academic, 2004), 544–46.

[10] Thomas Aquinas, *Summa Theologica* I–II, q. 94, a. 4, co.

INTRODUCTION

aspects of the Protestant tradition they are explaining! Certain chapters are predominately historical and descriptive. Others are more constructive. Some are critical. It is our hope that this approach will allow the actual truths of the tradition to speak louder than any individual voice, and that it will invite the reader into this critical engagement, so he can see which arguments truly persuade. Even so, we believe a basic and compelling unity is there to be seen.

In fact, readers will notice that the majority of our essays do not begin with the Protestant Reformation but rather the early church and even pre-Christian writers. In this, we are merely following in the example of our Reformation forefathers, for they too pointed beyond themselves to the older sources and ultimately to the truth and authority of God's Word. And so, at the end of all our studies, it is our goal to use the traditional interpretations and arguments to more clearly highlight the content of God's two books, the Holy Scriptures and the light of nature. As understood by its own articulators, Protestant Social Teaching is *merely Christian* Social Teaching. May our world discover it afresh.

PART ONE:

Law, Justice, and Punishment

I.

Law and the Christian

E.J. HUTCHINSON

THERE was a parable that Franz Kafka liked to tell, so much so that it appears in several different places in his works, most notably in *The Trial*. Titled "Before the Law," it is only about two pages long, and goes like this. A man comes from the country to "the Law" (*das Gesetz*), described as a sort of labyrinthine building. Outside the building is a doorkeeper, and the man asks him for permission to enter. The doorkeeper tells him that he cannot grant him permission now, so the man decides to wait. In fact, he waits there for the rest of his life. Shortly before he dies, old and frail, he "sees a radiance that streams forth inextinguishably from the door of the Law." He asks the doorkeeper why, given that "[e]veryone strives to reach the Law," no one else has come to ask to be let in. The doorkeeper replies, "No one else could obtain admission here, because this entrance was ordained only for you. I'm going now to shut it."[1] The precise meaning of this parable is mysterious and opaque, and it is debated among interpreters—even within *The Trial* itself. Still, at the very least the reader can draw from it the basic point that "the Law"—whatever it is precisely—is difficult to understand. This is certainly true in Kafka's stories and novels; but it is true of Scripture as well.

---

[1] Franz Kafka, *Der Prozess* (Berlin: Verlag Die Schmiede, 1925), 375–78. Unless otherwise noted, all translations are my own.

"The word 'law' is equivocal," says Martin Chemnitz (1522—1586).[2] We find it used in many different senses in Scripture, and it takes hard work to understand its precise denotations and connotations. For instance, Galatians 4:21 (ESV) uses "law" in two different senses *in the same verse*: "Tell me, you who desire to be under the law, do you not listen to the law?" Here, "law" first means a rigorous set of demands that must be met to achieve righteousness before God, and in the next breath it means the book of Genesis, as the following discussion of Abraham and his sons shows.

Consider further some of the many other ways in which the biblical authors use "law." In Romans 8:10, Paul says that "the law of the Spirit of life has set you free in Christ Jesus from the law of sin and death." Earlier in the same letter, he had already referred to "the law of faith" (Rom. 3:27). Is the gospel, then, a law? Some, like Thomas Aquinas, for example, have claimed that it is.[3] Sometimes "law" refers to the entirety of the Old Testament canon. Thus John writes in John 10:34 that Jesus said to the Jews, "Is it not written in your Law, 'I said, you are gods?'" where the quotation comes from Psalm 82:6. Perhaps, then, the Old Testament Patriarchs had no knowledge of the Gospel. Instead, God gave them promises concerning external things alone. So thought the Anabaptists. Or, consider when, in Matthew 11:13, Christ says that "the Law prophesied until John." Does this mean that the law has no positive function for the Christian? This the Antinomians and Libertines confessed.

Distinguo, "I distinguish," the medieval scholastic might interject—and so should we. Following Chemnitz, we can observe at least six different

---

[2] I will be plagiarizing Chemnitz's *locus* ("topic") "On the Law of God" (*De lege divina*) from his *Loci theologici* (*Theological Commonplaces*) liberally throughout this essay. Chemnitz (1522–86) was a Lutheran theologian and church leader, particularly in the Duchy of Brunswick-Wolfenbüttel.
For Chemnitz's *Loci*, I use the 1653 edition published in Frankfurt and Wittenberg: Martin Chemnitz, *Loci theologici* (Frankfurt and Wittenberg: Sumptibus Haeredum D. Tobiae Mevii et Elerdi Schumacheri, 1653), Tomus Secundus, 1–101. The quotation above is found on p. 2. An English translation of the majority of the work can be found in Martin Chemnitz, *Loci Theologici*, trans. J. A. O. Preus (St. Louis: Concordia Publishing House, 1989), 2 vols. See vol. 2 for Chemnitz's discussion of "The Divine Law." It should be noted that the *Loci* were originally lectures, and the published version is the product of Polycarp Leyser's editorial work on student notes. See William R. Russell's review of Preus's translation in *The Sixteenth Century Journal* 21, no. 4 (1990): 697–98.

[3] See Thomas Aquinas, *Summa Theologiae*, I–II, q. 106, arts 1–4.

semantic domains in which "law" is found in Scripture. Once we have set those out, we can zero in on a basic definition of the term as far as its moral, social, and spiritual functions are concerned.

First, "law" can mean a basic driving force. It is used in this way when Paul refers to the "law of sin and death" and "the law of the Spirit of life." These two oppose each other; the impulse to sin and the impulse to be obedient are contradictory motions in the same individual.

Second, "law" can refer to God's revealed teaching as a whole, and in this way can even include the gospel itself. One finds this in, for example, Isaiah 2:3: "[M]any peoples shall come, and say: 'Come, let us go up to the mountain of the LORD, to the house of the God of Jacob, that he may teach us his ways and that we may walk in his paths.' For out of Zion shall go the law, and the word of the LORD from Jerusalem."

Third, "law" can refer to the books in which that teaching is found. Sometimes that means the entire Old Testament (see, in addition to John 10:34, John 15:25, which quotes Psalm 35:19 or 69:4; or 1 Cor. 14:21, which quotes Isaiah 28:11–12: the Psalms and Isaiah are both referred to as "the Law"); sometimes it means the Pentateuch or books of Moses (see Luke 24:44); sometimes it means those books of Moses in which the laws of Israel are written (Exodus, Leviticus, Deuteronomy; see Luke 10:26).

Fourth, "law" can refer to the peculiar political and religious arrangements of the nation of Israel, or the shape of Israel's life before the coming of the Messiah. (This latter is preferable, because it allows for continuity within the changing form of Jewish life after the Exile.) This sense is in view when Jesus says that "all the Prophets and the Law prophesied until John" (Matt. 11:13). The last two divisions are best seen by opposition and are closely related to each other.

The fifth sense of "law" is as the antonym of the gospel or of faith. When used with this meaning, it refers to everything that God commands to be done, whether in the Old or the New Testament, whereas the gospel refers to what God has done for man.

In the sixth sense, "law" is opposed to grace. Here, "law" means the rigor of the law: its demand for pure, perfect, and perpetual obedience—or else. Both of these meanings are in view in Romans 10:4–5: "For Christ is the end of the law for righteousness to everyone who believes. For Moses writes about the righteousness that is based on the law, that the person who does the commandments shall live by them." He goes on to contrast "the righteousness that is based on the law" with "the righteousness based on faith." This distinction should not be confused with a rejection of the law. When Paul says (Rom. 6:14) that "you are not under law but under grace," he does not mean that disobedience to God becomes good, or at least indifferent, but that the Christian is free from the curse that results from disobedience.

Thus far the uses of "law" in Scripture. It is notable that some of these senses have immediate ongoing validity for Christians, while others are less directly relevant. It is also notable that we still do not have a sense of what "the law of God" in particular—my topic in this essay—*is*, both in itself and in relation to us. We therefore need to complement the above approach with a more direct definitional statement.

"LAW" AND THE LAW OF GOD

The modifier "of God" is important, because it reminds us of one of the major divisions of the law: divine and human; our concern is with the former. Therefore, out of the entire domain of law, our discussion picks out one type, the divine law. The reader might notice that I have already nudged the discussion in that direction, given that all six senses of "law" sketched above somehow relate to the law of God. But divine law or the law of God remains quite broad and can be further specified and distributed into three types via another standard distinction: God's law as one encounters it in Scripture is either moral, ceremonial, or judicial. The ceremonial law, which related to the worship of Old Testament Israel, and the judicial law, which related to the polity of Old Testament Israel, expired with the coming of the Messiah: under the old order, God gave detailed instructions about cultic, civic, and criminal matters to Israel as his covenanted nation, and that is a status that no longer obtains for any political entity. The moral law, on the other hand, which is summarized in the Ten Commandments, is the revelation of God's eternal wisdom and nature, and displays God's will for man as such, and not simply for one particular community of men, thereby establishing its permanent validity.

The ceremonial and judicial laws are, it should be noted, encountered *only* in Scripture, whereas the moral law is encountered both within and without the Bible. That distinction reminds us in turn of another important division, that between written and unwritten law. The former corresponds to revealed law, while the latter corresponds to natural law.[4] These are mediated to us in different ways, but, because their content is identical (see Rom. 2:1–16) they frequently can be treated interchangeably. Because the focus of the present discussion is on the law in theological perspective, I will mostly refer to the "moral law" as a shorthand for what God has revealed to us about ethical norms. Or, less elliptically: what we wish to define is divine moral law in its written form, and what we want to investigate is how that divine moral law relates to our lives before God and one another.

But I am, I fear, getting ahead of myself. Before we can think well about the law of God "in itself and in relation to us," as it was phrased above, we must have an idea in mind about law "in itself" *in general*. First, then, let us zoom out for a moment and think about "law" more broadly. At its most basic, "law" is *a directive rule telling us what we ought to pursue and what we ought to avoid*. Philosophers have given us various definitions of this law, and Johann Gerhard (1582—1637), the great Lutheran scholastic theologian, collects many of them in his *locus* "On the Law of God" in the *Loci theologici* (*Theological Commonplaces*).[5] Here are a few:

> Plato: "Law is right reason in governing, which is directed toward the best end through advantageous means, offering punishments to transgressors and rewards to the obedient."
>
> Aristotle: "Law is mind without appetite."
>
> Cicero: "Law is the highest reason implanted in nature, which commands those things that must be done and prohibits their opposites. This same reason, when it is strengthened and completed in the mind of man, is law."
>
> Cicero, again: "Law is reason in commanding and forbidding. It is a force of nature, the mind and reason of a prudent man, the rule of justice and injustice, the distinction of just and unjust

---

[4] There is, of course, a sense in which natural law is "revealed" via the conscience and widespread human institutions such as marriage (cf., for convenience and clarity, the discussion in C. S. Lewis's *The Abolition of Man*), but I mean the term here in the sense of what is usually called "special revelation."

[5] Johann Gerhard, *Loci theologici* (Berlin: Sumptibus Gust. Schlawitz, 1865), Tomus Tertius, 1–108. The ceremonial and judicial laws are treated in the following *locus*. An English translation of Gerhard's treatises on law in the *Loci* can be found in Johann Gerhard, *On the Law (Theological Commonplaces XV–XVIII)*, trans. Richard Dinda (St. Louis: Concordia Publishing House), 2015.

things, which afflicts the wicked with punishment and defends and protects the good."

Demosthenes: "Law is the discovery and gift of the gods, the teaching of wise men, the correction of voluntary and involuntary faults, the common convention of a city, according to which everyone in the city ought to live."[6]

These definitions are good in and of themselves. They do not, however, go far enough for our topic. The next step, therefore, is to build upon them to reach our goal, which is a self-consciously *theological* definition of "law" that will serve careful Christian reflection. What we want, in other words, is a definition in keeping with the basic thrust of these traditional definitions, but one that better specifies how the moral law provides a rule for pursuing and avoiding that reflects the nature and wisdom of the God whose law it is.

THE LEVELS OF THE LAW

The need to build up a more detailed account of "law" for theological purposes, one that explicitly foregrounds a Christian account of both the nature of God (a "theological theology", to borrowm from John Webster) and the nature of man (a theological anthropology), becomes evident if we reflect on the demands of the law and how those are handled at three different levels: the moral or natural law considered as a basis for human positive law; philosophy; and the law of God.[7] Philip Melanchthon (1497—1560) has given perhaps the best account of the fine distinctions in play. "Human laws," he writes in his *locus* "On the Law of God" in the final phase of the *Loci communes (Commonplaces)*, "demand or forbid only external works."[8]

---

[6] Gerhard, *Loci*, 3.

[7] The following discussion may call to mind the familiar distinction between the "letter of the law" and the "spirit of the law." This is an appropriate analog, with the caveat that the "spirit of the law" will turn out to have levels and contours of its own, rather than simply being the binary opposite of the "letter."

[8] Philip Melanchthon, *Loci theologici: Tertia eorum aetas* [hereafter *Loci* (3)], in *Corpus Reformatorum* [hereafter *CR*], ed. H. E. Bindseil (Braunschweig: Apud C.A. Schwetschke et Filium, 1854), 21:685–732. The quotation is from 686. The publication of the first version of Melanchthon's *Loci* occurred in 1521. The work subsequently went through two more major phases; the publication of the final version commenced in 1543 and was variously titled the *Loci theologici*, *Loci communes theologici*, or *Loci praeipui theologici* (*Commonplaces*, *Theological Topics*, *Theological Commonplaces*, or *Chief Theological Topics*). An English translation of the whole work

If there is a human law that I may not steal my neighbor's snow shovel, the law only goes so far as to say that I may not physically walk into my neighbor's garage without permission, pick up the shovel, and take it home.

But "philosophy," Melanchthon continues, "teaches something more, namely, that an honorable action is not only an external or pretended work. Instead, philosophy says, right judgment must be added in the mind and free choice or *proairesis* in the will in order to act rightly."[9] Philosophy, in other words, acknowledges an internal component in obedience to the law: to continue the example above, it is not enough, in philosophical terms, that I do not walk into my neighbor's garage and steal his snow shovel. Hypothetically, I might have wanted to steal the shovel, but was prevented by having a broken leg, or perhaps I was being held hostage by insane Beatles fans who were enraged by my opinion of their 1966 self-titled release commonly known as the "White Album." I have fulfilled the letter of the law, but I have not acted ethically, because my avoidance of theft was due to accidental circumstances rather than to a choice to act correctly based upon accurate judgment. Indeed, it is this very internal moderation that constitutes an action *as ethical*, and human law does not take it into account in assessing rewards and punishments.

Still, philosophy does not address human action at the deepest level. It has nothing to say about the initial impulse to steal, or the vitiating effect that the corruption leading to such an impulse has on all our actions before an omniscient God who exhaustively knows all the recesses of the heart.

Not so the law of God, which touches not only our external actions, not only our internal restraint from wrongdoing in external actions, but our nature in its totality. Melanchthon puts it as follows: "The law of God requires not only external deeds or the diligence in restraining the affections that philosophy speaks about, but commands that our nature as a whole obey God, and that it have a firm knowledge of and burning love for God." For Melanchthon, this is what Paul means when he says that "the law is spiritual" (Rom. 7:14). It is more than "political wisdom," because it demands "spiritual motions," that is, it demands that all our external actions originate in the unfeigned love and fear commanded in the first table of the Decalogue. To

---

can be found in Philip Melanchthon, *The Chief Theological Topics (*Loci Praecipui Theologici *1559)*, trans. J. A. O. Preus (St. Louis: Concordia Publishing House, 2011).

[9] Melanchthon, *Loci* (3), *CR* 21, 686.

obey the law truly in this sense, I may not even have so much as the passing desire to steal my neighbor's snow shovel.[10]

When the levels of the law, as it were, are set out in this way, we can see a couple of very significant features. First, notice that there is a sense in which the objective content of the law is the same at all three levels: "Do not steal." But it is applied to us with greater and greater subjective force as we move from human or civil law to ethical philosophy, until, in the law of God, it reaches and arrests our very nature in its totality. On the one hand, "Do not steal" is always the law of God; but, on the other, we are not treating it *as* the law of God most fully until we encounter it at the third level.

FINALLY, AFTER ALL THAT, A DEFINITION

Such clarifications allow us to come, at long last, to a detailed definition of the law of God, a definition that goes beyond the philosophical definitions—necessary but inadequate for our purposes—to a self-consciously theological one. As Chemnitz notes, Melanchthon has provided at least two different but complementary definitions in various places. If we look at them both together while attending both to the differences and complementarities, we will arrive at a good and fairly comprehensive understanding of how we might think about the law of God.[11]

The first comes from Melanchthon's 1543 *Loci*, referred to above. There, Melanchthon says that "the law of God is a teaching handed on by God, commanding what sort of people we ought to be and the things that

---

[10] Compare Martin Luther's comment on Galatians 3:10: "Even the sophists themselves are compelled to admit, and thus they also teach, that a moral work done externally, if it is not done with a sincere heart, a good will, and the right prescription of the reason, is feigned." Martin Luther, *In epistolam S. Pauli ad Galatas Commentarius ex praelectione D. Martini Lutheri (1531) collectus 1535*, in *D. Martin Luthers Werke: Kritische Gesamtausgabe*, ed. A. Freitag (Weimar: Hermann Böhlaus Nachfolger, 1911, 1914), Band 40.1 (chapters 1–4) and 40.2 (chapters 5–6). All quotations in this essay come from 40.1; the quotation above is found on 402. Melanchthon's discussion here is harmonious with Luther's discussion shortly thereafter of what "doing" means in nature, philosophy, and theology in *Ad Galatas*, 410–11. An English translation of the entire commentary can be found in Martin Luther, *Lectures on Galatians: Chapters 1–4* and *Lectures on Galatians: Chapters 5–6*, in *Luther's Works: American Edition*, vols. 26–27, trans. Jaroslav Pelikan (St. Louis: Concordia Publishing House, 1962 [vol. 26] and 1964 [vol. 27]).

[11] Chemnitz (*Loci*, 4) quotes both, but omits a couple of clauses in the second. For that reason, I will cite both as they are found in Melanchthon's own writings.

we ought to do and not to do; it requires perfect obedience toward God, and pronounces that God is wrathful toward those who do not offer perfect obedience and punishes them with eternal death."[12] In the *Examen ordinandorum* (*Examination of Ordinands*, 1554), on the other hand, he writes:

> The moral law is the eternal and immoveable wisdom and the rule of righteousness in God, distinguishing between what is right and what is not right, and exercising horrible wrath against the stubborn (or, put slightly differently, denouncing horrendous wrath against stubbornness that resists this ordinance of God); it was revealed to men in creation, and afterwards it was often repeated and declared by the voice of God, so that we might know that God exists, as well as what sort of a God he is, binding all rational creatures and demanding that they all be conformed to God, and condemning and destroying all who are not conformed to God unless remission and reconciliation should be made on account of the Son as Mediator.[13]

The first significant difference between the two definitions concerns *what is being defined*. The first speaks generally of the "law of God," while the second refers to the "moral law." The second term is to be preferred. Why? Because, as noted above, the "law of God" in one sense includes the ceremonial and judicial laws of the Old Testament as well. And whereas the ceremonial and judicial laws were temporary and are not in force today, the moral law is "eternal and immoveable" and remains in force everywhere. That such a law is Melanchthon's object of inquiry is clear from the discussion that follows in the *Loci theologici*, which is concerned exclusively with two forms of the moral law, the Decalogue and the law of nature. Or, as Melanchthon writes in the *Examen*, "The summary of this [moral] law is comprehended in the Decalogue; for that reason, we often use the word 'Decalogue' in place of 'moral law,' so that we might show, as it were, its chief heads."[14]

Although Melanchthon does not refer to the "law of nature" (*lex naturae*) in the *Examen*, he does do so in the *Loci*, where he asserts:

---

[12] Melanchthon, *Loci* (3), *CR* 21, 685.

[13] Philip Melanchthon, *Examen ordinandorum Latine*, in *CR* 23, ed. H. E. Bindseil (Braunschweig: Apud C.A. Schwetschke et Filium, 1855), 1–102.

[14] Melanchthon, *Examen*, *CR* 23, 8.

> [The] true definition of the law of nature is that the law of nature is the knowledge of the divine law implanted in the nature of man. For the reason that it is said that man was created according to the image of God is because in him was shining forth the image—that is, the knowledge—of God and a certain likeness to the divine mind (that is, the distinction between honorable and shameful things), and he had powers congruent with this knowledge.[15]

He then proceeds to give an account of the natural principles found in the commandments of the Decalogue. Perhaps, then, we could combine Melanchthon's two terms to say that what he is defining is the "divine moral law." So, to repeat, in terms of content, moral and natural law are the same; the distinction between the two terms has to do in large part with mode of delivery.

Another important detail which the second definition includes is the *permanence* of this divine moral law. It is both eternal in the divine mind, where it is synonymous with the divine wisdom (rather than a product of an arbitrary divine will), and perpetual and universal in the human mind, to which it was revealed concurrently with the mind's creation. Man, that is, knew the moral law long before Sinai. It was given to him internally when the Spirit of God breathed upon him, and was subsequently repeated externally in the Decalogue, as well as by the prophets and apostles.

The second definition also contains an important point of natural theology that is only implicit in the first, namely, that we know by nature both "*that* God exists" and "*what sort of* a God he is." On the other hand, the first definition is clearer about the demands of the law. It does not simply enjoin what we should or should not do, but "*what sort of* people we ought to be." This phrase better specifies the way in which the law searches hearts and character and not simply actions, and explicitly states—as the second definition does not—that our conformity must be "perfect." If we are not (and Melanchthon expects us to know we are not), we are lost without a Mediator. Both of these emphases—knowledge of who God is and knowledge of ourselves as those who ought to be righteous and yet are sinners and consequently in need of God's mercy—are necessary for what

---

[15] Melanchthon, *Loci* (3), *CR* 21, 712.

we might call an accurate "knowledge-of-self-in-relation" so that we can contemplate and use the law aright.[16]

Man's status as sinner helps to answer a question Chemnitz imagines an unpersuaded interlocutor raising at this point: Melanchthon says that the law threatens death against the disobedient, but why doesn't he say anything about the law's promise of life for the obedient? The reason is that the definitions he gives are indexed not to an abstract ideal of human perfection, but to the kind of creature man is in his corrupted state. The law offers eternal rewards for perfect obedience, it is true; but that ideal is unattainable for fallen man. For one to hold out such a promise to him, therefore, would be somewhat beside the point—unless the point were to show that the law accuses and condemns all men, so that all have need of a Mediator. This is a topic to which we shall return.

Though the comparison just carried out may seem excessive, it is heuristically useful for setting us on the path of determining and enumerating the elements that a properly theological definition of the moral law ought to include. Following Chemnitz, we can say that there are seven.

1. It is *divine*. The moral law is a teaching given to us by God.
2. It is *comprehensive*. The moral law addresses not just our actions, but our entire nature—and it addresses that nature in its state of corruption.
3. Its demands are *total*. The moral law requires perfect, perpetual, and pure obedience.
4. Its demands are *impossible*. Man, in a state of corruption, cannot fulfill the moral law.
5. It is therefore *paradoxical*. The moral law offers life *in se*, and yet we should not seek life and blessing in it.
6. For us, then, it is *deadly*. That is why Paul calls the law a "ministry of death" and says that the law "works wrath." In the first instance, the law teaches the knowledge of sin, and the wages of sin is death.
7. It is, therefore, a *John the Baptist*. I could not find a term with the desired meaning ("to point away from oneself to someone or something else"), so I stole one, despite my example about the

---

[16] I admit that the phrase is cumbersome—as well as redundant, since accurate self-knowledge is always knowledge of self in relation to God. But I hope that it at least gestures toward the synthetic point I am attempting to make.

snow shovel above: so inveterate is man's corruption.[17] The moral law in all its rigor makes possible the teaching of grace and faith. It points, that is, to Christ the Forgiver and Christ the Mediator, who is "the end of the law for righteousness to everyone who believes" (Rom. 10:4).[18]

The introduction of grace adds a further complexity to what we can say about the law in its theological function, for, viewed from the vantage point of grace, that function is manifold rather than singular. For those who "are not under law but under grace" (Rom. 6:14), the moral law—mysteriously—shows the way to walk in freedom. Chemnitz includes this guiding function in the seventh element of his definition; I have omitted it until we see why he does so. Our attempt takes us into the territory of the *uses of the law*, to which we now turn our attention.

THE LAW'S TWO (AND ALSO THREE) USES

Traditionally, Protestants have divided the law's uses or functions in a threefold manner called, conveniently enough, the "first use of the law" (the political use, sometimes referred to as "curb"); the "second use of the law" (the elenctic use, the one that reveals sin, sometimes referred to as "mirror"); and the "third use of the law" (the didactic use, sometimes referred to as "guide").[19] However, the threefold division in fact rests on a prior twofold division, and that is where we must begin.

The twofold division, whose explication derives especially from Martin Luther's 1535 Galatians commentary, distributes the law into a "civil" or

---

[17] Stolen from Luther, in fact, who uses the phrase in a similar way in other contexts.

[18] As is regularly the case, knowing a thing's final cause is essential for understanding it: what a thing is *for* tells us a lot about what it *is*.

Gerhard (*Loci*, 208) also includes seven parts in his definition. They link up with those of Chemnitz mostly but not exactly: for example, Gerhard divides the theological use into two parts (points six and seven, justification and sanctification), and combines the law's regulation of the inner man with its requirement of perfect obedience (separated in Chemnitz). He also includes a point (2) about the law's immutability. It is worth noting that Gerhard, too—like Chemnitz—endorses Melanchthon's definition from the *Examen ordinandorum*, with which he closes his discussion of the law of God.

[19] One occasionally encounters differences in the ordering of the uses (e.g., in John Calvin's *Institutes of the Christian Religion*, the first two uses are reversed), but the substance is the same.

"political" use and a "theological" use.[20] The political use of the law provides for the restraint and coercion of sinful man in the civil sphere lest he break out in unbridled wickedness to the detriment of his family, neighbors, and society in general. That is, this first use of the law takes account of post-lapsarian man's corrupted nature and places a check on his vice through threats of punishment. Luther puts it this way:

> [W]e must know that there are two uses of the law. The one use is civil: God has ordained civil laws—indeed, all laws—for restraining transgressions. Therefore, every law is passed for the purpose of hindering sin....Therefore, the first understanding and use of the law is to restrain the ungodly. For the Devil reigns in the whole world and drives men to all shameful acts. God has ordained magistrates, parents, teachers, laws, bonds, and all civil ordinances so that, if they can do nothing more, they might at least bind the Devil's hands so that he does not rage in accordance with his lust, etc. Therefore, just as bonds and chains are cast on possessed men in whom the Devil powerfully reigns so that they do not harm anyone, so the magistrate is present before the whole world, which is possessed by the Devil and carried headlong into all crimes, with his own bonds and chains, that is, with laws, restraining the world's hands and feet so that it does not rush headlong into all evils. If one does not allow himself to be kept in order in this way, capital punishment is the sentence.[21]

It is important to note that this function of the law does not justify, and does not make man better in any spiritual sense, even if it makes him less bad than he would be otherwise. As Luther notes, when we obey the law externally (by, for example, not murdering or committing adultery), we do so "not willingly or because of the love of virtue," but because we "fear the sword and the executioner." Because this is so, the law cannot provide righteousness; instead, it serves, according to Luther, as a "sign of unrighteousness."[22] We are "under" this sign as a hindrance to our vicious natures.

---

[20] He also refers to the civil or political as the "gentile" use. Luther, *Ad Galatas*, 528.
[21] Luther, *Ad Galatas*, 479–80.
[22] Luther, *Ad Galatas*, 479.

Nevertheless, the fact that the first use of the law is not theological does not mean that it has no *relation* to theology or to the theological use(s) of the law. As Luther goes on to say,

> This civil restraint[23] is absolutely necessary and has been instituted by God, both on account of public peace and on account of the preservation of everything, but especially so that the progress of the gospel will not be hindered by the disturbances and seditions of insolent men.[24]

The political use, then—the restraint of flagrant and violent sin—is ordered toward the creation of room for the gospel to do its work.

But that is not the only role the law has to play in relation to the gospel, and it is at this point in his Galatians commentary that Luther turns to "the other use of the law," which is "theological or spiritual": the revelation to man of "his sin, blindness, misery, ungodliness, ignorance, hatred and contempt of God, death, hell, judgment, and the well deserved wrath he has incurred before God," which is the law's "principal and proper use."[25]

Does the fact that the law cannot save and can only condemn sinful man mean that the law is somehow evil in itself? By no means. It is only through this chief use of the law that a place is made for the gospel to be truly good news to one's soul. Just as the political use of the law creates a civic environment in which the gospel can flourish corporately and externally, the theological use of the law creates a spiritual environment in which it can do so individually and internally.

Throughout this section of the commentary, it is clear that the doctrine of justification is Luther's chief concern. He repeatedly stresses that the law, in its accusatory function,[26] is directed against what Luther refers to several times as the *opinio iustitiae*, a phrase best rendered as "a self-satisfied opinion concerning one's own righteousness."[27] In order to strike this opinion down and destroy it, man must be made to see that his situation considered in itself

---

[23] *Cohercio*; the word could also be translated "coercion."
[24] Luther, *Ad Galatas*, 480.
[25] Luther, *Ad Galatas*, 480-481.
[26] This is the function that Gerhard, below, calls "theological elenctic."
[27] See Luther, *Ad Galatas*, 481, 482, 484, 488.

is irreparable: the law cannot offer "righteousness and life," but only wrath. It can only bring man to despair.[28]

But despair for its own sake is not God's goal. His goal is rather to turn our eyes from the law to grasp the grace of God in the gospel. As he puts it,

> The gospel is the light that illuminates and vivifies hearts; for it shows what the grace and mercy of God are, what remission of sins, blessing, righteousness, life, and eternal salvation are, and how we ought to obtain those things. By distinguishing law and gospel in this way, we give to each its own proper use and office.[29]

This, of course, is the standard law/gospel distinction. In confessional terms, then, the distinction between law and gospel, though it is true and pertinent whenever the law is spoken of, relates particularly to the second use of the law: salvation is found only through God's free gift of grace revealed to us in the gospel, once we have been convicted of sin by the demands revealed to us in the law. The law, used properly, should be found "with" the gospel. The two go together in such a way that the first reveals man's liability to judgment and condemnation, while the second reveals the remedy. But should one stop there? Does the law play any further role than to convict a person of sin?

Dogmaticians in the sixteenth and seventeenth centuries said "No" to the first question and "Yes" to the second; and here we come to the (puzzlingly) controversial third use of the law. This third use is found already formulated in the second period of Melanchthon's *Loci communes* (first published in 1535, the same year as Luther's Galatians commentary) and becomes standard in Melanchthon's writings. In the *Loci*, we find this:

> The third office (*tertium officium*) of the law, which is in those who are righteous by faith, is both to teach them about what good works are pleasing to God and to command certain works in which they may practice their obedience to God. For although we are free from the law as far as justification is concerned, the law nevertheless remains as far as obedience is concerned.[30]

---

[28] Luther, *Ad Galatas*, 485–86.

[29] Luther, *Ad Galatas*, 486.

[30] Philip Melanchthon, *Loci theologici: Secunda eorum aetas*, CR 21, 406. An English translation of the whole work can be found in Philip Melanchthon, *Common Theological*

Melanchthon would later make a similar statement in the aforementioned *Examen ordinandorum*, where he asserts that the "third use (*tertius usus*) is in those who have been reborn"; its purpose is "to teach what forms of worship are pleasing to God, because, although human reason in some way knows the difference between honorable and shameful things, it is still necessary to have an express testimony of God regarding what works are pleasing to him."[31] And yet, I note in passing, there is no tension between the rational and revealed aspects of the law's character: and not only that, but Melanchthon adds that the rational moral order of the revealed law will exist for eternity,[32] "in order that the rational creation may be subject to God the creator, and be conformed to him."[33] In that text, he notes that human reason does indeed know the difference between right and wrong, but we still need an "express testimony of God" to that effect, as Ezekiel 20:19 teaches. Though he does not say so here, such an emphasis on the need for a sure word from God in matters of divine obedience or Christian ethics can be easily harmonized with what Melanchthon says elsewhere about the darkness of corrupted human reason, especially in the things of God.

Similar to Melanchthon, Martin Chemnitz divides the second and third uses of the law between "those who *are to be* justified" (*iustificandis*) and "those who *have been* justified or reborn" (*iustificatis seu renatis*).[34] Perhaps most useful of all, however, is the formulation of Johann Gerhard. Like Luther, Gerhard distinguishes between the "political" and "theological" uses of the law. He then subdivides the "theological" use in two: what he calls the θεολογικὸς ἐλεγκτικός [*theologikos elenktikos*, "theological elenctic"] and the θεολογικὸς διδακτικός [*theologikos didaktikos*, "theological didactic"]. The purpose of the former is to "rebuke sin" (that is, the second use of the law), and the purpose of the latter is to "instruct those who who have been reborn about what the truly good works are in which they ought to walk and by which they can please God" (that is, the third use of the law). If, in the first use, man is

---

Topics (Loci Communes Theologici *[1535]*), trans. Paul A. Rydecki (Malone, TX: Repristination Press, 2020).

[31] Melanchthon, *Examen*, CR 23, 11.

[32] The phrase is mine (Melanchthon's words are, "This order will not cease to exist for all eternity"), and one could just as easily exchange the components to refer to "the revealed moral order of the rational law."

[33] Melanchthon, *Examen*, CR 23, 11.

[34] Chemnitz, *Loci*, 100.

"under" the law, and in the second use the law is found "with" the gospel in order for man to be reborn, here, in the third, we find the man who has been reborn "in" the law as his path in the Christian life.

In Gerhard's own view, he is drawing this distinction from Luther himself, namely, from—once again—the 1535 Galatians commentary. And, while Luther there restricts the term "theological use" to what we customarily call the second or accusatory use of the law, the substance of what Gerhard states about the third use is present. As Luther says (and as Gerhard quotes him as saying), "There is still a need for a pedagogue to train and trouble the strong ass, our flesh, so that by this pedagogy sins might be diminished and the way to Christ made manifest."[35]

Christians too, that is, must still contend with the flesh and its lusts, and this battle goes on as long as life does, until we finally put off the flesh.[36] For that reason, it is not, in my view, illegitimate to say that Luther's term "theological use" covers both the "second" and "third" uses in the formulation of Melanchthon, Chemnitz, and Gerhard. For in a sense, the third use paradoxically *is* the second use, but applied to Christians in so far as the old Adam, who must be daily drowned and put off, still persists. "Therefore," Luther writes,

> as long as we live in the flesh, which does not exist without sin, *the law continually returns and performs its office*, in one more, in another less—*not, however, for destruction, but for salvation*. For this training of the law is the daily mortification of the flesh, the reason, and our own powers, and the renewal of our mind.[37]

If we were wholly perfect, of course, we would have no need of the law;[38] but, for that matter, we would have no need of the gospel, the sacraments, or absolution, either.

---

[35] Luther, *Ad Galatas*, 537.

[36] Luther, *Ad Galatas*, 535–36.

[37] Luther, *Ad Galatas*, 537 (emphasis mine).

[38] This statement may seem to be in tension with what was said above, in reference to Melanchthon, about the order of the law existing for all eternity. But they can be easily harmonized. In glory, the law is not encountered as it is here below, for the perfected will not feel the sting of conscience or the law's accusations, nor will the old Adam need to be drowned daily any longer. But because the law simply is, at bottom, the rational divine order of all created being, it will necessarily exist for as long as created being will exist, i.e., forever.

Still, Luther has more than merely negative restraint and coercion in mind when he speaks of the law as it pertains to the Christian; that is, he means more than merely putting off the old Adam. For something must be put *on* as well: the second Adam, Christ. According to Luther, the putting on of Christ occurs in two ways, and here the law/gospel distinction reappears in a new light: for Christ must be put on according to both the law and the gospel.

Luther lays this out in his comments on Galatians 3:27, "For as many of you as were baptized into Christ Jesus have put on Christ." Luther remarks:

> "To put on Christ" is understood in two ways: according to the law (*Legaliter*) and according to the gospel (*Evangelice*). Romans 13:14 speaks according to the law: "Put on the Lord Jesus Christ," that is, "Imitate the example and virtues of Christ, do and suffer those things that he did and suffered....And we see in Christ the highest patience, the highest gentleness and charity and an admirable moderation in all things. We ought to put on this adornment of Christ, that is, to imitate these virtues of his. In the same way we are also able to imitate other saints.[39]

More succinctly, putting on Christ "according to the law" means imitating Christ, the one who shows us perfect obedience to the law.[40] The "virtues" of Christ, such as patience and moderation, are synonymous with obedience to the Decalogue. The moral virtues and the moral law are correlative concepts.

But to put on Christ "according to the gospel" is something quite different. Luther explains it like this: "[T]o put on Christ according to the gospel is not a matter of imitation, but of new birth and new creation, because

---

[39] Luther, *Ad Galatas*, 539–40.

[40] Compare Werner Jaeger's comments about Gregory of Nyssa in *Early Christianity and Greek Paideia* (Cambridge, MA: Harvard University Press, 1961): "The paideia of the Christian is *imitatio Christi*: Christ must take shape in him. This appears most clearly in the manner in which Gregory quotes the Bible as the supreme authority. Instead of saying, 'the prophet says' or 'Christ says,' as would be most natural for us, he writes innumerable times, 'the prophet Isaiah educates us' or 'the apostle educates us' (*paideuei*), implying that what the Bible teaches must be accepted as the paideia of the Christian. This very way of expressing, not so much the philological fact that this or that is written in the Bible, but the formative function of what is written, is indicative of his paideutic interpretation of the authority. It is not law but education."

I am clothed with Christ himself, that is, with his innocence, righteousness, wisdom, power, salvation, life, etc."[41] This is a much more radical change than putting on Christ "according to the law," and it is not something *we* do at all. Instead, it is done *to us* in baptism. Luther continues to describe the transformation that God works upon us:

> We were clothed with Adam's garment of skin, which is the garment of mortality and the clothing of sin. That is, we were all subject to and sold under sin; there was horrible blindness, ignorance, and contempt and hatred for God in us. At that time, we were full of evil concupiscence, uncleanness, greed, etc. This clothing, that is, this corrupt and sinful nature, we contracted from Adam via propagation; Paul customarily calls it the "old man." "He must be put off with his deeds" (Eph. 4, Col. 3), so that, from being sons of Adam, we might be made sons of God. This does not happen by changing our clothes, nor by any laws or works, but by the rebirth and renewal that is in baptism.[42]

And yet the grace of baptism is not disconnected from the imitation of Christ or virtuous living according to the pattern of Christ. Indeed, it is the very foundation of it. In other words, baptism is dynamic rather than static. Luther concludes the paragraph like this: "For in the baptized a new light and flame arises; new and godly affections come into being (fear, trust in God, hope, etc.); a new will comes into being. This, then, is to put on Christ properly, truly, and according to the gospel."[43]

All this comes, moreover, simply as a manifestation of grace. Luther is at pains to point out that the new birth of baptism is not a law or a work, but a gift. And it is this gift—this putting on of Christ "according to the gospel"—that is the source and necessary antecedent of putting on Christ "according to the law." As Luther remarks shortly afterwards, "When we have put on Christ as the garment of righteousness and our salvation, then we shall also put on Christ as the clothing of imitation."[44] Christians are no longer *under* the law's condemnation, but, having been freed from condemnation by the Gospel that must be found *with* the law, "God's

---

[41] Luther, *Ad Galatas*, 540.
[42] Luther, *Ad Galatas*, 540.
[43] Luther, *Ad Galatas*, 540.
[44] Luther, *Ad Galatas*, 541.

children," in the words of the *Epitome* of the *Formula of Concord*, "live *in* the Law and walk according to God's Law."[45]

It is no coincidence, therefore, that the two paragraphs in the commentary just discussed in some detail are perfectly harmonious with what Luther's *Small Catechism* says about baptism: on the one hand, it "works forgiveness of sins, rescues from death and the devil, and gives eternal salvation to all who believe this"; on the other, it "indicates that the Old Adam in us should by daily contrition and repentance be drowned and die with all sins and evil desires, and that a new man should daily emerge and arise to live before God in righteousness and purity forever."[46]

But it is also no coincidence that they are harmonious with the rest of the tradition of orthodox reflection on the law of God as found in Melanchthon, Chemnitz, and Gerhard. Though terminology and details differ from time to time, the basic thrust is clear and impressively coherent: there are three uses of the one law of God in order to facilitate civic life, show man the way of salvation, and guide him in how he should live as a child of God. The hinge for the proper understanding of these matters is Christ himself.

Or, perhaps "hinge" isn't the best metaphor. Instead, let us end where we began. For Kafka, before the law stood a mysterious and inscrutable doorkeeper. But for the Christian, before the law stands Christ, who is the door (John 10:9) to our proper understanding of the law. For Christ is the end of the law (Rom. 10:4) in at least three ways: He perfectly fulfills the demands of the law, and thus personifies the law's perfection; He is the one to whom the law points the accused conscience for justification and life, and thus is the end of the law's condemnation for all who believe; and his life's

---

[45] *Formula of Concord, Epitome* 6.6.5 (emphasis mine), in *Concordia: The Lutheran Confessions: A Reader's Edition of the Book of Concord*, ed. Paul Timothy McCain (St. Louis: Concordia Publishing House, 2006), 487. In reality, the situation is a little more complicated than I let on, for there is a sense in which we are still *under* the law civilly.

[46] It is worth noting that this "transtemporal dynamism," so to speak, is also reflected in Luther's thought about Christ's coming: "Christ came once at the appointed time; faith also came once, when the Apostles preached the Gospel through the whole world. Next, Christ also comes spiritually (*spiritualiter*) every day; faith also comes every day through the Word of the Gospel." Luther, *Ad Galatas*, 538.

pattern is the goal for the justified as they seek to walk in Christlikeness in this life.[47]

---

[47] Compare Melanchthon's different, but not incongruent, delineation of the four ways in which Christ fulfills the law (*Examen*, CR 23, 11): "Christ fulfills the law in four ways: First, by his own obedience; second, by taking the punishment for sin upon himself; third, by restoring righteousness and eternal life in us; fourth, by hallowing the law, as he says: 'I have not come to destroy the law,' etc."

II.

The Civil Magistrate

BRADFORD LITTLEJOHN

AN ALIEN WORLD

WHEN most of us think about politics in the Reformation (which, to be fair, is probably not often), we may be apt to think first of Luther's proclamation of "the freedom of a Christian" and his stirring defiance of the emperor: "here I stand, I can do no other." Or, conversely, we might have our imaginations darkened by thoughts of Henry VIII and his wives, or Calvin and the burning of Servetus, and dismiss the Reformation as a cruelly authoritarian age.[1] So which was it? The first stirrings of liberal individualism, a society reimagined around the autonomy of each conscience, or a time in which craven churchmen empowered a leviathan state?

The best answer, of course, would be "neither." Any attempts to read modern libertarian or statist paradigms onto the political theology of the sixteenth century are bound to lead us astray. The thought of the Magisterial Reformers comprised a coherent theological and political vision, but one whose assumptions and rhetoric can feel like an alien world to the twenty-first century reader. Despite the distance of five centuries, though, there is no question that the Reformers' understanding of the civil magistrate helped

---

[1] Michael Servetus (1511-1553) was a Reformation era polymath, burnt at the stake in Calvin's Geneva for denying the Trinity and infant baptism.

to shape the world we inhabit today and can continue to challenge and inform our own thinking.

In an age plagued by a crisis of authority, in which increasingly "every man does what is right in his own eyes," the Reformers' profound respect for the mystery of God-given political authority is a jarring but needed wake-up call, one that can help us question our own deep-seated individualism. However, in an age when political authority has become increasingly unmoored from any sense of accountability to an objective vision of the human good, the Reformers' insistence on the divine mission and religious vocation of the magistrate will appear as a sharp rebuke to the secularized, bureaucratized modern ideal of "the government" as manager of rival interests and manipulator of public opinion. For the Reformers, the magistrate's responsibility for the temporal common good was never separable from a concern for the final, spiritual good of his subjects. We may wrestle with how to apply such a foreign idea to an age of privatized and pluralized religion, but we can at least begin by seeking to understand it on its own terms.

"THE MOST SACRED OF ALL STATIONS IN MORTAL LIFE": THE REFORMERS' REVERENCE FOR CIVIL AUTHORITY

The alien character of Reformation political thought is liable to strike us first in the lofty rhetoric they used to describe their rulers. John Calvin (1509—1564), for instance, writes in the final chapter of his *Institutes*, "[N]o one ought to doubt that civil authority is a calling, not only holy and lawful before God, but the most sacred and by far the most honorable of all callings in the whole life of mortal men."[2] In the same year, his friend Peter Martyr Vermigli (1499—1562) greeted the accession of Queen Elizabeth in language borrowed from Luke 1 and 2: "Glory be now to God on high, Peace in the Church, and the good will of God towards the people of England, that by the guide and good government of this godly Queen, her subjects being adorned with righteousness and holiness, may walk always and innocently before Him."[3]

---

[2] John Calvin, *Institutes of the Christian Religion*, 2 vols., ed. John T. McNeill, trans. Ford Lewis Battles (Louisville: Westminster John Knox Press, 1960), IV.20, 2:1490.

[3] Peter Martyr Vermigli, "Epistle to the Princess Elizabeth," in W. J. Torrance Kirby, *The Zurich Connection and Tudor Political Thought* (Leiden: Brill, 2007), 196.

If any Christian today dared use such language, he might be described as "worshiping the state," guilty of political idolatry. For the Reformers, though, it was precisely because civil magistrates were under God—ordained and put in place by Him—that they could be spoken of in such strong terms. Romans 13, although always an important touchstone for Christian political thought, became the central pillar of the Reformers' doctrine of the magistrate: "there is no authority but from God, and those that exist have been instituted by God" (13:1, ESV). Civil magistrates held authority because they had been authorized by God, and were accountable to him to use that power for the good of their peoples, rather than for mere private benefit.

Moreover, Protestant moral theology routinely placed the respect owed to rulers under the heading of the fifth commandment (for Lutherans and Catholics, the fourth commandment): "honor your father and your mother." The Westminster Larger Catechism of 1647, for instance, following a pattern begun by Luther in his *Small Catechism*, stated, "By father and mother, in the fifth commandment, are meant, not only natural parents, but all superiors in age and gifts; and especially such as, by God's ordinance, are over us in place of authority, whether in family, church, or commonwealth" (Question 124). Kings, the Reformers pointed out, were often described in Scripture as "fathers" of their people, and "nursing mothers" of the Church, and thus were owed the respect and obedience that every child owes his parents:

> [W]illing obedience to their lawful commands and counsels; due submission to their corrections; fidelity to, defense and maintenance of their persons and authority, according to their several ranks, and the nature of their places; bearing with their infirmities, and covering them in love, that so they may be an honor to them and to their government (Question 127).

As this last clause makes clear, though, this high respect for civil authority did not entail naïvete about the virtues of princes. Quite the contrary. "A wise prince is a mighty rare bird," wrote Luther, "and an upright prince even rarer. They are generally the biggest fools or the worst scoundrels on earth; therefore one must constantly expect the worst from them and look for little good."[4] After all, concluded Luther with his typical cynicism, "[t]he

---

[4] Martin Luther, *On Temporal Authority: To What Extent It Should Be Obeyed* (1523), in *Luther's Works*, vol. 45, *Christian in Society II*, trans. J. J. Schindel, rev. Walther I. Brandt (Philadelphia: Fortress Press, 1962), 113.

world is too wicked, and does not deserve to have many wise and pious princes."[5] If anything, the Reformers were less apt than we are to have any illusions about the piety and wisdom of the ruling class, forced as they were to work in close proximity and strained partnership with greedy, petty, and incompetent kings, courtiers, or city councilmen. Calvin, whom we have quoted above on civil magistracy as "the most honorable of all callings in the whole life of mortal men," is famous for his regular wranglings with the Genevan city council.

The Reformers, however, were able to hold both of these things together—the lofty status of civil authority and the manifold vices of civil authorities—in a way that we often fail to do today: by clearly distinguishing the *office* from the *person*. The office was given by God, while the person was put into that office by man. The necessity for the office, the powers belonging to the office, and the respect due to it persisted in spite of the frequent abuses of authority or derelictions of duty by individual officeholders. Indeed, it was this very distinction that enabled rulers to be held accountable: were they carrying out their God-given functions, or not? If not, the same Reformers who preached devotion and deference to rulers did not hesitate to call them to account. Consider the case of Archbishop of Canterbury Edmund Grindal (1519—1583), forced into early retirement after he dared to write to Queen Elizabeth when ordered to act against his conscience,

> In God's matters all princes ought to bow their scepters to the Son of God, and to ask counsel at his mouth, what they ought to do.... Must not you also one day appear before the fearful judgment-seat of the Crucified, to receive there according as you have done in the body, whether it be good or evil? And although ye are a mighty prince, yet remember that He which dwelleth in heaven is mightier.[6]

The decrees of earthly rulers were always limited by God's own authority, as Calvin emphasized in the *Institutes*: "If they command anything against Him, let it go unesteemed. And here let us not be concerned at all about the dignity which the magistrates possess; for no harm is done to it

---

[5] Luther, *On Temporal Authority*, 114.

[6] W. Nicholson, ed., *The Remains of Edmund Grindal* (Cambridge: The Parker Society, 1843), 389–90.

when it is humbled before that singular and truly supreme power of God."[7] Still, in keeping with the principles of the fifth commandment and the necessity of maintaining social order, Christians should not lightly jump to this conclusion, but try wherever possible to give magistrates the benefit of the doubt. As Richard Hooker (1554—1600) argued, "peace and quietness are not possible unless the probable voice of an entire society or body politic should overrule all similarly probable private judgments within the same body."[8] Organized resistance to unjust rulers, then, while not ruled out by the Reformers, was only justifiable under extreme circumstances and was generally discouraged.

After all, most sixteenth-century societies were always teetering on the brink of potential chaos in a way that is difficult for us to imagine today. America has only experienced one civil war in its 250-year history, and bloody as it was, the ordinary structures of law and government continued to function remarkably well throughout the war in most of the country. England and France, however, each experienced thirty-year periods of intermittent civil war in the fifteenth and sixteenth centuries. To most Reformers, aware that the Reformation itself constituted a crisis of authority and social order throughout most of Christendom, the threat of anarchy was a greater danger than that of tyranny. While we today, able to take basic public order and national security for granted most of the time, might rail, "no justice, no peace," for them, the converse was clear: "no peace, no justice"; without some modicum of order, however oppressive at times, no one could enjoy secure possession of life and property.

Moreover, from the Reformers' standpoint, it was papists who were most apt to preach resistance to civil authority. The papacy, after all, had long claimed the role of arbitrating just and unjust claims to civil authority and just and unjust actions of princes, reserving the right to excommunicate or even depose rulers deemed unworthy. Reformation-era popes continued to invoke this authority, most famously in the case of Queen Elizabeth, excommunicated in 1570 by the papal bull *Regnans in Excelsis*, which went so far as to call on her subjects to rise up against her and on foreign Catholic powers to invade. In light of such teaching—and such concrete threats to the

---

[7] Calvin, *Institutes* IV.20.32, 2:1520.

[8] Richard Hooker, *The Laws of Ecclesiastical Polity in Modern English*, vol. 1, *Preface–Book IV*, ed. W. Bradford Littlejohn, Bradley Belschner, and Brian Marr (Landrum, SC: Davenant Press, 2019), Preface 6.6, 29.

safety and stability of Protestant polities—most of the Reformers preferred to err on the side of emphasizing the authority of rulers, and not the rights of subjects to rebel.

That said, the language of "rulers" and "subjects" might give the mistaken impression that the Reformers were all monarchists. Far from it. Although many key Protestant territories were under hereditary princes (like Luther's Saxony) or kings (like England or Denmark), the Reformation also thrived in republican city-states, like Zwingli's Zurich, Calvin's Geneva, or Bucer's Strasbourg. Indeed, the standard line from the Reformers on the proper *form* of government was pluralism: any of the standard regime types—democratic, aristocratic, monarchical—was in principle justified and might work well in different contexts, although the best governments were likely to be those which mixed all three elements in some measure. The same basic principles drawn from Romans 13 and the fifth commandment, however, applied regardless of whether one lived under an elected city council or a hereditary monarch. Heinrich Bullinger (1504—1575), for instance, who worked closely with the former in Zurich throughout his life, frequently advised fellow Reformers in England under Henry VIII, Edward VI, and Elizabeth I without any hint that the basic duties owed by and to the magistrate (which he described at length in a classic of Reformation political theology, Part II, Sermon 7 of his *Decades*) were any different in the two cases.[9]

That said, despite all the language of deference to "princes," the overall trajectory of Protestant political thought was toward increasingly popular government. This is a long story that cannot be told here, but the basic logic is clear. Under the medieval arrangement, rulers were accountable above all to the pope, an extra-national super-sovereign charged with ensuring that monarchs upheld justice and piety. The Reformers, recognizing the gross abuses in this arrangement, declared the independence of Christian commonwealths from papal authority, but not—in general—from any earthly accountability. In place of the papacy, the people themselves, conceived of no longer as passive subjects within the hierarchy of global Christendom, but rather as an active political and self-governing political nation, began to exercise increasing accountability over their rulers. This development is apparent already in the thought of Richard Hooker, whose

---

[9] Heinrich Bullinger, *The Decades of Henry Bullinger*, ed. for the Parker Society by Thomas Harding, 4 vols. (Cambridge: Cambridge University Press, 1849–52).

1590s defense of the church of England conceived of Parliament, not the Queen in her personal capacity, as the embodiment of the English nation and the appropriate instrument of legislation. Over the following two centuries it would come to dominate Protestant political thought and practice on both sides of the Atlantic.

At its heart, Reformation political theology was about the empowerment of the laity. Following from Luther's revolutionary proclamation of the "priesthood of all believers" and rejection of the millennium-long spiritual hierarchy of clergy and laity, the Reformers consistently emphasized the office of civil magistrate as a calling to lay leadership within the body of believers. The prince, wrote Melanchthon, was the *praecipuum membrum ecclesiae*, the "foremost member of the church," and as such called upon to use his position for both the temporal and spiritual common good of his people.[10] In this way, Reformation political theology set itself in opposition to the dual threats of papalism and Anabaptism, both of which denigrated the exercise of political authority by the Christian layman. For papalism, the unspiritual laity were to be firmly subordinated to the clergy, who had ultimate authority over civil magistrates. For Anabaptism, the dichotomy of clergy and laity was reframed as one of Church and world, but the upshot was the same: the dirty work of politics was sub-Christian. For some Anabaptists, like those who signed the Schleitheim Confession of 1527, true Christians must renounce all earthly government and refuse to use the sword; for others, like those who seized power in Münster in 1535, true Christians alone could exercise authority, superseding all earthly governments. Against all these, the Magisterial Reformers insisted that civil authority, as an office of leadership for lay Christians within society, was "not only holy and lawful before God, but the most sacred and by far the most honorable of all callings in the whole life of mortal men."[11]

---

[10] Quoted in James Estes, *Peace, Order, and the Glory of God: Secular Authority and the Church in the Thought of Luther and Melanchthon, 1518–1559* (Leiden: Brill, 2005), 128.

[11] Calvin, *Institutes* IV.20.4, 2:1490.

"NOT LESS THAN THAT OF BREAD AND WATER": PRESERVING THE TEMPORAL COMMON GOOD

If, then, the office of civil magistrate is so sacred, what is its purpose? What responsibilities did the Reformers assign to their rulers? Here again Calvin sums up the consensus well:

> [Its] function among men is no less than that of bread, water, sun, and air; indeed, its place of honor is far more excellent. For it does not merely see to it, as all these serve to do, that men breathe, eat, drink, and are kept warm, even though it surely embraces all these activities when it provides for their living together. It does not, I repeat, look to this only, but also prevents idolatry, sacrilege against God's name, blasphemies against his truth, and other public offenses against religion from arising and spreading among the people; it prevents the public peace from being disturbed; it provides that each man may keep his property safe and sound; that men may carry on blameless intercourse among themselves; that honesty and modesty may be preserved among men. In short, it provides that a public manifestation of religion may exist among Christians, and that humanity be maintained among men.[12]

The task of the civil magistrate, in short, is to secure and maintain the *common good*, a concept that the Reformers carried over unchanged from their classical and medieval forebears. And as man consists of both body and soul, this common good involves both a temporal and a spiritual dimension. We will consider each of these in turn.

Although the Reformers certainly believed that man's spiritual destiny was more important than his material wants, they also understood that material provision was a precondition for spiritual nourishment. After all, as Hooker pithily remarked, "we cannot live virtuously unless we first live."[13] Therefore, the first priority of any civil authority must be the physical protection of the lives and livelihoods of his citizens, and of the political stability of his own regime. This latter might seem self-serving, until we remember that *order* was sometimes in rather scarce supply in the sixteenth century, and even a somewhat corrupt regime, the Reformers recognized, was generally better than no regime. This explains in part most Protestants'

---

[12] Calvin, *Institutes* IV.20.3, 2:1488.
[13] Hooker, *Laws* I.10.2, 83.

support for Henry VIII's divorce from Catherine of Aragon. As Henry saw it, Catherine was clearly unable to produce a male heir, something England urgently needed in order to avoid another bitter dynastic dispute such as that of the disastrous Wars of the Roses (1455–85). The pope's refusal to grant an annulment (something that would ordinarily have been given as a matter of course in such circumstances) was seen as a form of foreign meddling in a matter of urgent English national security, provoking a fierce anti-papal backlash that sowed the seeds of the English Reformation.[14]

Another particularly unpleasant episode of the Reformation, the infamous Peasants' Revolt of 1525, highlighted the same concern for maintaining civil order. Martin Luther—though initially sympathizing with the impoverished peasants' grievances—soon sided unequivocally with the nobles who banded together to suppress the uprising. Although this suppression proved brutal and bloody, and we might wish Luther had maintained a more even-handed approach, his reasoning was sound enough. As he wrote the year following the revolt in *Whether Soldiers Can Be Saved*, "There is as great a difference between changing a government and improving it as the distance from heaven to earth. It is easy to change a government, but it is difficult to get one that is better, and the danger is you will not."[15] His fear of rebellion was based on a sober and realistic assessment that rebellions destroyed the social fabric of a society, unleashing the basest passions of our nature in acts of unrestrained vengeance, and were thus almost certain to do more harm than good. Indeed, he wrote in *Against the Robbing and Murdering Hordes*, "[R]ebellion is not just simple murder; it is like a great fire, which attacks and devastates a whole land. Thus rebellion brings with it a land filled with murder and bloodshed; it makes widows and orphans, and turns everything upside down, like the worst disaster."[16] Luther was thus emphatic in arguing not simply that the magistrates have a *right* to

---

[14] See further my "The English Reformation: England's First Brexit," *American Conservative*, January 15, 2020, https://www.theamericanconservative.com/articles/the-english-reformation-englands-first-brexit/.

[15] Martin Luther, *Whether Soldiers, Too, Can Be Saved* (1526) in *Luther's Works*, vol. 46, *Christian in Society III*, trans. Helmut T. Lehmann and Robert C. Schultz (Philadelphia: Fortress Press, 1967), 111–12.

[16] Martin Luther, *Against the Robbing and Murdering Hordes of Peasants* (1525), in *Luther's Works*, 46:50.

defend themselves, but that they have a *duty*, for the sake of the whole body politic, to suppress rebellion.

If the magistrate can justly use the sword against internal threats, all the more so can he use it against external enemies. Luther had little patience with the pacifism of some of the radical Anabaptists. In *Whether Soldiers Can Be Saved*, he writes that although slaying may not seem like a work of love, it can be—just as a doctor must sometimes amputate a limb to preserve the body, so a magistrate must sometimes kill an individual threatening to destroy the whole people under him.

> For if the sword were not on guard to preserve peace, everything in the world would be ruined because of a lack of peace. Therefore, such a war is only a very brief lack of peace that prevents an everlasting and immeasurable lack of peace, a small misfortune that prevents a great misfortune.... The small lack of peace called war or the sword must set a limit to this universal, worldwide lack of peace which would destroy everyone.[17]

The sword, in short, is what God has provided as a mercy, but precisely by being unmerciful when necessary:

> The Scriptures... see that out of great mercy, it [the sword] must be unmerciful, and from utter kindliness, it must exercise wrath and severity.... And beyond all doubt, these are precious works of mercy, love, and kindness, since there is nothing on earth that is worse than disturbance, insecurity, oppression, violence, and injustice.[18]

Such statements may shock us today, but this is partly because we are blessed enough to live in a society from which insecurity has been largely banished (though there are signs even now that it may not always remain so).

Since other essays in this volume address rebellion and just war at greater length, however, let us move on to other ways in which the civil magistrate was charged with protection of the temporal common good.

Second only to his people's lives, any good ruler must protect their livelihoods; economic issues will therefore always be front and center of the

---

[17] Luther, *Whether Soldiers Can Be Saved*, 96.
[18] Martin Luther, *An Open Letter concerning the Hard Book Against the Peasants* (1525), in *Luther's Works*, 46:73.

political agenda. In fact, the events that kicked off the Reformation itself—Luther's famous showdown with Tetzel over indulgences—can be described as something of a trade dispute. Ostensibly ordered to help finance the construction of St. Peter's Basilica in Rome, much of the money from Tetzel's 1517 indulgence campaign actually went into the coffers of Archbishop Albrecht of Mainz, who needed it to repay the Fugger banking family after they had funded his immense papal bribe a few years earlier. Since the most enthusiastic buyers of indulgences were the uneducated and gullible poor, Tetzel's indulgence campaign constituted an extraordinary redistribution of wealth upward from the poorest to the richest in Christendom—a social justice theme that, though largely forgotten, echoed loudly through the pages of Luther's *Ninety-Five Theses* and other sermons from the period.[19]

However, it also constituted an extraordinary redistribution of wealth out of certain German principalities, where Tetzel did most of his preaching, into the principalities of Archbishop Albrecht—and indeed on a larger scale out of the Holy Roman Empire into the Papal States. In modern terms, indulgences were the vehicle for perpetuating a large ongoing trade imbalance between Germany and Italy. Tired of having his impoverished subjects pay their last farthing for dubious spiritual benefits that materially benefited his rivals, Frederick the Wise banned Tetzel from preaching in his territory.[20] Tetzel did what every good gambling tycoon has learned: set up shop right on the borders of the banned territory. So effective was his propaganda that commoners from around Saxony flocked to the border to buy remittance for the penalties of their sins and those of their relatives. It was these events that directly precipitated Luther's *Ninety-Five Theses*, and the eventual break with Rome that followed.

Once the authority of the Roman church had been cast off, however, Reformation leaders were left with important questions of how to care for the poor within their communities. In medieval society, wealthier monasteries had often played a crucial role in poor relief, although others contributed to the problem, as men and women took vows of poverty for their spiritual benefit and lived off of the resources of surrounding

---

[19] See for instance Theses 43–45, 50–51, 86.

[20] For more background, see Timothy J. Wengert, *Martin Luther's 95 Theses with Introduction, Commentary, and Study Guide* (Minneapolis: Fortress Press, 2015), xix–xxvi, 27–28.

communities. It was not easy to tell the difference between a pious mendicant and a shiftless panhandler, and many Christians, taught that their almsgiving earned them spiritual merits, did not ask too many questions. Accordingly, a priority for many Reformation civil magistrates was to tackle the problem of beggars and establish coordinated programs of poor relief that could distinguish between those who deserved assistance and those who should be able to earn their own keep. Such programs required a strong partnership between civil authorities and local church leaders, with Calvinist churches rediscovering the biblical diaconate as a vocation of service chiefly focused on caring for the needy in the community. Calvin's work with the Genevan city council on the "General Hospital" that provided both healthcare and poor relief was one influential model.[21] Another, attempted on the scale of an entire kingdom, was Martin Bucer's (1491—1551) proposal to King Edward VI of England in his 1550 treatise *On the Kingdom of Christ*.

To cut down on the problem of beggars and their well-intentioned enablers, Bucer went so far as to propose a ban on private charity, with poor relief centered in local churches, overseen and coordinated by the central government. Each church should be equipped with as many wise and godly deacons as possible, who would be responsible, first, to "investigate how many really indigent persons live in each church for whom it is equitable for the church to provide the necessities of life." They should exclude from this number any who could "sustain themselves by their own powers" but do not, preferring idleness.[22] If possible, they should identify family members of the impoverished person who could care for them; otherwise, the diaconate should ensure their support. The government, for its part, should ensure that churches allocate sufficient resources to diaconal funds (even if it meant cutting down on the salaries of overpaid pastors in some cases), and that excess resources be regularly transferred from wealthier parishes to needier ones.

Bucer was also aware that the best way to tackle poverty was to cut it off at its source, by ensuring that the society had thriving industry and good employment for all of its citizens. Accordingly, in one particularly intriguing chapter of *On the Kingdom of Christ*, "On the Restoration of Various Crafts,"

---

[21] See Jeannine E. Olson, *Calvin and Social Welfare: Deacons and the Bourse Francaise* (Selinsgrove, PA: Susquehanna University Press, 1989).

[22] Martin Bucer, *De Regno Christi* (1550), reprinted in *Melanchthon and Bucer*, trans. and ed. Wilhelm Pauck (Louisville: Westminster John Knox Press, 2006), 307.

Bucer encourages King Edward to oversee thoroughgoing economic development that will overcome the problem of idleness and put all the people of England to work in profitable labor to both provide for themselves and enable the whole kingdom to prosper. Remarking that "it is apparent that this island has been adorned by the Lord with such good soil and climate that it should be able to produce far richer farm products than it now does," Bucer argues that England has a God-given responsibility to develop its natural resources as fully as possible.[23] The goal of this cultivation, however, should be maximal human flourishing, not private profit. The land, he says, "should be cultivated on its own merits and for the good of the commonwealth, at the expense (at least partial if not entire) of the profit in wool. Insofar as this profit provides only harmful pomp and luxury, it should be turned over to the purpose of giving sustenance to human beings who are the sons of God."[24]

On this basis, Bucer recommends curtailing the then-common practice of enclosing farmland for sheep-grazing, which enriched the landlords but put numerous rural Englishmen out of work and deprived them of access to the traditional agricultural commons to raise food for their own families. For Bucer, this situation was an urgent moral and theological concern because the flourishing of human life, not the pursuit of private profit, is the ultimate purpose of an economy. "But what person not completely destitute of the mind of Christ," he fumes, "can fail to acknowledge that Christian princes must make it a major project that there should be as [many] good men[25] as possible everywhere who live for the glory of God." Economic policies that fail to promote population growth, he goes on, "rob the state of its greatest riches and ornaments, namely, good citizens, and deprive the Church and heaven of worshipers praising God."[26]

Thus the responsible magistrate must see to it that his nation's natural resources are used for the long-term economic benefit of the whole population, rather than to maximize short-term profit. This didn't make Bucer a Luddite, however. While concerned that England was growing more raw wool than was good for it, he thought it was processing too little; instead,

---

[23] Bucer, *De Regno Christi*, 338.

[24] Bucer, *De Regno Christi*, 338.

[25] *Plurimi* (very many) appears in the Latin text but is omitted by oversight in the English translation.

[26] Bucer, *De Regno Christi*, 338.

it was exporting raw materials to Catholic Antwerp and then buying back the finished products. Accordingly, Bucer exhorted the king that "an effort will have to be made to develop all possible wool-making techniques in this realm, through hiring technicians from wherever this is permitted and entrusting to them... young men who are found to be gifted by the Lord for these skills."[27] All such economic policy should serve the fundamental goal of national self-protection; by developing national industry, Bucer argued, "the commonwealth will obtain in this one operation the means of feeding itself, and, when necessary, of defending itself."[28]

Whether because of Bucer's advice or because the intellectual currents of the time were already running in the same direction, Tudor England enacted policies not dissimilar to his recommendations, both for poor relief and for trade and economic development. England was hardly unique in either respect; many Reformation polities pursued similar agendas, but England enjoyed greater success, surging past its economic rivals by the eighteenth century. Indeed, so pervasive and deep-seated was this vision of the magistrate's responsibility for national economic development that even the text we now today think of as the bible of *laissez-faire* economics, Adam Smith's *The Wealth of Nations*, started from the premise that it was the state's job to ensure the development of its natural resources to support the largest possible population. Smith simply argued that this would be better achieved through free trade than through protectionism.

"NO BLASPHEMY AGAINST THE NAME OF GOD": ADVANCING THE SPIRITUAL COMMON GOOD

If Reformation ideas about the magistrate's care for the temporal common good remain at least relatively intelligible today, the same can hardly be said of their vision of his care for the spiritual common good. In early Protestant Social Teaching, it was a virtual truism that "the charge of religion belongeth unto princes," and indeed, we see this prominently highlighted in the quotation from Calvin above.[29] Although Calvin is famous among the Reformers for being particularly concerned to guard the independence of the institutional church, note his insistence that "no

---

[27] Bucer, *De Regno Christi*, 337.

[28] Bucer, *De Regno Christi*, 340.

[29] Peter Martyr Vermigli, quoted in Kirby, *Zurich Connection*, 59.

idolatry, no blasphemy against the name of God, no calumnies against his truth, nor other offenses to religion, break out and be disseminated among the people." In short, he says, the magistrate must ensure that "a public manifestation of religion may exist among Christians."[30]

How could this be? Well, the phrase "a *public form* of religion" is the crucial one. Calvin never believed for a moment that the civil magistrate could be in the business of saving souls; he could neither preach the Word nor administer the sacraments, nor could he try to "make windows into men's souls" (as Queen Elizabeth I famously put it, acknowledging the limits of her authority) in order to determine who was and was not a member of Christ's body. All of these things belonged to what Luther called the *geistliche Reiche*—the "spiritual kingdom," and were either the business of ordained ministers or of Jesus himself. This did not mean, however, that the ruler should be entirely oblivious to what was going on in the Church, which in its visible form as an organized institution fell within what Luther called the *weltliche Reiche*—the "earthly kingdom."[31] For one thing, even the magistrate's bare responsibility for national security required him to exercise some oversight of religious matters in a society where everyone claimed to be Christian and where such matters could easily be the occasion for violence. Throughout Reformation Europe, religious changes were often accompanied by violent social upheavals, as angry mobs destroyed churches belonging to "idolaters" or "heretics," and sometimes even assaulted their fellow citizens. The prudent ruler might recognize the need to moderate the pace of reform, establish uniform standards of worship, and punish acts of public blasphemy simply to prevent chaos and bloodshed. Moreover, if it was indeed the case, as Scripture taught, that God blessed righteous nations and brought judgment down on ungodly, idolatrous nations, then it simply stood to reason that any sensible ruler, tasked with protecting his people from invasion and plague, would have an interest in restraining the public practice of idolatry. Certainly there was ample biblical precedent in the form of godly kings like Hezekiah and Josiah.

Beyond all this, however, lay a deeper rationale for the magistrate's care for religion: namely, a conviction that since man consisted of body and soul

---

[30] Calvin, *Institutes* IV.20.3 (2:1488).

[31] See further my *Two Kingdoms: A Guide for the Perplexed* (Landrum, SC: Davenant Press, 2017).

together, the common good of society must be spiritual as well as temporal. As often, Richard Hooker put it best:

> A gross error it is to think that regal power ought to serve for the good of the body and not of the soul, for men's temporal peace and not their eternal safety; as if God had ordained Kings for no other end and purpose but only to fat up men like hogs and to see that they have their mash?[32]

The Reformers often attributed this gross error (so central to modern Western liberalism) to the teachings of Roman Catholicism, with its tendency to demote civil authority and exclude Christian laity from spiritual concerns. To rebut such teaching, one did not even need Scripture; as Peter Martyr Vermigli put it, "the very Philosophers do not so absurdly judge. Aristotle in his *Politics* says, that the office of a Magistrate is, to provide that the people may live well and virtuously. And no greater virtue there is, than Religion."[33]

In other words, the good of the body exists above all for the good of the soul; therefore, good rulers should, as much as in them lies, seek to promote the edification of their citizens' souls, even if they could only do so indirectly. Indeed, the two goals go hand in hand, inasmuch as those with well-formed souls will also be those most likely to materially bless their neighbors. Accordingly, writes Bucer, "the kings of this world ought also to establish and promote the means of making their citizens devout and righteous who rightly acknowledge and worship their God and who are truly helpful toward their neighbors in all their actions."[34] The Reformers' passionate commitment to education lay at the center of this virtuous circle. Godly rulers ought to invest public resources in the education of young people, both so that these might be equipped to better serve their

---

[32] W. Speed Hill, Georges Edelen, and P. G. Stanwood, eds., *The Folger Library Edition of the Works of Richard Hooker*, vols. 1–3, *The Laws of Ecclesiastical Polity* (Cambridge, MA: Belknap Press of Harvard University Press, 1977, 1981), VIII.3.5 (3:352), spelling modernized. Cf. Peter Martyr Vermigli: "neither must Princes have only a care over the bodies of men, and neglect their souls. For we do not imagine that a Prince is a neteherd [cowherd] or swineherd, to whom is committed a care only of the flesh, belly, and skin of his subjects, yea rather he must provide that they may live virtuously and godly." *The common places of the most famous and renowned diuine Doctor Peter Martyr [...]*, trans. and ed. Anthonie Marten, 4 vols. (London: Henry Denham and Henry Middleton, 1583), IV.13.10 (4:231), spelling modernized.

[33] Vermigli, *Common Places*, IV.14.2 (4:246–47), spelling modernized.

[34] Bucer, *De Regno Christi*, 180.

communities, but also because education in basic literacy was necessary to read the Bible. This was one of the best examples of how, according to Reformation political thought, the civil magistrate could use his God-given office to indirectly aid the saving work of the Church. And indeed, Protestant polities across Europe soon boasted the most literate populations in world history, a legacy of the Reformation that continues to bear fruit down to the present day.

Still, while we might be able to get on board with the idea of state-supported literacy education as a way of promoting Christianity, we're likely to have a much harder time with the idea of government-appointed bishops, government-licensed prayer books, and government suppression of unorthodox religious groups. And what about that whole Servetus affair?

There is no space for a full answer to such questions here. Suffice to say that if the Church is to exist as a legal institution within society, it must ultimately fall under the supreme oversight either of the pope or of the king (or Parliament, etc.). The former was no longer an option for the Reformers; *ergo*, inasmuch as the good of the society was at stake, territorial churches should be accountable to the territorial sovereign.[35] Given how deeply religion penetrated everyday life, he could hardly afford to ignore theological or liturgical questions, and given the propensity for religious conflicts to end in violence, he could not simply leave the churches to figure things out on their own. Moreover, if he was indeed, as Melanchthon had said, "the foremost layman in the church," why should he not want to use his supervisory role to promote orthodoxy and right worship? This was never understood, however, as authorizing the civil magistrate to engage in religious persecution. Luther had drawn a firm line against such a confusion of spiritual and temporal tasks at the very outset of his career and, even when the boundaries were sometimes blurred, his followers never lost sight of the basic distinction. But the distinction is still quite different than our contemporary ideas of religious freedom.

Thus, for instance, Johannes Althusius (1563—1638) would write in his *Politica* (1603/1614), "Whoever therefore wishes to have a peaceful realm

---

[35] Indeed, the same Protestant legal principle is operative today in most Western countries, where churches remain juridically accountable to the civil authority, although in general, they are left the freedom to determine their own internal affairs. See further my essay, "We're All Marsilians Now," *Breaking Ground*, October 2, 2020, https://breakingground.us/were-all-marsilians-now/.

should abstain from persecutions. He should not, however, permit the practice of a wicked religion lest what occurred to Solomon may happen to him."[36] To us, these two sentences seem to stand in bald contradiction. To Althusius, however, "persecution" meant something quite specific: using coercive force for the express purpose of making someone change his or her religious beliefs. This was, after all, what the Roman Catholic Church not merely practiced but positively defended, justifying the torture and burning of heretics on the reasoning that it is better to lose the body than lose the soul. Protestants, armed with Luther's two-kingdoms distinction, never countenanced this idea. They did, however, believe that the *overt teaching or practice* of false religion could be restrained and punished, for the sake of others within the society (whether for the sake of their souls, to guard against divine judgment on society, or to prevent civil disorder). In an extreme case, even the death penalty could be applied for this purpose, as in the case of Servetus, although this case is so famous chiefly because it was such a rare exception.

These principles remained operative until well into the eighteenth century; writing in 1757 for the Enlightenment monarch Frederick the Great of Prussia, the Swiss Reformed jurist Emer de Vattel (1714—1767) summarized,

> In religious affairs a citizen has only a right to be free from compulsion, but can by no means claim that of openly doing what he pleases, without regard to the consequences it may produce on society.... If all men are bound to serve God, the entire nation, in her national capacity, is doubtless obliged to serve and honor him. And as this important duty is to be discharged by the nation in whatever manner she judges best,— to the nation it belongs to determine what religion she will follow, and what public worship she thinks proper to establish.[37]

But since the rationale of such religious laws was the preservation of society, the godly magistrate should *not* make such laws if they would do more harm than good. Thus, immediately after saying that a ruler should not permit the practice of a wicked religion, Althusius had continued, "But if he cannot

---

[36] Johannes Althusius, *Politica*, ed. and trans. Frederick S. Carney (Indianapolis: Liberty Fund, 1964), 173.

[37] Emer de Vattel, *The Law of Nations*, ed. Bela Kapossy and Richard Whatmore (Indianapolis: Liberty Fund, 2008), 157.

prohibit it without hazard to the commonwealth, he is to suffer it to exist in order that he not bring ruin to the commonwealth."[38] This grudging concession would be progressively expanded upon over the next two centuries as religious diversity increased in Protestant nations, and their populations became more accustomed to peaceful coexistence. So Vattel would write 150 years later,

> Do but crush the spirit of persecution,—punish severely whoever shall dare to disturb others on account of their creed,—and you will see all sects living in peace in their common country, and ambitious of producing good citizens. Holland and the states of the king of Prussia furnish a proof of this: Calvinists, Lutherans, Catholics, Pietists, Socinians, Jews, all live there in peace, because they are equally protected by the sovereign; and none are punished, but the disturbers of the tranquility of others.[39]

In other words, although within the Reformation era, Protestant principles may have dictated enforced religious conformity, those same principles would dictate greater religious liberty within more mature Protestant societies. Even today, it remains true that the civil magistrate should seek to promote right religion, but up to a point at least, we now deem that this can be accomplished by encouraging independent religious denominations to engage in friendly competition. Certainly this approach helped make nineteenth-century America into one of the most devoutly religious societies in history, although it was also fraught with dangers that have undermined the health of the Church today. In any case, though, the very success of Reformation-era education initiatives helped Protestant societies transcend in some measure the need for the kind of paternalistic government that Reformers like Martin Bucer had advocated. A highly-educated, highly religious population can often be better trusted to advance the common good through its own voluntary activities than through the top-down regulation of the civil magistrate.

---

[38] Althusius, *Politica*, 173.

[39] Vattel, *Law of Nations*, 162.

CONCLUSION

This last observation is a crucial one if we are to make the Reformation doctrine of the civil magistrate relevant today. For the attentive reader—indeed, pretty much any reader!—will surely have noticed by now that the Reformers' political theory was hardly one of libertarian minimalism. Not only was the office of civil magistrate sacred or honorable, but its duties were manifold: to protect against external and internal threats, preserve order, care for the poor, stimulate and regulate the economy, promote education, and even promote right religion and suppress (in some measure) bad religion. With the restraint of an independent church hierarchy removed, what was to keep this newly-empowered civil authority from growing into an unaccountable leviathan state?

Certainly it is true that the Reformers, with their eye on the threats of anarchy, Anabaptism, and papal interference, were more concerned about the civil magistrate being too weak than being too strong. But they were hardly oblivious to the latter threat, and the legacy of Protestant political thought contained within it three powerful antidotes to the rising threat of statism.

First, while in one way declaring the office of the magistrate "sacred," in another way the Reformation profoundly desacralized politics. Luther's two-kingdoms distinction made clear that while the state might indirectly support the work of the Church, it could never be an agent of the Church's work. The firm Protestant stand against outright religious persecution set Protestant polities apart from their Catholic rivals France and Spain, where it was understood to be the king's royal duty to enforce the Catholic faith at sword-point if need be. This fusion of religious and civil horizons reached its apogee in the reign of His Most Christian Majesty Louis XIV, the "Sun-King" of France, who cruelly persecuted the Protestant Huguenots, and believed that the universality of the Roman Catholic Church demanded political expression in a "universal monarchy" under his rule. Louis XIV's France was the closest approximation to Hobbes's "Leviathan," and it provoked a strong reaction in defense of liberty in neighboring England and the Netherlands.

Second, as noted earlier, by rejecting the idea that civil rulers were ultimately accountable to the pope, Protestants paved the way for the growth of representative institutions whereby they could be held accountable to their people. For Richard Hooker, the best realms were those where the people are in no subjection but such as willingly themselves have condescended unto for their own most behoof and security. In Kingdoms therefore of this quality the highest Governor hath indeed universal dominion, but with dependence upon that whole entire body over the several parts whereof he hath dominion.[40]

Such ongoing dependence ensures a limited monarchy. However, says Hooker, in one of his pithier remarks:

> I am not of (the) opinion, that simply always in Kings the most, but the best limited power is best, both for them and the people. The most limited is that which may deal in fewest things, the best that which in dealing is tied unto the soundest, perfectest, and most indifferent rule, which rule is the law.... Happier that people, whose law is their King in the greatest things than that whose King is himself their law.[41]

Hooker thus articulated an ideal in which the civil magistrate rules on behalf of God but in dependence on the consent of his people, given through representatives and formalized in the rule of law; an ideal that was to profoundly shape the evolution of the modern world.

Finally, though the civil magistrate held final sovereignty over all temporal concerns within his territory, this hardly meant that he should personally oversee every aspect of society. Nor did it mean that the structures of everyday life derived their being from the state. Far from it. As the great Johannes Althusius argued, "politics is the art of associating men for the purpose of establishing, cultivating, and conserving social life among them," and this social life takes a rich and diverse institutional form that precedes the state and retains its own integrity. His *Politica* traces the various forms of human association from the family, to the *collegium* (a club, guild, society, or educational institution), to the city and the province, before rising to consider political sovereignty in its fullest form. His point is that the well-ordered society is one in which the various constituent parts exercise as much self-rule as possible, with the civil magistrate serving merely to coordinate their activities toward a shared common good. This principle, which has come to be known as "subsidiarity" and popularized in Catholic Social Teaching over

---

[40] Richard Hooker, *Of the Laws of Ecclesiastical* Polity, VIII.3.2 (FLE 3:341), spelling modernized.

[41] Hooker, *Of the Laws*, VIII.3.2 (FLE 3:341–42), spelling modernized.

the past century, was a core contribution of Protestant Social Teaching long before.

Together, these three principles—the desacralization of politics, the accountability of the magistrate to the rule of law and the consent of the governed, and a decentralized ideal of federalism and subsidiarity—came together in the more conservative strands of the American Founding as a great fruition of Protestant political thought. Despite the profound changes to society since and the dangers inherent in our increasingly centralized and bureaucratized politics, these principles, together with the Reformational vision of the God-given calling of the civil magistrate to protect and advance the common good, remain the best hope and surest guide for the task of Christian citizenship today.

III.

Resistance and Rebellion

GLENN MOOTS

INTRODUCTION

AS THE Reformation took hold throughout Europe, much ink and blood was spilt over the question of what is right to do when what the government is wrong. As a movement that challenged Roman Catholic civil authorities and established Protestant ones, the Reformation prompted many occasions to consider the who, what, when, and why of disobeying, resisting, or replacing civil authorities. Armies were raised and polemics written in this cause. The impact was felt centuries later—even into the American Revolution.

But disobedience and resistance aren't just historical curiosities for Protestants, something that concerns generations past. These ideas are arguably as relevant as ever. Recurring rhetoric about abuse of power, whether in the context of COVID-19 policies, taxation, gun control, or a host of other controversies, should force us to take a step back and think seriously about what Protestantism has to say about disobedience and resistance.

WHAT IS PROTESTANT IN PROTESTANT POLITICAL THOUGHT?

By the time of the Reformation, there was already a long tradition of Christian thinking about politics. Insofar as the Reformers considered themselves to be restoring and conserving Christendom or an existing Christian tradition, they did not presume to reinvent political theology. The intellectual context of Protestant arguments for disobedience, resistance, and revolution therefore owe quite a bit to the preceding Western Christian tradition: John of Salisbury (d. 1180), John Parvus (c. 1360—1411), Thomas Aquinas (1225—1274), and the Conciliarist movement, for example, all took up these questions prior to the Reformation.

Furthermore, all Christian higher education at the time of the Reformation was "humanist," which means the Reformers had deep appreciation for the traditional methods and content of what is now called "Western civilization," including its long tradition of philosophy, jurisprudence, and history. John Calvin's (1509—1564) first scholarly work was on the Roman philosopher Seneca, for example. Peter Martyr Vermigli (1499—1562) wrote a book appreciating and critiquing Aristotle's *Nicomachean Ethics*. It should not surprise us, therefore, to see familiar ideas from history, explicitly or implicitly, in Protestant political thinking. Some Reformers also had formal legal training emphasizing canon or church law rooted in Roman jurisprudence. Protestants therefore freely borrowed from the traditions they inherited, often without attribution. Samuel Rutherford's (1600—1661) *Lex, Rex*, for example, drew from over 700 authors both pagan and Christian.[1]

In deploying relevant ideas for politics, centuries of Reformers did not use a "sacred" versus "secular" dichotomy more familiar to us today. Nor did they feel hostility or suspicion toward natural law or humanist learning, as one finds in modern Protestants like Karl Barth (1886—1968) and Cornelius Van Til (1895—1987). Instead, they considered themselves part of a long intellectual tradition carrying forward many older ideas without hesitation. All Reformers did consider Scripture the most authoritative source they could use, even for politics, but the Reformers were not "fundamentalists" or "biblicists." Likewise, they did not disqualify the use of non-biblical sources by any presumption of "total depravity," a concept that some Calvinists misunderstand (and some non-Calvinists misunderstand with regard to Calvinists). Calvin himself argued that politics and other salutary

---

[1] John Coffey, *Politics, Religion and the British Revolutions: The Mind of Samuel Rutherford* (New York: Cambridge University Press, 1997), 70.

pursuits of earthly life could be rightly informed by human reason and experience.[2]

This essay will take its cues from the Reformers and eschew tracing ideas or influence, who first said what, or who influenced whom. "Protestant" will mean only those ideas articulated by Protestants in a Protestant context: a Protestant author writing to a Protestant audience or in defense of Protestants.

Some of the ideas presented in this chapter were articulated from Scripture or included Scripture proofs, but not always. Some of our authors were theologians, and their ideas presented in a theological context—Calvin's *Institutes*, for example—and this context enables us to also use the term "political theology." We will be careful not to make too much of Scripture being used in argumentation—to consider its use necessarily "theology" however. At the time of the Reformation, and for centuries afterwards, Scripture was deployed by all educated persons. Using it to defend a conclusion gave added authority to any argument, and it was a source most reliably familiar to laypersons. Even Thomas Paine (1737—1809), an infamous deist sharply critical of orthodox confessional believers, deployed Scripture throughout *Common Sense* (1776), the most popular tract of the American Revolution. Sources in this chapter will not be confined to theologians, and we will give consideration even to authors like Hugo Grotius (1583—1645), for example. Though Grotius rejected certain points of confessional Protestantism, he used Scripture and presumed to be writing as a Protestant to a largely Protestant audience.

One last preliminary note is necessary. A lot of suppositions have grown up around Protestant political ideas because of the American Revolution. Given the overwhelmingly Protestant character of early America, including how patriots hearkened back to classical Protestant statements about resistance and revolution, presuming on the significance of Protestantism for American independence is reasonable. However, this chapter does not presume a "Whig history" wherein America, or any other revolution, is necessarily the progressive fruition or fulfillment of Protestant revolutionary ideas. There were faithful Protestants on both sides of the American Revolution, just as there were faithful Protestants on all sides of

---

[2] John Calvin, *Institutes*, 2.2.13. All citations refer to the 1559 edition.

the Wars of the Three Kingdoms (i.e., British Civil Wars). Protestants have disagreed about if and when it is right to resist authority.

RAISING THE STAKES OF CIVIL OBEDIENCE

Many passages of Scripture seem to take a high view of government. David refuses to kill Saul in 1 Samuel 24. Paul tells us to obey the governing authorities in Romans 13, as does Peter in 1 Peter 2:13. Civil disobedience in many forms, including revolution, may therefore appear to take a *low* view of government. After all, if government and its accompanying goods (e.g., the rule of law or social order) are so important, why would anyone disrupt or threaten those benefits? Consider, for example, an ancient text such as Plato's *Crito*. Socrates, convicted and sentenced to death, is offered an escape by his friends. In an imaginary dialogue with the laws of Athens, the laws tell Socrates that he has agreed to obey the laws and that they have provided him with many goods. Anyone who would subvert the laws not only betrays that arrangement but also, in subverting the benefits of political community, becomes an enemy of human flourishing. Even pagans understood the importance of civil authority, therefore, and shouldn't Christians demonstrate more wisdom than pagans?

For a Christian, however, there are goods much higher than earthly goods, even the benefits of social or political stability. This higher view of flourishing is essential to Christian life, and it is reinforced in Protestant catechisms.[3] Such a sentiment is reflected in the popular hymn "A Mighty Fortress is Our God" by Martin Luther, which concludes with this stanza:

> Let goods and kindred go,
> This mortal life also;
> The body they may kill:
> God's truth abideth still,
> His Kingdom is forever.

One might conclude from this verse that there is no mortal good, including allegiance to government or our country, that supersedes our obligations to

---

[3] For example, the first question of the Heidelberg Catechism tells us that we belong, "body and soul, in life and in death," to Jesus Christ. The Westminster Shorter Catechism tells us that our chief "end" (or purpose) is "to glorify God and enjoy him forever."

God and the happiness he intends for his people. After all, Luther himself defied both ecclesiastical and civil authorities to do what is right.

Furthermore, when Luther defined the duties of a Christian, he argued that our duties to God under the "First Table" of the Ten Commandments oblige disobedience to anyone who demands anything contrary to our duties commanded by God. In articulating the duties of a Christian, Luther was explicit that we must disobey unjust commands from not only ecclesiastical authorities but even parents, arguing that "we sin also if we follow and obey, or even tolerate" those who would command us to disobey God.[4] Given this radical vision of life calling people to disobey *any* authority that acted contrary to God, presented at a tumultuous time of political upheaval, it is no coincidence that Protestantism is associated with revolution. Many notable scholars (e.g., Quentin Skinner, Michael Walzer, Francis Oakley, John Witte) have demonstrated how revolutionary ideas proliferated either during, or in the wake of, the Protestant Reformation.

However, in examining Luther's *Treatise on Good Works* further, we find something that might surprise us. Citing Romans 13, Titus 3, and 1 Peter 2:1, Luther also urges *submission* to authority, especially civil authorities. Not only should we not deceive or be disloyal to civil authorities, Luther says we also shouldn't even curse them or grumble against them in secret. Heinrich Bullinger (1504—1575) and other Reformed Protestants agreed with such strict proscriptions.[5] Not even the harm civil authorities can do to us should drive us to chafe against their rules if those rules aren't unjust. A malicious ruler cannot, after all, harm the soul but only the body and property. If protecting our body and property motivates us to sin by disobeying authority when we ought not to, we harm our souls; and Luther argues that our greater concern should be for the soul. Such warnings should undermine any hasty interpretation of Luther's hymn. So long as the civil magistrate does not presume ecclesiastical or spiritual power, Luther says, we should even be prepared to suffer wrong at his hands. Suffering wrong might even do us

---

[4] Martin Luther, *A Treatise on Good Works* (1520), https://www.gutenberg.org/files/418/418-h/418-h.htm.

[5] Heinrich Bullinger, *The Decades of Henry Bullinger*, ed. Thomas Harding for the Parker Society, 1849–52, 2 vols., reprint, with new introductions by George Ella and Joel R. Beeke, Parker Society Edition (Grand Rapids: Reformation Heritage Books, 2004), II.v, 280; II.vi, 311.

good, he argues, because such suffering can be good for our souls. It certainly is better, from a spiritual perspective, to suffer evil than to commit it.

Luther is so insistent on civil obedience that in his *Larger Catechism* he goes so far as to call the civil ruler a father over many people—equating the civil ruler with parents whom the Decalogue commands us to obey. Those who complain against a bad ruler, Luther says, are often selfish; and God uses bad rulers to punish such vice. When we resist them as God's instrument, we suffer many unpleasant consequences.[6] So whereas pagan societies emphasized civil obedience out of a sense of reciprocity, usefulness, or reverence for tradition or ancestors, Protestant Christians raised the stakes. They emphasized that obedience was a Christian duty under the Ten Commandments.

But if we do not resist sinful rulers, then who will punish them? Luther says that God will punish them. This does not mean that we shouldn't care about our rulers, however; they must still be held to the highest standards for their political and personal moral conduct. The New England Puritans, for example, set high expectations for civil rulers in regular "election" sermons preached to rulers and laypeople. If ministers are called to resemble Old Testament prophets and warn political leaders (and citizens) about God's judgment if they do not conform to the highest biblical standards, that constitutes a very *high* view of government and not a low one at all.

Other Reformers besides Luther drew from the fifth commandment ("honor your father and mother") to prescribe civil obedience. In doing so, they continued the example of medieval Catholic theologians Bonaventure (1221—1274) and Thomas Aquinas. William Tyndale (1494—1536), for example, takes up the question of civil obedience by first asking about the duties of children to their elders, then the duties of wives and servants. He devotes considerable attention to the blessing and benefit enabled by civil rulers, yoking them together with "mother, master, husband" and comparing the duties of a father to the duties of a magistrate.[7] He even goes so far as to write, "Though he be the greatest tyrant in the world, yet is he unto thee a great benefit of God and a thing wherefore thou oughtest to thank God

---

[6] Martin Luther, *Larger Catechism* (1529), https://bookofconcord.org/large-catechism/part-i/commandment-iv/.

[7] William Tyndale, *The Obedience of a Christian Man*, ed. David Daniell (New York: Penguin Books, 2000), 37.

highly."[8] Likewise, Calvin's exposition of the fifth commandment was applied to rulers as readily as parents.[9]

WHEN TO RESIST? HISTORICAL CIRCUMSTANCES AND CONTEMPORARY APPLICATIONS

This call to obedience is an essential starting point, but to go further we need to revisit the context of the Reformation. Understanding the context in which Protestants formulated their political ideas is essential, though this shouldn't "historicize" them, however. We don't want to make the ideas of the earliest Protestants seem antiquated or anachronistic because their context is several centuries old. Rather, the historical context of the sixteenth century helps us understand how Protestant Social Teaching departed from Roman Catholic precedent, what new challenges it created, and how we might think about them today. Also, by investigating historical circumstances, in the context of ideas about civil *obedience*, we can better understand and apply ideas about civil *disobedience*.

First, Protestants rejected altogether the spiritual authority of the pope and Roman Catholic hierarchy. Because Protestants valued authority, and understood it to be established by God, this rejection of a centralized *ecclesiastical* authority necessitated greater emphasis on *civil* authority—especially given that coherent denominational structures were slow in developing and the concept of an independent congregation-governed church would not be accepted by any Protestants until the seventeenth century. In other words, the idea of churches independent of civil authority was not popular with anyone. Everyone expected civil authorities to take an interest in the Church, and Protestants expected them to take an interest in church reform. This became what is called "Magisterial Protestantism."

Protestant countries all had some form of what we would (anachronistically) now call "state churches." It took a long time even for Protestants in colonial America to approve independent self-governing churches not supported or protected by civil authorities. Early Protestants therefore had to figure out how to make formerly Roman Catholic ecclesiastical structures Protestant while cooperating with civil authorities for

---

[8] Tyndale, *Obedience of a Christian Man*, 41.
[9] Calvin, *Institutes*, 2.8.35. Calvin makes similar applications in his *Commentaries on the Last Four Books of Moses* (1563).

legal and financial support. To undermine civil authorities, or even appear to, would be to leave churches without support and protection. Furthermore, religious quarrels, even if not directed at the magistrate, caused civil disturbances that concerned civil authorities.

Just because most Protestant countries no longer have state churches, however, we shouldn't treat civil authority any more lightly than the Reformers did. Civil authority's divine institution is clearly stated in Scripture, and the Reformers' association of civil obedience with the fifth commandment is important. Though churches no longer rely on the civil government for direct financial support, lawmakers and enforcers are no less essential for enabling Christians to practice their faith peaceably. What's more, it is also as true now as it was then that antagonistic religious opinions, where spiritual matters are not at stake, can prompt antagonism from our neighbors. In democratic forms of government, now accentuated by democratic vehicles for self-expression and debate such as social media, offending one's neighbor is arguably equivalent to offending those in charge and will most certainly result in civil strife.

We must offend where God's Word obliges us to offend, especially given Jesus's words in Luke 12:51. But we should not offend our neighbor unnecessarily, nor should we take a low view of political community and concord. Protestants have typically had a high view of civic life. It is not merely a necessary evil. We should therefore examine ourselves closely with prayer and study before disobeying or railing against civil authorities, including our neighbors, or causing civil strife.

English Bishop John Ponet (1514—1556) said as much in 1556 when considering whether or not to act against a tyrant: "It is the matter that will accuse thee, and defend thee: acquit thee, and condemn thee: when you shall come before the throne of the highest and everlasting power, where no temporal power will appear for thee, to make answer or to defend thee: but you yourself must answer for yourself, and for whatever you have done."[10] We must remember that if we are going to challenge God's appointed authority, it should be on grounds that God himself would approve.

---

[10] John Ponet, *A Short Treatise on Political Power, and of the true obedience which subjects our to kings and other civil governors, with an Exhortation to all true and natural English men* (1556), Chapter 4, https://constitution.org/1-Constitution/cmt/ponet/polpower.htm#chap4.

Another important point of context for the Reformers is that they were quick to distance themselves from radical groups (e.g., Anabaptists in the sixteenth century, and Quakers in the seventeenth century) who sometimes engaged in disruptive and violent civil conduct. Anabaptists, for example, thought that as a community of believers they were separate from the secular world, and therefore could not and should not be subjected to its rules and obligations.[11] Though neither of those groups is politically disruptive today, the lesson for Protestants remains: association with radical groups, in the service of questionable protests against authority, can undermine a righteous cause and tempt sinful conduct.

There was an additional motivation for supporting civil authorities during the Reformation: Rome excommunicated some Protestant leaders and thereby declared them open season for Roman Catholic revolutionaries. In 1570, the papacy excommunicated Elizabeth I, for example, in the hope of restoring a Catholic monarch. Protestants did not want to imitate the papacy and presume to assert authority over civil rulers. To avoid any similar contest between ecclesiastical and civil authority, they articulated a coherent "Two Kingdoms" doctrine.[12]

All of that said, it wouldn't be correct to call Two Kingdoms doctrine "separation of Church and state," especially a modern American judicial interpretation of that phrase.[13] Though Protestants disagreed on the particulars, they were generally in agreement that spiritual affairs should be more independent of politics than they were under Roman Catholic authorities. Conversely, spiritual leaders were often restrained from asserting secular authority. In Puritan New England, for example, clergy did not hold civil office as they did in Anglican Britain. Most Protestants were wary of having civil authority appear subordinate to the Church, or vice versa.

Despite all of these caveats, Protestants social teaching is emphatic that *our duty to God is higher than our duty to any other authority*. That is, after all, why Luther or Zwingli were willing to disobey Rome: it commanded duties

---

[11] See the Anabaptist Schleitheim Confession, for example.

[12] For an excellent introduction to the much misunderstood doctrine of the "Two Kingdoms" see W. Bradford Littlejohn, *The Two Kingdoms: A Guide for the Perplexed* (Landrum, SC: 2017).

[13] For the complications concerning this, see, for example, Daniel Dreisbach, *Thomas Jefferson and the Wall of Separation between Church and State* (New York: New York University Press, 2002).

contrary to Scripture, just like (in Luther's example) bad parents commanding children to do ungodly things. If civil authorities did likewise, they tempted righteous disobedience as well. Luther said that any ruler presuming to govern matters of faith becomes a tyrant. He called those authorities who confiscated New Testaments from the people, for example, "tyrants."[14] He added that "where secular authority takes it upon itself to legislate for the soul, it trespasses on… God's government, and merely seduces and ruins souls."[15] Even the Protestant church that gave the most religious authority to civil magistrates, the Church of England, denied to its civil rulers "the ministering either of God's word or of sacraments" in its Thirty-Nine Articles.[16]

Protestants have all agreed that the Church alone has authority over the soul. And though it is true that boisterous heretics or heterodox persons were pursued by civil authorities in the first two centuries of Protestantism, the state was never presumed to be working under the authority of the Church (as if the Church were sovereign over it) nor was the state presumed to have authority over souls. Civil action against heresy was usually understood to be only for preserving civil peace or concord while protecting (rather than administering, directing, or evangelizing for) the Church. Though the question of the conscience for the Reformers, especially in a political context, can be complicated and confusing—even appearing to be contradictory—the conscience was still assumed to be dissuaded rather than forced.

REBELLING AS A CHRISTIAN

If there are therefore biblical grounds for resisting authority, as Reformers like Luther claimed, how does one keep such a potentially dangerous idea from being deployed recklessly? Protestant political thinkers offered some solutions to blunt such a danger. One way is to prioritize legal justifications in addressing the "why?" of disobedience or resistance. Closely related to this is the "who?" Protestants have preferred to take the responsibility for

---

[14] Martin Luther, *On Secular Authority: How Far Does the Obedience Owed to It Extend?* in *Luther and Calvin on Secular Authority*, ed. Harro Hopfl (New York: Cambridge University Press, 1991), 29.

[15] Luther, *On Secular Authority*, 23.

[16] Articles of Religion (39 Articles), Article 37, http://www.eskimo.com/~lhowell/bcp1662/articles/articles.html.

resistance out of the hands of individuals, if possible, and assign it to other civil authorities. This inhibits every person's judgment of his own conscience from becoming a potential catalyst for political upheaval.

Ideally, a political leader opposes another on behalf of the people or God. As we will see later in the chapter, this does not mean that civil authority is merely a servant of the people. Rather, God is the chief authority over civil rulers, though he may covenant with both the people and the ruler. Nor is the magistrate necessarily preserving the "rights" of the people. Though the Reformers did express concern for the rights of citizens, Protestant social thought does not often fit neatly with liberalism and its concern for "rights." A Protestant understanding of rights would be more traditional, rooted in the rule of law. *Natural* rights and liberties, though important, would likely be subordinated by Protestantism to *civil* rights and liberties: those afforded by particular polities and their laws, not abstractions now popular in modern American or European political reasoning, for example. Using the vernacular of the first few centuries of Protestantism, it would be better to talk about the "common weal" or common good of the people, or the rule of law, and the rights and duties associated with them than it would be to talk about individual rights in any abstract sense.

Since a magistrate defending the people would probably be opposing another magistrate with greater authority, power, or sovereignty, such resistance came to be called the "doctrine of the lesser magistrate." These lesser magistrates would also serve as mediating authorities. Today in America, for example, a governor or state legislature might oppose federal authorities, or a sheriff might refuse to enforce a state law.

Another way to approach this idea of magistrates acting on behalf of the people is to consider the doctrine of vocation or "calling," a theological and social idea exposited by both Luther and William Perkins. Not everyone is *called* to lead an action against bad rulers, especially if one is not already in a position of authority. Only rulers, those God has installed with civil authority per Romans 13, can safely be said to have a charge to punish wickedness; tyranny is, after all, no different from other forms of wickedness.[17] When Calvin refers to the possibility of God sending "avengers" of the oppressed, he says that while those avengers could be

---

[17] Luther, "Admonition to Peace: A Reply to the Twelve Articles of the Peasants in Swabia," in *Luther: Selected Political Writings*, ed. J. M. Porter (Philadelphia, PA: Fortress Press, 1974), 72. See also, "Whether Soldiers, Too, Can Be Saved."

foreign princes, they should also be domestic magistrates whom Calvin says have a duty to check kings taking license with their power.[18] Those who do not exercise their authority to guard the liberty of the people, Calvin argued, are traitors.[19]

However, both magistrates and the people are also reminded that all civil action—especially rebellion—has to be approached using prudence. If one replaces a bad ruler only to then find himself under the authority of a worse one, or in a state of anarchy, or subject to the terrors of civil war, one has made matters worse. Tyndale argues that a passive and effeminate ruler who doesn't punish evil at all is worse than a tyrant who imperfectly punishes evil.[20] Luther likewise cautioned against substituting a war for a tyrant, especially when there is no guarantee of a better replacement.[21] Prudence in such cases is not just a question of self-interest or expediency, however. There is a moral dilemma at work: if in the quest for relief or even righteous justice, the circumstance of others is made worse, we tempt sin through that harm.[22]

Another way of slowing down hasty disobedience was to emphasize the Lord's secret purposes in visiting his people with suffering. While one should resist anyone who forces us to sin, tyranny may be an occasion to discern sin among those oppressed (rather than just among the leaders). Calvin, for example, argued that tyranny is chastisement.[23] For example, God may be chastening his people for vices like pride or spiritual declension. If so, then relief should come first through repentance rather than rebellion. Calvin went so far as to argue that even if people are tormented, robbed, persecuted, or neglected, they should try to remain obedient and instead look to God for deliverance.[24] In other words, the same justified concern for one's soul that

---

[18] Calvin, *Institutes*, 4.20, 30, 31.

[19] Calvin, *Institutes*, 4.20.8.

[20] Tyndale, *Obedience*, 41–42. *Effeminate* here would mean a ruler lacking in courage or resolve, especially when it comes to punishing lawbreakers.

[21] Luther, "Whether Soldiers, Too, Can Be Saved," in *Luther: Selected Political Writings*, 109.

[22] This emphasis on prudence demonstrates the long influence of the classical world, carried forward in the Catholic precedent of Aquinas. R. W. Dyson, ed., *Aquinas: Political Writings* (Cambridge, UK: Cambridge University Press, 2000), 250.

[23] For example, see Calvin, *Institutes*, 4.20.29.

[24] Calvin, *Institutes*, 4.20.29.

would prompt rebellion should just as readily prompt reflection on God's Word and confession of sin. God may even bless the sufferer, Luther argued.[25]

To borrow the words of a famous American revolutionary, then, do we have a *right* or do we have a *duty* to disobey or resist a ruler? *May* we resist, or *must* we resist? Are we to (again, recalling Thomas Jefferson's Declaration of Independence) "suffer while evils are sufferable?" For the individual believer, at least, there is no question about spiritual tyranny: we must disobey it. But whether the believer *may* or *must* do more than disobey a spiritual tyrant remains in doubt. Some Reformers such as John Knox, Christopher Goodman, and John Ponet were read by scholar Quentin Skinner to say that resistance is a duty.[26] If one reads Ponet carefully, however, one doesn't find this to be the case at all. Ponet does emphatically condemn those who refuse to *disobey* spiritual tyranny because it will result in the loss of one's soul in disobeying God. But he explicitly says, "There is no express positive law for punishment of a tyrant among Christian men."[27] In other words, while there is a *duty* to disobey a spiritual tyrant, there is only a lawful *right* to rebel against him. That right may or may not be exercised, as prudence dictates, even to the point of tyrannicide.

REBELLING AS A CITIZEN

So much for spiritual tyranny, at least, but what about other kinds of tyranny? Tyrants willing to usurp unjust authority over the soul are likely willing to abuse power over body and property as well. Per Two Kingdoms theology, the Christian isn't just a spirit but remains a citizen endowed by God's providence with life and goods. Under Two Kingdoms theology, and its high view of political society, Protestants have a view of tyranny not confined merely to the soul.

First, concerning the doctrine of the lesser magistrate, a lesser magistrate should ask if a higher authority neglected a constitutional duty to the common good generally. Such legal ground would not be confined to

---

[25] Luther, *On Secular Authority*, 29.

[26] Skinner reads them to argue that those who fail to resist tyrants would be damned. Quentin Skinner, *The Foundations of Modern Political Thought*, vol. 2, *The Age of Reformation* (Cambridge: Cambridge University Press, 1978), 234–37.

[27] Ponet, *Short Treatise*, Ch. 6.

spiritual abuses but could concern life or property generally. Calvin, for example, explicitly cited Greek, Roman, or medieval precedent.[28] Calvin's citation was not just bolstering a point with historical or legal erudition. Greek or Roman authors would not have shared Christian concerns about one's soul or conscience before God. Their concerns included harm to life, property, or the rule of law. Hence, Calvin's citation of them in support of interposition implicitly recognizes those broader common categories of tyranny and abuse of power that any reasonable society could recognize.[29]

Second, moving from the rights and duties of magistrates, citizens have a right to self-defense under the law. While one cannot oppose a legitimate magistrate, one can oppose a magistrate who through abuse of power abdicates his legal and moral authority *de facto*, if not *de jure*. Such an abdicating ruler then becomes an equal or peer of the citizen, no different than an outlaw: literally someone who acts outside the law. Here we can look to Hugo Grotius, a Protestant founder of international law. Fighting a tyrant is not rebellion because a tyrant loses legitimate authority when he becomes an enemy of his own nation. Such hostile action is no different than if he abdicated or handed over power to someone holding no legal right or claim.[30] Protestant legal theorist Samuel Pufendorf (1632—1694) made a similar argument but confined it to a ruler's inaction to protect the people against domestic or foreign enemies. Such neglectful rulers, Pufendorf argued, "plainly abdicated the government."[31] Another Protestant founder of international law, Emer de Vattel (1714—1767), made a similar case in arguing that political sovereignty is for the sake of the people's good and not their ruin. Sovereigns who act against the public good become public enemies.[32]

---

[28] Calvin, *Institutes*, 4.20.8.

[29] Recall the depth of learning concerning legal authority and jurisdiction. One finds the most elaborate and impressive constitutional scheme articulated by a Protestant author in Johann Althusius's *Politica*, demonstrating the level of political sophistication that existed among Protestant intellectuals and statesmen (Althusius was both).

[30] Hugo Grotius, *The Rights of War and Peace* (1625), 1.4.4.9–11.

[31] Samuel Pufendorf, *Of the Law of Nature and Nations* (1672), 7.8.4.

[32] Threats against the public good include violations of natural law, unjust threats against life, or anything essential for life. Emer de Vattel, *The Law of Nations* (1758), 1.4.51, 54. Citing the arguments of these three prominent legal theorists is important not because they used theological/biblical arguments but because their positions

Nevertheless, violent resistance remains a judgment call. For example, we know that Scottish reformer John Knox (1514—1572) approached both John Calvin and Heinrich Bullinger—arguably the most important Reformers on the continent at that time—for approval of armed resistance by Protestant nobles against Catholic rulers. Given the status of the nobles as "lesser magistrates" and the abuse of spiritual power by Catholic rulers who had persecuted and martyred Protestants, one might have expected enthusiastic approval. However, both Bullinger and Calvin gave tepid and cautious replies to Knox.[33] Was it because they didn't think Knox met an appropriate threshold for spiritual or legal tyranny that justified resistance (rather than merely disobedience)? Did they think that Knox lacked constitutional grounds? Or was this simply a judgment of prudence based on circumstances? They didn't say.

An additional consideration that parallels this idea of constitutional violation or abdication can be found in the Reformed Protestant idea of politics built on covenants. The *Vindiciae, Contra Tyrannos* (1579) was the first extensive expression of this idea, though it is implied in other Reformed political theology as well.[34]

Covenantal politics can be interpreted as providing both a mechanism and a sanction. As a mechanism, covenants suggest that polities gain their legitimacy from a solemn and enforceable agreement made between parties. As a sanction, the covenant enforces penalties on those who violate such agreements.[35] In politics with a covenantal framework, there is a double

---

succinctly reflect (and distill to great effect) a longstanding legal tradition favored by Protestant political theologians and statesmen.

[33] Jane Dawson, *John Knox* (New Haven, CT: Yale University Press, 2015), 86. Calvin likewise discouraged acts of rebellion by others in almost every other case—including some by Huguenots threatened with persecution. His only exception appears to be a rebellion with clear constitutional authority. See John Calvin, *Homilies on the First Book of Samuel*, in *Opera Omnia*, ed. G. Baum et al., 29:552; "To the Admiral De Coligny," April 16, 1561, DLXXXVIII, 175–76.

[34] Another excellent example is Johannes Althusius's *Politica* (1614), which does does not confine a covenantal structure to Christian polities and elaborates on the idea of "federal" government—federal being a word derived from the Latin word for "covenant."

[35] It is important not to confuse the idea of covenanting with social contract theory—as one finds in John Locke, for example. None of the early Reformers could be called social contractarians because none believed that government was formed, or

covenant. The first is between the ruler and the people, holding rulers accountable to the citizens (or their representatives such as the lesser magistrates) and vice versa. The second covenant exists between God, the ruler, and the people. This obliges both ruler and citizen to maintain moral standards within the polity, most of all not to transgress God's law. A polity that violates God's law, whether the law is violated by the people or the ruler, tempts moral sanction from God. This can therefore be a criteria for action by the people or their representatives to avoid such moral sanction. It can also add a legal dimension. The tyrant becomes a "covenant breaker" for breaking his agreement with the people, and thus their right to disobey or resist him becomes enforceable.

ROMANS 13

But what about Romans 13:1–7? Isn't talk of disobedience and resistance made moot by Paul's command to obey the governing authorities? Protestant advocates of disobedience and revolution have always anticipated the objection. Ponet, for example, characterized his opponents to say, "Such a one (they say) must be obeyed in all things, not may speak against his proceedings, for he that resists the power, resists the ordinance of God, and he that resists, purchases for himself damnation." Ponet then replies sharply, "Thus they go about to blind men's eyes to confirm and increase their devilish kingdom."[36] In other words, interpreting this passage as a command to unconditional obedience is a smokescreen used by tyrants.

If, as Protestant Social Teaching argues consistently, disobedience to spiritual tyranny is obliged by God, then this must mean that Paul's command that we obey is necessarily conditional. Calvin concluded as much, arguing that our obligation to political rulers is but a species of the genus, the genus being our obligation to God. Our obligation to rulers is likewise just a subset of our obligation to God. The command of God binds the conscience unconditionally and defines the scope of all subordinate obedience.[37] Samuel Rutherford likewise argued that civil subjection was conditional: "It is evident from Rom xiii. that all subjection and obedience to higher powers

---

authority granted, simply by agreement of the people. Nor could the people dissolve the government except under exceptional circumstances.

[36] Ponet, *Short Treatise*, Ch. 4.

[37] Calvin, *Institutes*, 3.19.15; 4.10.3, 5.

commanded there, is subjection to the power and office of the magistrate in abstracto, or, which is all one, to the person using the power lawfully, and that no subjection is due by that text, or any word of God, to the abused and tyrannical power of the king."[38] If tyranny is the work of the devil, and lawless, as Rutherford and other Protestants argue, then it cannot command unconditional obedience. Resisting tyranny is therefore resisting Satan while being obedient to God.

All of that said, however, tyranny of any kind should drive Christians first to self-examination, prayer, and repentance. God's ultimate purposes remain part of his inscrutable wisdom (Isa. 55, Rom. 11), and we are still endowed by reason and blessed with the Word of God to discern God's reason and Scripture, must carefully be brought to bear on and enlighten any decision to disobey or resist political authority.

---

[38] Samuel Rutherford, *Lex, Rex, or The Law and the Prince* (Harrisonburg: Sprinkle Publications, 1982 [1644]), 144.

IV.

Just War

MARC LIVECCHE

ON A cold, gray, January day in Poland in 1995, I attended ceremonies marking the fiftieth anniversary of the liberation of Auschwitz-Birkenau, the former Nazi concentration camp in the southern Polish town of Oświęcim. Following the formal observance, the names of all the dead began to be read over loudspeaker; one, by one, by one. I toured the camp for several hours and, all the while, the names continued. When I departed, heading toward town on foot along the hated rail line until it bent away, I could still hear the names—name after name after name—as they faded into the growing distance. Later that evening, sitting soul-worn in a village pub, I worked out how long that recitation must have continued. Imagining we had the names of all the estimated 1.2 million people murdered at Auschwitz, and supposing that it took a single second to read each name, it would have taken 13.8 days to read the names entirely. Two weeks, without pause, of an unbroken litany of stolen lives.

As a military ethicist and a Christian, I am sometimes asked, given both the dominical prescriptions of neighbor love and the implications of divine love that ground human dignity, how I can sanction killing someone made in the *imago Dei*. On these occasions, I admit that I never would. Not unless the real question is, "What am I supposed to do when one *imago Dei* is kicking apart the face of another *imago Dei*—without justification—and he won't stop?" I do know that I am supposed to love both my victim-neighbor as well as his aggressor—let us call him my enemy-neighbor. I also know it's insufficient to say that I love the victim-neighbor *now*, and the enemy-neighbor later. But it's also clear that I cannot love both of them in precisely the same way in precisely the same moment. But I am to love them.

From her earliest days to the present times, such conundrums always burdened the Christian church. Happily, also from her earliest days, the Church has never been without answers. Although its roots are grounded in the wisdom of ancient Greco-Roman and Hebraic thought, it was from within a predominantly Christian civilization—one that operated within a Christian, sometimes theological, cultural framework—that the just war tradition first took its characteristic shape. Speaking to the confusion surrounding morality, ethics, and the use of force in his own day, Thomas Aquinas (1225—1274) wrote, "For a war to be just, three things are necessary": sovereign authority, just cause, and right intention.[1] These terms correspond directly to what Augustine earlier identified as the three goods of the political community: order, justice, and peace. Just war historian James Turner Johnson makes much of this, observing that the tradition is set within a larger moral framework of good politics oriented to a just and peaceful order in which "the use of armed force is a necessary tool to be used by responsible political authority to protect that just and peaceful order in a world in which serious threats are not only possible but actual."[2] The just war tradition serves as a way to prevent a fourteenth day of names.

The particular stream of just war thought to be elucidated here traces back at least to the Christian realist headwaters of Augustine of Hippo (354–430). This is directly consequent to the neighbor-love conundrum regarding the tension between killing and Christian love. To ground the just war moral framework in Augustinian soil is to assert that there is no necessary disharmony between the requirements of Christian love and killing a man. This grim compatibility between love and war, and the corresponding affirmation that a Christian soul can be both loving and martial, is, Augustine insisted, necessary if one is to respond appropriately—both *faithfully* and *responsibly*—to the conditions of the world. Contrary to the platitude that love conquers war, and to its cynical converse that all is fair in love and war, the

---

[1] Thomas Aquinas, *Summa Theologiæ*, II-II, q. 40, a.1.

[2] James Turner Johnson, *The War to Oust Saddam Hussein: Just War and the New Face of Conflict*, 1st ed. (Lanham, MD: Rowman & Littlefield Publishers, 2005), 36.

Augustinian just warrior, recognizing basic distinctions between an external action and internal intent—which in turn support other distinctions between killing and murder, justice and vengeance, and the like—sees no necessary contradiction between a Christian engaging in warfare and loving the enemy you war against. For the Augustinian, as when a parent disciplines a disobedient child with a "benevolent harshness," one can resolutely punish an enemy that deserves to be punished while having the enemy's good in mind and with a manifest regret that the punishment is required.[3]

Just war's Christian underpinnings grew out of Augustine's maturing theory of politics first outlined in *The City of God*, which characterized the good society as one embodying a just order and, therefore, enjoying peaceful relations—both internally among its own people and externally with similarly fashioned societies.[4] That said, important as his early role was, the popular casting of Augustine as the father of just war tradition is something of an overstatement. Besides the tradition's ideas already being in—albeit prenatal—circulation in the classical Greco-Roman thought of thinkers such as Aristotle and Cicero, Augustine offered no organized treatment of his own. Rather, his numerous contributions to just war thinking were scattered through a number of works whose primary focus lay elsewhere. The forging of an organized, consolidated conception of just war would be the achievement of a later era.[5]

Beginning around the middle of the twelfth century, this more systematic framework began to emerge with the *Decretum* by the Bolognese canon lawyer Gratian (359—383). This systematization took theological form in Thomas Aquinas (1225–74). Significantly, in the *Summa Theologiae* Thomas followed Augustine's emphasis on love by placing his own discussion of just war in the midst of his wider treatment of *caritas*, or charity.[6] Later in the

---

[3] Augustine, "Letter 138 (to Marcellinus)," in *Political Writings*, ed. E. Margaret Atkins and Robert Dodaro (Cambridge: Cambridge University Press, 2001).

[4] Augustine, *The City of God*, trans. Henry Bettenson (London; New York: Penguin Books, 2003), Bk. XIX, esp. chs. 13–17.

[5] Johnson, *War to Oust Saddam Hussein*, 16.

[6] Aquinas, *Summa Theologiæ*, II–II, q. 40. Thomas might have taken his cue from the Apostle Paul. In his Epistle to the Romans, Chapter 12, verse 9, Paul implores the Christian to "love without hypocrisy," and in the verses immediatly following he explains what this means. Later, in Chapter 13, verse 10, he again directly picks up the theme with his proclamation that "Love does no wrong to the neighbor." In between, he discusses human government and affirms that God has ordained

Middle Ages, particularly during the Hundred Years War, this "canonical and theological conception of just war was further elaborated by incorporation of ideas, customs, and practices from the chivalric code and the experience of war."[7]

It was into this growing tradition that the great Protestant Reformers made their own contributions while standing in general continuity with the heritage that had come before. Martin Luther (1483–1546) and John Calvin (1509–1564), the towering figures of the Magisterial Reformation, stand also as the most significant early Protestant thinkers on war.

While Martin Luther departed from certain traditional tenets of just war tradition, he improved the tradition in other ways. Regarding the former, Luther, ever bombastic, tended "to dispense with traditional subtleties and distinctions," thereby giving an account of war marked in some ways by considerably less nuance than earlier writers.[8] Before looking at this directly, we should note that the vigor of Luther's assertions about war rests in the favor with which he viewed the magistrate's calling. Setting the stage in "On Temporal Authority," Luther insists the civil law—and the force with which the magistrate administers it—are in the world by God's will and decree. Following Paul, Luther averred that law and the magistrate's sword pose no threat to the righteous—who, guided by the Word of God through the Holy Spirit, do not need civil law to be moral. But law—and law enforcement—serve as necessary goads to the unrighteous, who, comprising an admittedly large percentage of mankind, require coercion to goad them into right behavior. This division of human beings in turn signals Luther's famous bifurcation of human governance:

> God has ordained two governments: the spiritual, by which the Holy Spirit produces Christians and righteous people under Christ; and the temporal, which restrains the un-Christian and wicked so that—no thanks to them—they are obliged to keep still and to maintain an outward peace.[9]

---

government to use "the sword" to curb wrongdoing. Here, as in Aquinas's *Summa Theologiae*, deliberation on the use of force occurs in the midst of a discussion of love.

[7] Johnson, "Just War, As It Was and Is," 14.

[8] David D. Corey and J. Daryl Charles, *The Just War Tradition: An Introduction* (Wilmington, DE: ISI Books, 2014), 100–101.

[9] Martin Luther, "On Temporal Authority," in *Martin Luther's Basic Theological Writings*, ed. Timothy Lull (Minneapolis: Fortress Press, 1989), 665.

For Luther, this two kingdoms distinction offers a resolution to the question about neighbor-love and war identified above. This is because in order for the law and the sword to function as they ought, it is incumbent upon Christians to set an example by obeying the temporal authorities as an act of charity.

> Because a true Christian, while he is on the earth, lives for and serves his neighbor and not himself, he does things that are of no benefit to himself, but of which his neighbor stands in need…Now, the Sword is indispensable for the whole world, to preserve peace, punish sin, and restrain the wicked. And therefore, Christians readily submit themselves to be governed by the Sword.… All this even though Christians do not need it for themselves, but they attend to what others need.[10]

This charitable obligation runs deep. With the love-war conundrum in view, it may mean that the Christian is called upon by the secular authority to commit a deed that is ostensibly sinful—such as killing an enemy in war. However, it not the "Christian qua Christian who is called upon but the Christian qua obedient subject of the temporal powers."[11] In Luther's view, the Christian does what ought never to be done as a work of love to his assailed neighbor.

How this is a work of love is seen in Luther's stark image of a world without strong ruling authorities. He asks us to imagine herding together wolves, lions, eagles, and sheep into a single pen, letting them mix freely, and bidding them to feed and live peaceably. In such a scenario, goodwill and the gospel alone would be insufficient. Without enforced security, the strong would simply prey upon the weak. For these reasons, Christians should seek to serve in governing authority if they have the necessary skills, whether as court official, judge, or even hangman.[12]

At the heart of it all is Luther's concern for order. In *Whether Soldiers, Too, Can Be Saved*, Luther expounds on questions of rebellion, sedition, and disobedience. With the ghastly Peasants' Revolt in view, Luther offered plain talk on the importance of submission to authority—even tyrannical ones. Subjects cannot exist, in the same moment, in conditions of "obedience" and

---

[10] Luther, "On Temporal Authority."
[11] Corey and Charles, *The Just War Tradition*, 89–90.
[12] Lull, *Basic Theological Writings*.

"resistance." Subjects cannot at the same time be judges of their government.[13] Even when a ruler proved tyrannical, a single tyrant was preferable to the "rule of many tyrants."[14] This fear of anarchy remains cogent to this day. Nevertheless, Luther would, over time, develop a deeper and more subtle position on resistance to government. Indeed, this can be seen in nascent form in Luther's allowance that, on certain very narrow occasions, Christian soldiers can disobey a ruler's command to fight. This could only be done when it became clear that obeying a ruler would result in clear disobedience to God. "If you know for *sure* that [your ruler] is wrong, then you should fear God rather than men, and you should neither fight nor serve," Luther instructed. However, in cases in which you cannot know whether the ruler is wrong, then "you ought not to weaken certain obedience for the sake of an uncertain justice."[15]

Where Luther broke with the just war tradition up to that point includes his view of what justified war in the first place. Whereas just war's traditional three just causes—protection of the innocent, requiting injustice, and punishing evil—offered defensive, restitutive, and retributive motivations, Luther allowed for only defense against an outside attack (with the one exception that God could directly command war for other reasons). One upshot is that it is harder, in the Lutheran view, to justify one nation coming to the assistance of another in order to repel an attack. A second is that Luther was among the first major Christian thinkers on war to clearly condemn holy war. In *On War against the Turk*, for instance, Luther stresses that Christians qua Christians are to fight against the devil—or the infidel—with prayer, not the sword. So while Luther's comparatively thin doctrine of just cause omits many situations in which the tradition allows for force, his corrective position against holy war would become the standard.

Luther's second major break with the tradition is his more permissive view of appropriate tactics. Soldiers, Luther warned, are "not playing games." They are not to be quick to draw their sword, but, when they do—beware! Couple this with his lack of any reference to love for the enemy and one finds little in Luther of any restrictions on *how* one fights once the threshold to war has been crossed. Soldiers were "to kill enemies without scruple, to rob and

---

[13] Corey and Charles, *The Just War Tradition*, 99.
[14] Martin Luther, "Whether Soldiers, Too, Can Be Saved," *Luther's Works* (Philadelphia: Fortress Press, 1955–86), 46:105–6.
[15] Luther, "Whether Soldiers, Too, Can Be Saved," 130–31.

to burn, and to do whatever damages the enemy, according to the usages of war, until he is defeated."[16] Luther's earnestness in this regard is nowhere better seen then in his *Against the Murderous and Thieving Rabble of the Peasants* in which he bade the ruling princes to crush the peasant revolt and to "stab, kill, and strangle" them like dogs.

Being the center of gravity that he was, Luther would have occasionally far-reaching influence, affecting the just war tradition—and those who fight within it—in sometimes unforeseen and startling ways.

Following Luther, John Calvin marked in many ways a substantive return to earlier emphases, illustrated by his grounding of the coercive powers of the state in natural law, which linked civil and moral law in the pursuit of justice.[17] This gestures again to Augustine's distinction—amplified in Aquinas, especially in his doctrine of double effect—between internal dispositions and external acts, resulting in our ability, *pace* Luther, to both love and kill the enemy,[18] in the same moment, as we distinguish between the sinner and the sin.[19]

Calvin's handling of the moral conundrums of war relies heavily on his understanding of the life of Christ and in his insistence on the unity of the Old and New Testaments. This continuity of the Scriptures, as depicted in Christ's work, teaches us that it is part of God's character to use force—including lethal force—against evil, and that he uses human beings—including Christians—to wield this force against the evil actions of other human beings.

Taking his cue from Paul's letter to the Romans, Calvin understands soldiers to be agents of God's wrath. This wrath, however, is an expression of—not a contradiction *to*—God's love.[20] In his explication of Paul's teaching, Calvin recognizes there is only so much the Christian can do in terms of living in peace with others. Everything hinges on the qualifications

---

[16] Luther, "On Temporal Authority."

[17] John Calvin, *Institutes of the Christian Religion*, trans. Ford Lewis Battles (Louisville, KY: Westminster John Knox Press, 1960), 4.20.11.

[18] Calvin, *Institutes*, IV.20.20.

[19] Letter to the Duchess of Ferrara, January 24, 1564, trans. M. R. Gilchrist, in *The Letters of John Calvin*, ed. Jules Bonnet (New York: B. Franklin, 1973), 4:356–57.

[20] John Calvin, *Commentary on St. Paul's Epistle to the Romans*, 13:8.

of Paul's exhortation, "*If* possible, so far as it depends on you, live peaceably with all." Calvin understands it is not, in fact, always dependent upon us.

> [C]ourteousness should not degenerate into compliance, so as to lead us to flatter the vices of men for the sake of preserving peace. Since then it cannot always be, that we can have peace with all men, he has annexed two particulars by way of exception, *if it be possible*, and, *as far as you can*. But we are to conclude from what piety and love require, that we are not to violate pace, except when constrained by either of these two things.[21]

Inherent within Calvin's sanctioning of the use of force is his assertion that when a Christian employs lethal force—in the last resort—he is not repaying evil for evil. Unlike Luther, Calvin insists that a just act is *not* an evil act.

Calvin offers counsel to the Christian soldier in that he illuminates an important continuum: because God's character is reflected in his moral law, Christians who obey the moral law are being made increasingly fit for union with God—because we are being made more like him.[22] Soldiering, properly motivated and pursued, can develop in Christians a taste for Heaven, a desire for fellowship with God. The moral law, offering prescriptions for the development of virtue and not simply proscriptions for the avoidance of vice, instructs the just warrior. The commandment "Thou shall not murder" includes the positive obligation to exercise care for our threatened neighbors. Calvin writes:

> We are accordingly commanded, if we find anything of use to us in saving our neighbors' lives, to faithfully employ it; if there is anything that makes for their peace, to see to it; if anything harmful, to ward it off, if they are in danger, to lend a helping hand.[23]

This is not merely permission to employ force to protect the innocent, it is a mandate. To not come to the aid of the innocent is a violation of charity because it ignores the desecration of the *imago Dei*.

---

[21] Calvin, *Commentary on Romans*, 12:18

[22] John Calvin, *Commentary on Galatians*, 5:5.

[23] Calvin, *Institutes*, III.8.39.

Scripture notes that this commandment rests upon a twofold basis: man is both the image of God, and our flesh. Now, if we do not wish to violate the image of God, we ought to hold our neighbor sacred. And if we do not wish to renounce all humanity, we ought to cherish his as our own flesh.[24]

So, in answer to the earlier question about what the Christian is supposed to do when one *imago Dei* is unjustly kicking apart the face of another *imago Dei*, Calvin insists that failing to use even lethal force to stop the assault is not a solution, for "he who has merely refrained from shedding blood has not therefore avoided the crime of murder."[25] In other words, "there is no moral difference between murder and failing to save an innocent person from being murdered that you could have saved."[26] This obligation carries forward into battle. A Christian does not offend God by going to war, for soldiering can be a godly vocation.

Like Luther, Calvin relied heavily on his understanding of the Scriptures and on the insistence that Christian duty mirror Christian doctrine. Unlike Luther, Calvin more willingly relied on Catholic intelligence, thereby fusing tradition and reform.

This primarily Christian theological content of just war tradition had begun to wane by the seventeenth century. While some early modern just war thinkers were theologians and continued to utilize Christian Scripture, texts, and arguments, they each also attempted to present just war principles more exclusively on the more universal ground of natural law. In doing so, they developed arguments both more comprehensive as well as more widely applicable beyond the Christian West. Others at that time, however, would strip just war thinking of its Christian motivations entirely—and indeed of any explicit religious language of any kind—even as they maintained traditional moral attitudes.

In the 1960s, however, Paul Ramsey (1913–1988) pioneered a revival of specifically Christian, Augustinian—or, better, classical—just war thinking, which has been kept alive since in the work of figures like Jean Bethke

---

[24] Calvin, *Institutes*, III.8.40.

[25] Calvin, *Institutes*, III.8.40.

[26] Alexander F. C. Webster and Darrell Cole, *The Virtue of War: Reclaiming the Classic Christian Traditions East and West* (Salisbury, MA: Regina Orthodox Press, 2004), 161.

Elshtain (1941–2013), Oliver O'Donovan (b. 1945), Nigel Biggar (b. 1955), and others.[27]

JUST WAR

Over the 1500 years of its development, just war tradition has evolved into two primary sets of criteria, one pertaining to the justice of going to war in the first place (*jus ad bellum*) and the other addressing justice in the course of fighting (*jus in bello*).

In what follows, I will explain the component parts of this classical just war framework and will then defend it from the insistence that Christian love mandates a prohibition against the use of lethal force. In so doing, I will argue strongly against the view espoused by figures like Protestant ethicist Reinhold Niebuhr (1892—1971), who, following a Lutheran line, dangerously—if inadvertently so— stressed the tension—really, for him, a contradiction—between Christian love and Christian duty.

Jus ad Bellum
Sovereign Authority

Rightly understood, the sovereign is identified as the one over whom there is no one greater charged with the preservation of the order, justice, and peace of the political community. Because of this, "the natural order," Augustine writes, "which seeks the peace of mankind, ordains that the monarch should

---

[27] See Paul Ramsey, *War and the Christian Conscience* (Durham, NC: Duke University Press, 1961), *The Just War: Force and Political Responsibility* (Savage, MD: Rowman & Littlefield, 1968); Jean Bethke Elshtain, *Just War against Terror* (New York: Basic Books, 2003); Johnson, *War to Oust Saddam Hussein* and *Just War Tradition and the Restraint of War* (Princeton, NJ: Princeton University Press, 1983), among others; Oliver O'Donovan, *Peace and Certainty: A Theological Essay on Deterrence* (Oxford: Clarendon, 1989), *The Just War Revisited* (Cambridge: Cambridge University Press, 2003); and Nigel Biggar, *In Defence of War* (Oxford: Oxford University Press, 2013). See also, Eric Patterson, *Just American Wars: Ethical Dilemmas in U.S. Military History* (New York, Routledge, 2019), and Marc LiVecche, *The Good Kill: Just War & Moral Injury* (Oxford: Oxford University Press, 2021).

have the power of undertaking war if he thinks it advisable."[28] Johnson elaborates:

> Within this conception of politics, the ruler's right to rule is defined by his responsibility to secure and protect the order and justice, and thus the peace, of his own political community and also to contribute to orderly, just, and peaceful interactions with other such communities… The use of armed force in this conception was thus both strictly justified and strictly limited: it might be undertaken only on public authority and for the public good.[29]

This conception of sovereign rule as defined by sovereign responsibility takes its bearings from Romans 13:4: "For the one in authority is God's servant for your good. But if you do wrong, be afraid, for rulers do not bear the sword for no reason. They are God's servants, agents of wrath to bring punishment on the wrongdoer" (NIV).

Only those in a position of responsibility for the upkeep of the political community may authorize the use of the sword. Except in rare exceptions of extreme emergency, anyone else who deploys the sword—usurping the proper function of an existing sovereign—is guilty of disturbing the peace and order of the political community, no matter the cause. While a wise ruler will consider the counsel of well-informed advisors, the ultimate responsibility for the decision to use force rests with the sovereign.

Just Cause

The fundamental question is, "When ought just societies employ force against evil?" In response, the just war framework envisages three causes: protection of the innocent, recovery of what has been wrongly taken, and the punishment of evil.

The qualifier in each of these causes—'innocent,' 'wrongly,' 'evil'—is crucial. The reason for each is most easily seen by examining the first cause. It would be insufficient to name—as positive international law names—self-defense against attack as a just cause. When commenting on just cause,

---

[28] Augustine, "Contra Faustum," in *Nicene and Post-Nicene Fathers*, ed. Philip Schaff, trans. Richard Stothert, vol. 4 (Buffalo, NY: Christian Literature Publishing Co., 1887), XXII.75.

[29] Johnson, "Just War, As It Was and Is," 14.

Aquinas lists only recovery of what has been wrongly taken and punishment of evil. It is not that he does not believe a sovereign has the right to defend his realm against attack. On the contrary, Thomas makes a greater allowance than Augustine for private self-defense.[30]

In the classical just war view, the defense of the common *good* is the central rationale for just war as a whole. Insofar as the need for defense provides a just cause, it does so on the basis of the sovereign's responsibility to protect order and justice.[31] The reason that the qualifier in "protect the *innocent*" is so important is now clear: only the innocent have a right to be defended. To insist otherwise, to propose national sovereignty without qualification as a human good, and thereby to make national self-defense *simply* the model of justified war, is amoral. It ignores questions of motive, intention, cause, and the moral quality of the regime. It implies, for example, that as soon as the Allies invaded the borders of Germany in 1945, Hitler's belligerency became self-defensive and so justified, and the Allies' war-making became aggressive and so unjustified.[32]

A Christian realist view of just war refuses to take national self-defense as its paradigm. The Christian view is that since justified war is always a response to a grave injustice, it must always aim to rectify that injustice. This response may take defensive *or* aggressive forms. It may move seamlessly from defense to aggression, or it may begin with aggression. Justified aggression is what so-called "humanitarian intervention" is all about. The doctrine of the Responsibility to Protect (R2P) is, in effect, an attempted reassertion of the Christian paradigm of justified war.[33] Luther's—and others'—cautions against making matters worse, often through unintentionally swapping tyranny for anarchy, remain important considerations.

In any case, this responsive, reactive posture is essential. The just war view can never countenance the initiation of violence; force, justly deployed, can only ever be reactionary—never inaugural. When given a simple choice between violence or non-violence, in which either will equally effectively

---

[30] Aquinas, *Summa Theologiæ*, II.II.Q 25, a. 5, resp.; Q 64, a.3, resp.; a.7, resp.

[31] Johnson, "Just War, As It Was and Is," 17.

[32] Nigel Biggar, "In Defence of Just War: Christian Tradition, Controversies, & Cases," *Providence: A Journal of Christianity & American Foreign Policy* 4 (Summer 2016): 14.

[33] Biggar, "In Defence of Just War," 15.

requite an injustice, protect the innocent, or mete out appropriate punishment, the just warrior will always choose non-violence.[34] The point is that just war analysis kicks in only when violence or the clear and credible threat of violence is already unjustly perpetrated, and the only thing now in question is the manner of response.

Put another way, the Christian view of just cause allows that a war is justified only when it intends to stop and correct a grave injustice that threatens genuine and important human goods[35] or those social and political matrices upon which the flourishing of individual persons depends.[36] Because it reacts against injustice and defends justice, the just war use of force is also, in essence, punitive. This makes war a necessarily *moral* enterprise. It is not about defending, without evaluation, "whatever borders history or positive law happens to have posited, nor about maintaining a stable regional status quo, regardless of the evils behind those borders or the justice that could be done in transgressing them."[37]

Some argue that such a view of war risks fostering moral self-righteousness and loosening the reins of war. It is true that the Christian just war tradition has most often encouraged intervention, but it is untrue that it encourages conflict. The fact that there is cause to intervene in the first place means that the opportunity to avoid conflict is already past. But there is no necessity that conflict be violent. Intervention can begin and end with a rebuke. Escalation will depend almost entirely on whether and at what point the aggressor is willing to stand down.

While it is also true that this will require some to make moral judgments over others, this ought not to deter us. The political ethicist Jean Bethke Elshtain once quipped that "human nature is a complex admixture… good Harry Potter with a bit of evil Voldemortian temptation thrown in."[38] Knowing something about the poor condition of their own souls, Christians, above all others, should be allergic to simple binaries, in thinking that the just

---

[34] LiVecche, *The Good Kill*, 94.

[35] Biggar, *In Defence of War*, 212.

[36] Biggar, *In Defence of War*, 201–2.

[37] Nigel Biggar, "Natural Flourishing as the Normative Ground of Just War," in *Just War: Authority, Tradition, and Practice*, ed. Anthony Lang et al. (Georgetown University Press, 2013), 52.

[38] Jean Bethke Elshtain, "Peace, Order, Justice: Competing Understandings," *Millennium: Journal of International Studies* 36, no. 3 (May 2008): 422.

warrior stands against the unjust perpetrator as simply righteous against unrighteous, clean against unclean.[39] In fact, the punitive nature of just war is grounded in the recognition of the dignity of those punished. To respond appropriately to the moral choices of others is to take their status as moral beings seriously. It is to acknowledge that what they decide to do actually matters. It says they and their choices are significant.

Right Intention

What is the goal of a just war? Negatively, the intention must be to avoid evils. As Augustine puts it: "The real evils in war are love of violence, revengeful cruelty, fierce and implacable enmity, wild resistance, and the lust of power, and the like."[40] Positively, as already noted, war is waged to punish these "real evils." But there is more.

From Augustine to Luther to Calvin and onward, the purpose of war is always primarily to restore a disordered peace. In his letter to Boniface, the Roman military tribune in north Africa, Augustine insisted: "Peace should be the object of your desire; war should be waged only as a necessity…in order that peace may be obtained."[41] This peace is desired first for the innocent victims under unjust assault. But second, this desire for peace extends to the enemy—toward the restoration of the enemy into the fellowship of peace. Naturally, you cannot reconcile with someone who has not seen the error of his ways, repented, and given you solid reasons to trust that he will not seek to harm you again. There is therefore more to say about this than can be said here. For now, let's summarize the point this way: right intention casts warmaking as peacemaking. Just war is the initiation of the process of forgiveness.[42]

With this admonition there is a caution. As Elshtain reminds us, Augustine is talking about the peace of the *Pax Romana*—a compelled or ordered peace. However unjust in the full light of eschatological *shalom*—that

---

[39] Biggar, "Natural Flourishing," 52.

[40] Augustine, "Contra Faustum" XXII.74.

[41] Augustine, "Letter 189, To Boniface," in *Nicene and Post-Nicene Fathers*, ed. Philip Schaff, trans. J. G. Cunningham, vol. 1 (Buffalo, NY: Christian Literature Publishing Co., 1887).

[42] To explore this in more detail, the best starting point is Biggar, "Natural Flourishing as the Normative Ground of Just War."

heavenly state of wholeness, harmony, and completeness—this imperfect peace was nevertheless real and significant. More than any competitor then on the market, the Roman *Pax* kept neighbor from eating neighbor, and preserved the interconnected web of culture, civilization, art, and tradition that, by Augustine's day, was in jeopardy. As Luther aptly insisted, the imperfect good of ordered peace is much preferred to anarchy.

Better still is what Augustine calls *tranquilitas ordinis*—"the tranquility of order." Such peace is not externally forced but rather wells up from inside, prompted by love of God and neighbor. This peace, Augustine writes in *The City of God*, is born of a commitment that "one will be at peace, as far as lies in him, with all men." The basis of this commitment is "the observance of two rules: first, do no harm to anyone, and, secondly, to help everyone whenever possible."

There's an additional implication of the right intent requirement: if it is just to fight a war, it is just to fight that war to win it. Per Luther, this is not for the sake of chest-thumping, patriotic bravado. In the first place, the just cause requirement necessitates the offending wrong be requited. Per Calvin, to not try to do so, barring profoundly prudential excuses, is to hold the violated goods in contempt. Victory is, in most cases, the means to vindicate the innocent, to take back what's been wrongly taken, or to appropriately punish evil.[43]

Decisive victory is sometimes a bridge too far, and, therefore, it is a strong presumption based on prudent reasoning rather than a categorical imperative. But for both strategic as well as moral reasons, we should lean toward clean margins and err in the direction of thoroughness, just as we would in cancer surgery. It is because we desire the good of concord that we fight for a decisive end to conflict, one that secures and allows the enforcement of a durable peace.[44]

---

[43] On the importance of bringing wars to decisive conclusion, see Geoffrey Blainey, *The Causes of War*, 3rd ed. (New York: Free Press, 1988). See also my chapter "Grim Virtue: Decisiveness as an Implication of the Just War Tradition," in *A Persistent Fire: The Strategic Ethical Impact of World War 1 on the Gloval Profession of Arms*, ed. Timothy Mallard and Nathan White (Washington, DC: National Defense Univeristy Press, 2019), which can be freely downloaded: https://ndupress.ndu.edu/Publications/Books/A-Persistent-Fire/.

[44] Not incidental to the "right intent" requirement is consideration of what happens after the fighting stops. Durable peace does not simply emerge whole cloth after the smoke clears. Contemporary scholars often speak about *jus post bellum*—justice *after*

Taken together, right authority, just cause, and right intent are the primary criteria regarding when it is justified to use force. Deontological in nature, they impose the burden of duty on those bearing ultimate responsibility for the good of the political community and for good relations among political communities. Otherwise put, the *jus ad bellum* requirements, if satisfied, do not point to when it is merely *permissible* to consider force but rather when it is *obligatory*.

Secondary, prudential considerations regarding the proportionality of ends, probability of success, last resort, and the like serve as cautionary filters. It may be that simply because something is right to do, it remains unwise to actually do it. In such cases, when proper prudence dictates that we stand down despite the just cause arrayed before us, the decision not to fight should register as a tragedy. It can only mean that, for now, some innocents will not be protected, some injustice will remain unrequited, some great evil will go unpunished.

Jus in Bello

Following the *ad bellum* requirements, the *jus in bello* criteria tell us how it is that we ought to fight that fight that's right to fight. In its Christian outline, *jus in bello* has traditionally consisted of two primary requirements: justified actions in war must be both proportional and discriminate.

Proportionality

In everyday parlance, for something to be said to be proportional it must correspond in size or amount in relationship to something else. In our thinking about war, the principle of proportionality has suffered under this like-for-like presumption and has often resulted in confused moral reasoning. The problem begins with the lack of agreement as to what proportionality actually means. One claim, taking its cue from the common usage, suggests

---

war. I agree that victors—and victims—have responsibility for helping build—when possible—just conditions, including relations, following conflict and that it's helpful to articulate a criterion for what that might look like. I'm unsure we need a formal third category. One fear is that motion, once started, is sometimes difficult to arrest. Indeed, one already hears rumblings about adding a *fourth* category—*jus* ante *bellum*!

proportionality requires opposing force with similar force. This, as Jim Johnson quips, is to make war akin to a football game.[45]

Better is the suggestion that proportionality calls for ensuring that only the minimum amount of force is used to achieve the objective and to avoid harming noncombatants. Still, there are two immediate problems with this. First, in practice, it tends to issue in the assumption that any action entailing great destructive power is inherently disproportionate. Second, it is simply a mistake to conceive of proportionality's primary imperative as restraint.

It is true that a number of international agreements as well as customary international law point both to using only that amount of force as is proportionate to the injury received and only as much as required to reinstate the *status quo ante*. And it's also true that combatants are required to employ only as much force as is necessary to achieve legitimate military objectives and as is proportionate to the importance *of* those objectives. The just warrior must be neither gratuitous nor excessive. But casting the doctrine of proportionality in this way both demands something that is probably impossible to deliver as well as omits something that is essential to obtain.

The requirement to employ "no more force than necessary" will in many cases—especially in the time-constrained, high-stakes context of battle—be impossible to determine. It's right that one should attempt to limit violence to only what is deemed necessary, but it is also true, as we have seen stressed in Luther and others above, that when we are trying to make this determination our sense of proportionality should be leavened by a commitment to decisiveness and, with it, that preference for hedging against falling short, even as we limit this by considerations of discrimination and proportion.

If the basic imperative of proportionality is not restraint, what is it? Classically understood, proportionality has at its core the requirement to calculate gains and losses. Proportionality is about determining when a particular use of force—whether a weapon or a tactic—is likely to produce more harm than good. This is done by focusing on the aim of restoring a justly ordered peace and considering the measure of good intended to be achieved against two measures of harm: that which will likely occur if a particular act of force is used, and that which will likely be done if such force is not used. The operational interpretation of this would include targeting for

---

[45] Johnson, *War to Oust Saddam Hussein*, 47.

air strikes in an effort to maximize good results—defeating the enemy, shortening the conflict, force protection—over negative results—noncombatant harm, unnecessary destruction, etc.

The Swiss international lawyer Emer de Vattel (1714–1767), recognizing that, even here, our enemy has a say in how we fight, observes that an enemy who "observes all the rules of regular warfare" can be dealt with in more proportionate ways than can an enemy who does not.[46] Against those who do not observe the laws of war, Vattel's reasoning begins to reflect the gloves-off approach of Luther. Against some enemies—particularly those who ruthlessly make war for no justifiable reason or apparent motive—the rules simply do not apply: "When we are at war with a savage nation, who observe no rules, and never give quarter, we may punish them in the persons of any of their people whom we take…and endeavor… to force them to respect the laws of humanity."[47]

Discrimination

The moral reasoning associated with the principle of discrimination, or civilian or noncombatant immunity, is well contested. Not the least contentious issue, as scholar A. J. Coates reminds us, has to do with the moral status on which the principle rests. "Traditionally," he writes, "distinction is seen to arise out of the moral prohibition on the taking of innocent life."[48] The hangup is on precisely what constitutes innocence.

Because so much of what delineates between guilt and innocence has to do with the interior moral state, assessment quickly becomes difficult, so much so that the personal guilt or innocence of those whom they subject to attack is essentially impossible for warfighters to determine. In practice, therefore, the principle has come to be understood in a non-subjective moral sense. Coates writes:

> The logic of just war theorizing points to such an understanding of "innocence," since the use of force in the first instance is seen to be justified only in response to an attack or threatened attack. In line with its etymological derivation from the Latin *nocere* ("to

---

[46] Emer de Vattel, *The Law of Nations* (Indianapolis: Liberty Fund, 2008), 591.

[47] Vattel, *Law of Nations*, 487.

[48] A. J. Coates, *The Ethics of War* (Manchester: Manchester University Press, 1997), 235.

harm"), "innocent" in this context means "harmless" rather than "blameless."[49]

This emphasis links us to "forfeiture," the idea that one renders himself liable to harm on account of the unjustified threat he poses. One is not liable to harm when he does not pose, or no longer poses, harm to others. The operative moral term, then, is *noncombatant*, as opposed to *combatant*, both of which follow from direct involvement in prosecuting the war. Those rather easily classified as noncombatants include the very young, the very old, the infirm, and all those who lack the capacity or will to engage in fighting, including surrendered troops.[50] Not directly and intentionally harming noncombatants is in most instances defined as an exceptionless moral rule.

Nevertheless, the ambiguity surrounding who is or is not a noncombatant, amplified by the confusion as to what helping to prosecute a war really means, and what exactly is meant by *"intentional* harm," has led to continued debate. Mechanisms such as the doctrine of double effect—which allows unintentional, if foreseeable, harm to noncombatants—have been applied to aid moral deliberation, although these additional tools too have themselves become focal points of intense argument.

Vattel, for example, has made keen observations regarding the tension between necessity—doing what is required to achieve legitimate war aims—and deference to the humanity of the enemy. His assertion of the morality of necessity permits a broad assortment of actions and admits of occasional exceptions to sometimes commonly accepted restraints.

For instance, the doctrine of discrimination includes not only respecting the lives of noncombatants, but also observing restraints against destroying infrastructure essential to maintaining human welfare. Nevertheless, it may be that extreme necessity—often because of nefarious enemy tactics—requires destroying things—temples, tombs, public buildings and works—that normally ought to be spared.[51] In other cases, it may be even surrendered enemy fighters ought not to be spared:

> There is, however, one case, in which we may refuse to spare the life on an enemy who surrenders, or to allow any capitulation to a town reduced to the last extremity. It is when that enemy

---

[49] Coates, *Ethics of War*, 237.
[50] Coates, *Ethics of War*, 237.
[51] Vattel, *Law of Nations*, 571–72.

has been guilty of some enormous breach of the law of nations, and particularly when he has violated the laws of war.[52]

Nevertheless, in the main, it is essential to Vattel that the common humanity even of one's enemy is recognized.

> Let us not forget that our enemies are men. Though reduced to the disagreeable necessity of prosecuting our right by force of arms, let us not divest ourselves of that charity which connects us with all mankind. Thus we shall courageously defend our country's right without violating those of human nature. Let our valour preserve itself from every stain of cruelty, and the luster of victory will not be tarnished by inhuman and brutal actions.[53]

The Problem of Paradox

As I bring this overview of war to a conclusion, it is important to recognize that while the long tradition of Christian just war tradition acknowledges that there are times in which neighbor-love can be compatible with killing our neighbor, it has always also recognized that killing our neighbor ought not to be a light nor easy thing. Killing comes at a cost.

This is, of course, clear to those who do not, even at the outset, agree with the tenets of just war morality. Pacifism, whether in its secular or religious mode, is most fundamentally the renunciation of war in any form. This can be for either moral or practical reasons, or both. Unsurprisingly, there aren't many pacifists in the profession of arms nor among many just war scholars whose vocation is in service to the profession. Yet there is a species of pacifism that is endorsed by many in the military—including, most especially, many Christians. It is a kind of pacifism that was also held by the American Protestant theologian Reinhold Niebuhr. To link Niebuhr with pacifism will be surprising to some. Niebuhr, after all, is probably best known as the steadfast defender of democracy against the twentieth century's totalitarian regimes. He came to prominence in the lead up to World War II by making the case for American intervention against Nazism. To help do so, he inaugurated a publication, *Christianity & Crisis*, which he committed to the proposition that "the Christian faith offered no easy escape from the hard and sometimes cruel choices of such a world as ours; but that it did offer

---

[52] Vattel, *Law of Nations*, 544.

[53] Vattel, *Law of Nations*, 563–64.

resources and insights by which our decisions could be made wisely and our responsibilities borne courageously."[54]

Shortly after Japanese Zeros dropped from the December skies over Hawaii, Niebuhr published an editorial suggesting it was to America's own good that we had been "finally forced to be loyal to interests beyond our own." National threats had at last "strengthened our reluctant will and overruled our recalcitrant will," goading Americans to now do what they ought already to have done. "We have been thrown into a community of common responsibility," Niebuhr suggested, "by being engulfed in a community of common sorrow."[55]

While Niebuhr approved the moral rousing of American power, he did not rejoice in it. Harboring no illusions that the grim task ahead would be characterized by anything other than "blood, sweat, and tears," Niebuhr knew that if the totalitarian monsters were to be defeated, it would require "every resource" of the free world to gather against them. Such a conclusion wasn't a given for Niebuhr. The advent of World War II found him, again, needing to shed his own rather cyclical fidelity to pacifism, which ebbed and flowed in successive undulations since before the First World War. Now, against idealist sentiments and calls for dovish isolationism dominant among his fellow Christians, Niebuhr championed a realistic response to the political crisis, one willing to dirty its hands to overcome evil.

While much of this rightly positions Niebuhr within the Christian realism in which this essay is grounded, it is against his notion of "dirty hands" that my concluding thoughts are pitted. Rooted in Niebuhr's dialectic between love and justice, alternatively cast as the contradiction between a law of love and a law of responsibility, the Niebuhrian current of Christian realism results in a catastrophic paradox.[56]

Opposite his call for political responsibility, the second horn of Niebuhr's paradox is found in his contention that war, however rightly prosecuted, always exacts a terrible theological price: the at least partial

---

[54] Reinhold Niebuhr, "Our Responsibility in 1942," *Christianity and Crisis* 1, no. 24 (1942): 1–2.

[55] Niebuhr, "Our Responsibility in 1942," 1–2.

[56] See Marc LiVecche, "Reinhold Niebuhr and the Problem of Paradox," *Providence: A Journal of Christianity & American Foreign Policy* (Winter 2017); and LiVecche, *The Good Kill: Just War and Moral Injury* (Oxford: Oxford University Press, 2021).

renunciation of the ethics of Christ, which he insisted calls uncompromisingly for love without qualification:

> It is very foolish to deny that the ethic of Jesus is an absolute and uncompromising ethic. It is… an ethic of "love universalism and love perfectionism." The injunctions "resist not evil," "love your enemies," "if ye love them that love you what thanks have you?" "be not anxious for your life," and "be ye therefore perfect even as your father in heaven is perfect," are all one piece, and they are all uncompromising and absolute.[57]

For Niebuhr, love means not simply nonviolence (*pace* most species of pacifism) but non*resistance* to evil altogether. "There is not the slightest support in Scripture for [the] doctrine of non-violence," Niebuhr insists. "Nothing could be plainer than that the ethic uncompromisingly enjoins non-resistance and not non-violent resistance."[58] In practical terms, love means the rejection of all forms of self-assertion or coercion in human relationships. The ideal of love, fueled by the "sublime naiveté of the religious imagination," relinquishes moral judgment to look with impartiality toward the evil and the good.[59] While Niebuhr endorsed this ideal, he rejected the consequent belief that, because of love, there is ultimately "no conflict of interest which cannot be adjudicated" and, therefore, violence is never necessary.[60]

Against such wishful thinking, Niebuhr denied that "pure moral suasion could [solve every]… problem." Considering the circumstances of the day, Niebuhr contended that "if we believe that if Britain had only been fortunate enough to have produced 30 percent instead of 2 percent of conscientious objectors to military service, Hitler's heart would have been softened and he would not have attacked Poland, we hold a faith which no historic reality justifies." Therefore, the continued presence of recalcitrant injustice

---

[57] Jean Bethke Elshtain, *Just War against Terror: The Burden of American Power in a Violent World* (New York: Basic Books, 2003), 106.

[58] Reinhold Niebuhr, *Christianity and Power Politics* (New York: Scribner's, 1940), 9–10.

[59] Reinhold Niebuhr, *Moral Man and Immoral Society* (New York: Scribner's, 1960), 53.

[60] Niebuhr, *Moral Man*, 53.

"requires discriminate judgments between conflicting claims."[61] Failure to provide such judgments, attempting to universalize Christian benevolence despite the malevolent insistence of some to do violence against the innocent, is to abandon the requirements of concrete neighbor-love.

In summary, the Niebuhrian paradox, drawing on his Lutheran roots, maintains that the moral vision of the New Testament, specifically as revealed in the life of Christ, declares the law of love to be the normative ideal for Christian behavior. Given the conditions of history, however, again in line with Luther, this norm is impossible to follow. Alongside the impossible *ideal*, the law of responsibility allows at least the possibility of approximating those ideals. Given these options, in the face of sufficiently grave political evil, the law of love requires that we overrule love. This tragic paradox is of immense consequence for the just warrior.

Jean Elshtain, one of Niebuhr's leading interpreters, frequently reflected on this tragedy. "The world of political action," she wrote of the Niebuhrian compromise, "is one that may give rise to moral regret as we confront... the problem of 'dirty hands,' for we cannot remain pure in a difficult and dangerous world."[62] On the battlefield, the consequence is made most clear: "It is not possible to move in history without becoming tainted with guilt."[63]

In light of new understandings of combat trauma, this sentiment is disastrous. Many will already be familiar with moral injury, a proposed subset of PTSD that manifests not in symptoms associated to life-threat—such as hypervigilance, paranoia, and the like—but in symptoms such as shame, remorse, guilt, sorrow, and despair.[64] Over time, clinicians have pointed toward several causes, including doing or allowing to be done something that goes against deeply held moral beliefs. The number one predictor for moral injury is having killed in combat, and there is no statistically significant

---

[61] Andrew Flescher, "Love and Justice in Reinhold Neibuhr's Prophetic Christian Realism and Emmanuel Levinas's Ethics of Responsibility: Treading between Pacifism and Just-War Theory," *The Journal of Religion* 1 (2000): 28.

[62] Elshtain, *Just War against Terror*, 107.

[63] Reinhold Niebuhr, "The Bombing of Germany," in *Love and Justice: Selections from the Shorter Writings of Reinhold Niebuhr* (Louisville, KY: Westminster John Knox Press, 1992), 222.

[64] See Timothy S. Mallard, "The (Twin) Wounds of War," in *Providence*'s Fall 2016 issue; and Marc LiVecche, "The Fifth Image: Seeing the Enemy with Just War Eyes," Summer 2016, and "Kevlar for the Soul: The Morality of Force Protection," Fall 2015.

distinction between the accidental killing of a non-combatant and the killing of an enemy within the laws of armed conflict and the framework of the just war tradition.[65] The problem is that the number one predictor of suicide among combat veterans is moral injury. That's to say, a bright line can be drawn from having killed in battle—regardless of the morality of the kill—to combat veterans killing themselves, even long after those battles have ended.

Thus, my primary critique of Niebuhr is that by insisting that killing is always, simply wrong—even when necessary to do—he wrongly renders the very business of warfighting morally injurious. This, in turn, is killing those who fight our wars. Happily, there are other ways of understanding the business of warfighting. The particular current of just war tradition I have advocated above, flowing from its Augustinian and Thomistic headwaters, does not see a necessary contradiction between loving a man and killing him. It makes room to maintain that while unjust killing *should* be morally injurious, there are other kinds of killings that ought not to be. Indeed, it posits the grief-filled reality that sometimes war is the *manifestation* of love in the last resort.

None of this is to suggest easy solutions for warfighters who grieve their warfighting duties. But it does allow for the Christian, or moralist, to justify use of lethal force on grounds other than dirty hands. At the very least, it allows us to distinguish between different kinds of dirt—some might mar your hands but not stain your soul. Classical just war morality, in disentangling the very business of warfighting from moral injury, has helped to unburden warfighters from unnecessary burdens of guilt. At the very least, in distinguishing actions that issue in sorrow from those that issue in sin, we may uncover different sets of remedies to address different kinds of wounds.[66]

Just as essentially, the Christian just war tradition has relieved the tension between neighbor-love and the use of lethal force. It has demonstrated how war can be a godly vocation. It has put steel in the spine—and the spirit—of Christian warfighters so that they can go happy into battle. Not happy that they *get* to fight. But happy that they are the kinds of people who live in the kinds of nations fortified by the kind of faith *willing* to fight

---

[65] The one qualification is that many who suffer moral injury *have* experienced, directly or not, the accidental killing of civilians. The question then is to what degree such accidental killing grounds one's perception of all lethal combat action.

[66] LiVecche, *The Good Kill*, 202.

when fighting is necessary to protect the innocent, to overturn injustices, and to punish evil. And to prevent a fourteenth day of names.

PART TWO:

Marriage, Life, and Death

V.

Procreation and Children

MATTHEW LEE ANDERSON

IT IS remarkable that Protestant Social Teaching on contraception and fertility could be divided into two eras without significant oversimplification. Prior to the Anglican acceptance of contraception at the Lambeth conference of 1930, Protestants were unequivocal in rejecting the practice: Luther denounced Onan's sin as "far more atrocious than incest and adultery," and explicitly ties it to the avoidance of procreation.[1] Calvin's judgment is the same: "Deliberately avoiding the intercourse," he writes, "so that the seed drops on the ground, is double horrible," as it means that "that one quenches the hope of his family, and kills the son, which could be expected, before he is born."[2] He goes on: "When a woman in some way drives away the seed out the womb, through aids, then this is rightly seen as an unforgivable crime."[3] Now that we are almost a century out from Lambeth, though, every Protestant denomination has made its peace with contraception—either explicitly, or through a quiescent willingness to regard it as a matter for

---

[1] Martin Luther, "Lectures on Genesis," in *Luther's Works*, vol. 7, *Lectures on Genesis, Chapters 38–44* (St. Louis: Concordia, 1965), 20–21.

[2] John Calvin, "Commentary on Genesis 38:10," https://biblehub.com/commentaries/calvin/genesis/38.htm.

[3] To be clear, Luther concludes: "Onan was guilty of a similar crime, by defiling the earth with his seed, so that Tamar would not receive a future inheritor."

Christian debate.[4] By 1979, Calvin's views on the matter were so offensive that Baker Books quietly excised his commentary on Onan from their edition.[5] Protestantism has fractured into no end of denominations: yet they show a curious consistency at just this point.

The trajectory is all the more remarkable considering that the Anglicans' affirmation of contraception was qualified: the encyclical letter accompanying the resolutions worried that the standard for Christians has too often been assimilated to the "spirit of the age," nominally maintaining Christian distinctiveness in the face of widespread social pressures to endorse contraceptive use.[6] The formal resolution suggested only that contraception might be licit when couples have a "morally sound reason" (whatever that is!) for avoiding complete abstinence, and warned they must avoid motives of "selfishness, luxury, or mere convenience." The Communion made clear that there was dissent, noting in the report that it was carried by 193 votes to 67.[7] Yet the limitations of this formal concession were also belied by stronger affirmations of contraception at work in the deliberating body: the task force on the question proposed that there "exist moral situations which may make it obligatory" to use methods besides total abstinence in order to avoid conception. Such an "obligation," they went on to say, is "to a certain extent… affected by the advice of medical and scientific authority." The language is nebulous—but outsourcing such authority to the scientific establishment went hand-in-hand with the reification of private consciences,

---

[4] In the United States, the Orthodox Presybeterian Church does not take a formal position on the question of contraception, but clearly regards it as a matter for private judgment: https://opc.org/qa.html?question_id=13. The LCMS makes no official objection to contraception, though it does oppose voluntary childlessness: https://web.archive.org/web/20031226232737/http://www.lcms.org/pages/internal.asp?NavID=2122. Interestingly, this question is missing from its website—though the formal position is still the same; see https://www.lcms.org/about/beliefs/faqs/lcms-views#family. The LCMS has given guidance on contraceptive methods, which raise worries about the abortificient mechanisms at work in them—but which does not object to such methods *per se*. See https://files.lcms.org/file/preview/KBAHUMzlvxRPqQ9LyWKidfiW0ngUQgoc?. It has most recently published a task force report by Gilbert Meilaender that endorses the use of contraception: https://files.lcms.org/f/1A306E78-215D-4C26-B2D4-2D1BD510010E.

[5] John Calvin, *Commentary on Genesis* (Grand Rapids: Baker, 1979), 281.

[6] Lambeth Report 1930, 21.

[7] Lambeth Report 1930, 43–44.

and the exaltation of 'conscientiousness': "Each couple must decide for themselves," they wrote, "as in the sight of God, after the most careful and conscientious thought, and, if perplexed in mind, after taking competent advice, both medical and spiritual."[8]

Never has such a significant sea-change in faith or morals been enacted with such nebulous moral reasoning. Yet the ambiguity was part of the point: the unequivocal judgment of Scripture's clarity on the question by the Reformers gave way in the face of modern advancements of technology, leaving confession and uncertainty in its wake. By 1958, the Lambeth conference had embraced the language of "responsible procreation," and brought widespread social considerations of poverty and "overpopulation" into Christian deliberations about whether and how to conceive—and gave, again, qualified endorsement to sterilization provided that couples give the question "deepest and most conscientious thought" and give "adequate appreciation of its gravity as a moral decision."[9] Such heightened rhetoric has proved an impotent barrier against the ease of outsourcing procreative "control" to technological means. And once the negative form of "birth control" was asserted, the positive form of "family planning," with its acquiescence to forming human life in laboratories and all its attendant wrongs, became inevitable.[10]

The question for reviving Protestant social ethics in this area is simple, yet bracing: how did this state of affairs come about, and should we continue

---

[8] Lambeth Report 1930, 91. Other problems abound. Against the encyclical letter's cautions about the "spirit of the age," the task force resists the question of contraception "with a full appreciation of the facts and conditions which were not present in the past, but which are due to modern civilisation" (p. 90). While the task force report resists the use of contraception to address social problems like poverty, its considerations of the question were inextricable from this self-consciously "modern" awareness. Additionally, it is worth noting that the task force suggests that the prohibition on contraception "is not founded on any directions given in the New Testament" (p. 90). Such a stance effectively undermines the Hebrew Bible as an authoritative source for Protestant moral reasoning on procreation.

[9] Lambeth Conference 1958, 149.

[10] The Committee Report of the Anglican Communion in 1958 suggested that the "Christian rightly accepts the help of responsible physicians in making conception possible, where it may be prevented by some physical or emotional abnormality." This was a vague endorsement, but must be understood as broad given that the only negative qualifier the report offered was against artificial insemination by third parties. See: The Lambeth Conference 1958, 148.

to accept it as the status quo? Protestant moral theology has proved incapable of resisting our increasing willingness to subordinate our fertility to a technological logic. Why this is the case should give every Protestant pause, and prompt us to seriously consider whether this weakness is a momentary forgetfulness of our Protestant heritage or whether there are pressures within the Reformers' thought that generate such implications.

CALVIN ON PROCREATION

Behind Calvin's denunciation of Onan's avoidance of fertility lies a doctrine of procreation that is intertwined with the uniqueness of divine action in creating human life and God's providential care for creation. In his reading of Genesis 1:28, Calvin observes that the blessing of God is the source of human generation—which has implications not only at the level of the species, but for each individual act of generation.[11] Specifically, Calvin attributes fertility (or its absence) to divine action: "For we are fruitful or barren in respect of offspring," he writes, "as God imparts his power to some and withholds it from others."[12] However "natural" fecundity might seem, the "birth of every child is rightly deemed the effect of divine visitation."[13] As fertility is governed by God's providence, it is in His prerogative to leave some infertile—and to give children to fornicators and adulterers, even when such births are a corruption of God's ordination of procreation to marriage.[14]

Children born to parents are thus God's peculiar "gift," as Calvin names them in his commentary on Psalm 127.[15] There, Calvin reiterates that the power of God at work in procreation descends to each particular case, rather than being simply a general motion. Such an account allows Calvin to subvert what might be called (anachronistically) eugenic ideals. Calvin notes that stronger men might be thought better fitted for procreation, but "Solomon declares on the contrary, that those become fathers to whom God vouchsafes

---

[11] It is worth noting that this is the very inverse of Oliver O'Donovan's argument permitting contraception in *Begotten or Made*. O'Donovan objects to the act-oriented objection to contraception as falsifying the "true nature" of marital love. Oliver O'Donovan, *Begotten or Made?* (Oxford: Clarendon Press, 1984), 76–78.

[12] Calvin, *Commentary on Genesis*, 54–55.

[13] Calvin, *Commentary on Genesis*, 415.

[14] Cf. *Institutes*, 1.16.7; *Commentary on Genesis*, 54–55.

[15] John Calvin, *Commentary Upon the Book of Psalms: Psalms 93—150*, trans. Rev. James Anderson (Grand Rapids: Baker Books, 2003), 103-112. .

that honor."[16] The honor of receiving such a gift generates a task for parents: Calvin thinks that such knowledge is conducive both to bringing up children well, and to being settled about the continuance of God's grace.[17]

It is notable that Calvin does not often invoke his doctrine of sin in discussing the nature and significance of procreation, but steadfastly emphasizes the presence of divine action in making human life. Calvin notes that it would be better to have no children than children who lack virtue, and intimates that the children who are born to adulterers and fornicators will "tend to their greater destruction."[18] Yet his account of procreation remains relatively optimistic. Calvin notes that God formed Adam and Eve to people the earth, and formed *only* Adam and Eve to do so in order that "our desire of mutual concord might be the greater, and that each might the more freely embrace the other as his own flesh." While sin might generate inequalities from the expansion of humanity across the earth, Calvin is insistent that the "benediction of God so prevails that the earth everywhere lies open so that it may have its inhabitants, and so that an immense multitude of men may find, in some part of the globe, their home."[19]

Despite his emphasis on the uniqueness of divine action in procreation, Calvin also seems to regard those who do not receive such a gift as deficient in some way—a position animated by the general orientation of humanity toward having a lineage. In his commentary on Psalm 127, he suggests that those who are given posterity are given a new strength, in which they "may begin as it were to live a second time." Those who are childless, by contrast, are simply "solitary."[20] Such an extension of the language used for Adam is animated by Calvin's reading of Genesis 2:18, where he suggests that the description of Adam's aloneness marks a principle that humanity is "formed to be a social animal."[21] Elsewhere, commenting again on Genesis 38, Calvin argues that because every human is born "for the preservation of the whole

---

[16] Calvin works from the traditional assumption that Psalm 127 is a Psalm of Solomon. Cf. *Commentary Upon the Psalms*, 110.

[17] Calvin, *Commentary Upon the Psalms*, 111.

[18] Calvin, *Commentary on Genesis*, 55; cf. *Commentary on Psalms*, 111.

[19] Calvin, *Commentary on Genesis*, 54–55.

[20] Calvin, *Commentary Upon the Psalms*, 111.

[21] Calvin, *Commentary on Genesis*, 79.

race," there "seems to be... some defect of nature" if "anyone dies without children."[22]

LUTHER ON PROCREATION

While Luther shares the insistence on the "gift" of procreation, his account has a very different tenor than Calvin's. Luther also regards the "blessing" as the unique presence of divine action in fertility, which is necessary for the generation of life. While philosophers point to natural causes for new life, theologians know that "these events take place through the working of the Word." The Word is present within hens who lay eggs, and in all living creatures, as otherwise nature would be without effect. "Therefore," Luther writes, "because of this miraculous creation God adds the blessing of fruitful bodies."[23] In his denunciation of avoiding fertility, Luther describes procreation as the "greatest work of God."[24] Children "are a gift of God and come solely through the blessing of God.[25]

At the same time, Luther frames the solitude of Adam in terms that move procreation—rather than marriage *per se*—to the forefront. Luther suggests that Adam's deficiency is one of the "common good or the good of the species," rather than his personal good. Such a reading has much in common with Calvin: yet while Calvin emphasizes the good of *sociality* as the fundamental meaning of Adam's solitude and emphasizes the value of marriage *vis a vis* celibacy, Luther directly focuses on procreation, which limits the scope of the "sociality" the verse endorses to marriages that in fact generate children. While he has the good of innocence, he lacks the "common good which the rest of the living beings who propagated their kind through procreation had." The "good" in the passage thus "denotes the increase of the human race."[26]

Luther is emphatic, though, that the "blessing" of procreation has been transfigured by sin. In "The Estate of Marriage," Luther suggests Genesis 1:28 is "more than a command, namely, a divine ordinance which it is not

---

[22] Calvin, *Commentary on Genesis*, 281.

[23] Martin Luther, *Lectures on Genesis* in *Luther's Works: American Edition*, vols. 1—8,, trans. Jaroslav Pelikan (St. Louis: Concordia Publishing House, 1955), 1:53.

[24] Luther, *Lectures on Genesis*, 1:118.

[25] Luther, *Lectures on Genesis*, 2:132.

[26] Luther, *Lectures on Genesis*, 1:116.

our prerogative to hinder or ignore." It is as necessary to humanity as eating and sleeping.[27] In his later lectures on Genesis, Luther embraces the claim that "Be fruitful" is a command—but immediately pivots to a lament about what has been lost to humanity as a result of sin. Where humanity might have procreated in such a manner that is linked with the knowledge of God, now in procreating the "body becomes downright brutish and cannot beget in the knowledge of God." The perils of pregnancy and burdens of nature all "point out to us the enormity of original sin"—which renders the blessing of God a "cursed and debased blessing," a "marred blessing." While we must gratefully acknowledge it, as God still preserves it, procreation is burdensome in a way that it would not have been otherwise.[28] At the same time, Luther is explicit that original sin's structuring of the generative act and the product of creation should be kept distinct: "The work of procreation is something good and holy that God has created," he writes, which "would have been a very pure and honorable work" had not sin intruded.[29] Luther is unusually attentive to the burdens women face in giving birth and nurturing children, and is explicit that in the state of innocence they would have "given birth without pain"—a position shared with Calvin.[30]

Behind Luther's account of procreation lies an Augustinian affirmation of the goods of the body in the original creation, and the corruption of those goods through lust. Yet unlike Augustine, Luther extends this framework to regard aversion to procreation as itself intertwined with sin—implicating, it would seem, both the practices of clerical celibacy and monastic life that Luther inveighed so heavily against. That is, Luther's account of procreation commits him to a particular type of pro-natalism which lacks the qualifying, spiritualizing dimensions that Augustine's emphatic defense of celibacy preserves. Luther is explicit that in the state of innocence the fertility of

---

[27] Martin Luther, "The Estate of Marriage," in *The Christian in Society* in *Luther's Works: American Edition*, vols. 44—47, trans. Jaroslav Pelikan (St. Louis: Concordia Publishing House, 1955) 2:18.

[28] Luther, *Lectures on Genesis*, 1:71.

[29] Luther, *Lectures on Genesis*, 1:237.

[30] Luther, *Lectures on Genesis*, 1:118. On Calvin, see his acknowledgement that it would be "credible that the woman would have brought forth without pain, or at least without such great suffering, if she had stood in her original condition." Calvin, *Commentary on Genesis*, vol. 1, ch. 3, sec. 16.

women "would also have been far greater."[31] Luther is so insistent on the anti-natalist thrust of original sin that he queries whether it is a punishment for a woman to only give birth once a year. His answer is that if there were not sin, "women would have given birth to a much more numerous offspring." The failure to do so is intertwined with the "enormity of sin."[32] The fact that, in this life, many turn away from procreation is "the pope's and the devil's doing." It is specifically a feature of woman to have a womb that is "insatiable," such that it is "impossible for her not to desire increase."[33] While Calvin had regarded the birth of children to fornicators as contributing to their destruction, Luther uses it in a polemical context to defend the value of procreation to God.[34]

Yet Luther's intensification of procreation's value over and against the putative papist abrogation of procreation introduces elements into his theological ethics that ought give us pause. While Calvin had used the imagery of the gift to overturn the eugenic dimensions of marriage and procreation, Luther embraces them. In his discussion of Jacob and Rachel, Luther defends Jacob from committing a sin for wanting a beautiful wife, or for hoping "for offspring from a woman of outstanding beauty and strength of body." Luther contends that when marriages are a matter of choice (as they were not always in his day), "the strong should be chosen and united with the strong, the industrious with the industrious." While that might be innocuous as a matter of preference, Luther extends the principle by suggesting that "strong persons are united with those who are weak on account of original sin," an evil that must be counteracted by upholding fidelity within marriage.[35] More astoundingly, Luther simply *rejects* fictive forms of kinship outright. In "The Estate of Marriage," Luther argues that a prohibition on marrying an adopted sibling is a "worthless human invention," as "in the sight of God this adopted

---

[31] Thomas A. Fudge, "Incest and Lust in Luther's Marriage: Theology and Morality in Reformation Polemics," *The Sixteenth Century Journal* 34, no. 2 (2003): 319–45.

[32] Luther, *Lectures on Genesis*, 1:217.

[33] Luther, *Lectures on Genesis*, 2:16–17.

[34] "And, what is more, He seems to emphasize procreation to such an extent that children are born even to adulterers and fornicators contrary to their wish." Luther, "Lectures on Genesis," 4:04.

[35] Luther, *Lectures on Genesis*, 5:289–90.

person is neither your mother nor your sister, since there is no blood relationship."[36]

Despite their overlap, then, Calvin and Luther present two distinct conceptions of the place of procreation within a theological anthropology and ethics. Calvin's account of the "gift" of procreation underscores divine agency in a way that is commensurate with Luther's view: yet his endorsement of procreation's value does not generate the oppositional, emphatic pro-natalist fervor that one can read out of Luther's account. Moreover, while Calvin undoubtedly frames procreation as a unique work of divine action, his account of providence and procreation's value prior to the Fall does not become entwined with the type of pro-natalist framework that Luther seems to develop. For Luther, the impetus to procreate is not only grounded as a natural proclivity or tendency, but rises to the level of necessity—and that, seemingly, not only at the level of the species, where it had been regarded by both Augustine and Aquinas, but at the level of individuals and their own somatic constitutions. While Luther could offer nominal concessions to Paul's endorsement of celibacy as a gift in 1 Corinthians 7 (even while unequivocally rejecting monastic communities and the practices of vowing), the thrust of his account of procreation naturalizes sexuality to such a degree that even ascribing legitimacy to adoptive bonds becomes problematic—a position that would nullify the genealogies that Christ himself was born into.

CONCLUSION: REVIVING A PROTESTANT ETHIC OF PROCREATION

It is ironic that matters between Protestants and Rome stand in the exact reverse position today than they did for Luther. Luther's repudiation of the 'spiritual siblinghood' that the monastic orders enacted was personal: his marriage to a former nun, Katherine von Bora, was widely criticized by his Roman Catholic foes for being incestuous. His own emphasis on the naturalness of procreation was intertwined with his rejection of just such a framework: on his view, the papal structures of monasticism and celibacy entailed a repudiation of the "nature" that makes procreation necessary for individuals and, not surprisingly, led to fornication and other iniquities among priests and monastics. For Luther, the pope signified an opposition to the value of sex and, with it, procreation. The advent of contraception has

---

[36] Luther, "The Estate of Marriage," 2:25.

reversed the situation: while pro-natalist pockets of Protestant communities still exist, it is far more common to regard the Roman Catholic rejection of contraception as engendering a pro-natalism. Karl Barth (1886—1968), for instance, very likely associated (putatively) Jewish pro-natalist attitudes with Roman Catholicism.[37]

While Luther and Calvin are heirs of Augustine's account of sex and marriage, their approach to procreation is largely extricated from the theological framework that Augustine builds around his—one which both affirms procreation as a good of marriage, but also offers an ecclesiastically-centered way of living out the 'fruitfulness' we are called to as human beings *without* generating new human life directly. In his exposition of Psalm 127, Augustine contends that interpreting the psalm to refer to "this-worldly blessings"—i.e., physical children—would be disgraceful to the martyrs. Moreover, he suggests that it would be to say to any faithful childless follower of God that he "clearly does not fear the Lord," as "if he did, his wife would be like a fruitful vine in his house, not a barren woman unable to bear him children."[38] Such talk indicates that a person is "carnally-minded, with no sensitivity to anything that concerns the Spirit of God."[39] Thinking that way might lead one to expect "hordes of children and grandchildren, and a wife who is fertile and frequently pregnant."[40] But in a striking line, Augustine unequivocally rejects such pro-natalist implications: "these are not the good things of the eternal Jerusalem; they are the good things that belong to the land of the dying."[41] Those who are given children should give more thought to raising them rather than having more—and those without children should give thanks for their lack of troubles. More than that, childless couples *can* be fruitful—it may be, Augustine argues, "that some of those young olive saplings crowding round the Lord's table are your spiritual children, borne to

---

[37] William Werpehowski proposes that "one basis of Barth's limited treatment" of parents and children, "is a reluctance to endorse any but the most qualified 'pro-natalism' as over against, by his (perhaps mistaken) lights, Roman Catholic and Jewish thought." William Werpehowski, "Reading Karl Barth on Children," in *The Child in Christian Thought*, ed. Marcia J. Bunge (Grand Rapids: Eerdmans, 2001), 404. This is exactly right.

[38] Augustine, "Psalm 127," in *Expositions of the Psalms Vol. 5*, trans. Boniface Ramsey and Maria Boulding (New York: New City Press, 2004), 100

[39] Augustine, "Psalm 127", 100.

[40] Augustine, "Psalm 127", 101.

[41] Augustine, "Psalm 127", 101.

you by mother Church."[42] Augustine's willingness to read the Scriptures allegorically and metaphorically might lead him into trouble at points—but it also offers him a path toward consecrating nature without capitulating to it.

The question of contraception is centrally about the moral status of the nature of our own bodies and their inherent teleology toward reproduction. It is a curiosity that a movement founded upon Luther's reification of the body has now turned against it. How this happened is a question beyond the scope of this chapter. One worries, though, that Protestantism's theological imagination was not robust enough to resist the technologization of nature wrought in the early modern world, precisely because the Reformers had invested so deeply in sanctioning nature over and against institutional structures that had become too otherworldly. Yet when the goods of nature are dislocated from a context in which their significance is routinely and regularly referred beyond nature itself, toward God, other problems are likely to emerge—precisely because the suffering involved in fertility that an industrialized world imposes is so overwhelming, and the sorrow of childlessness that a world of technologized infertility evokes is so acute.

The task for renewing Protestant accounts of procreation is to recognize that, once again, anti-natalist attitudes and ideologies are on the insurgence—and that the remedy against them might not to be adopt the Reformers' account of procreation, but to embrace their theological method and retrieve the fullness of Augustine's ethics for our own time.

---

[42] Augustine, "Psalm 127," 112.

VI.

Sex, Marriage, and Divorce

ONSI AARON KAMEL & ALASTAIR ROBERTS

LIKE THE great reformers of the Western Church before them, Protestants carried out their task with the works of St. Augustine in one hand and the Bible in the other. Although John Calvin no doubt overstepped in claiming that Augustine's theology belonged exclusively to the Reformation in its conflict with Rome, it is true that the Reformers inherited, revived, and built upon the insights of Augustine in the realm of marriage and family life. At the same time, they allowed the Scriptures, and particularly the gospel of Christ's triumph over the forces of sin and death, to speak to them afresh. At their best, the Reformers offered an account of marriage and family that successfully synthesized the insights of St. Augustine with the teachings of the Scriptures, ultimately affirming both the severe reign of the flesh with its lusts and Christ's victory over it.

This account of Protestantism's teachings on marriage and family begins with St. Augustine's understanding of sex, marriage, and family after the Fall; turns subsequently to the Scripture's teachings on the same themes; and finally concludes by examining the synthesis of the Reformers.

ST. AUGUSTINE ON SEX, MARRIAGE, AND THE FAMILY

Marriage was as fraught a topic in Augustine's day as it is in ours, albeit for very different reasons. For Augustine's Christian contemporaries (as for

Augustine himself), celibacy was considered a higher vocation than married life; those who devoted themselves to celibacy freed themselves for unceasing prayer and singleminded devotion to the things of God. On this, the early church was in agreement. But some Church Fathers regularly went beyond this, insinuating that celibacy was the only morally respectable vocation. More radical champions of virginity, including St. Jerome, claimed that there was no sexual intercourse before the Fall; indeed, in his *Letter 22* to the wealthy Roman woman Eustochium, Jerome wryly claimed, "I praise marriage, I praise wedlock, but it is because they give me virgins."[1] Often attending the elevation of virginity and celibacy over marriage was the denigration of marriage and family life. In that same letter to Eustochium, Jerome writes mockingly of the "drawbacks of marriage, such as pregnancy, the crying of infants… the cares of household management, and all those fancied blessings which death at last cuts short." In one of his more generous moments, Jerome grants that married women "are not as such outside the pale; they have their own place." But ultimately, Jerome enjoins Eustochium to refrain from associating with married women and even widows who refused celibacy while their husbands lived.

It is in this context that St. Augustine's contributions to the debates of his day should be understood. For Augustine, the fundamental problem facing marriage after the Fall is the problem of the passions or "concupiscence" (fallen desire). In reflecting upon our passions after the Fall, Augustine took as his point of departure biblical texts such as Romans 7, in which St. Paul remarks that, despite his mind's submission to the law of God and his will's desire to follow the law of God, nevertheless "I see in my members another law waging war against the law of my mind and making me captive to the law of sin that dwells in my members" (Rom. 7:23, ESV). For Augustine, this text indicated that, after the Fall, human passions had become a law unto themselves, insubordinate to the will and the intellect, and that these sinful passions act, mysteriously, *even against man's will*.[2]

---

[1] St. Jerome, Letter 22, trans. W. H. Fremantle, G. Lewis, and W. G. Martley, in *Nicene and Post-Nicene Fathers, Second Series*, vol. 6, ed. Philip Schaff and Henry Wace (Buffalo, NY: Christian Literature Publishing Co., 1893). Revised and edited for New Advent by Kevin Knight, https://www.newadvent.org/fathers/3001022.htm.

[2] Onsi A. Kamel, "The Beloved Icon: An Augustinian Solution to the Problem of Sex," *Scottish Journal of Theology* 73, no. 4 (November 2020): 318–29, 319, https://doi.org/10.1017/S0036930620000642.

Sex was a paradigm case of this phenomenon for Augustine. For, in sex, the passions act independently of the mind and the will (Augustine gives the common example of being aroused against one's will). And crucially, this is a feature of sex itself after the Fall, not only a feature of unmarried or adulterous sex. In other words, the problem of lust does not simply go away once one is married.[3]

This position might seem to have radical implications for marriage, from a contemporary point of view. Can married sex really be *sinful*? Or to put our question more pointedly: given Augustine's claim that sex is always compromised by sin, how can we conclude marriage is not likewise fundamentally compromised? Does not the Apostle Paul say that one of the goods of marriage is precisely that those without self-control have a means not to burn with passion (1 Cor. 7:9)?

Augustine, far more than many of his contemporaries, realized that marriage and family are not evil, but are great goods. As he wrote in *On Marriage and Concupiscence*, "Matrimony, therefore, is a good, in which the human being is born after orderly conception; the fruit, too, of matrimony is good, as being the very human being which is thus born; sin, however, is an evil with which every man is born."[4]

Augustine carefully distinguishes between sex before the Fall (sinless because there was no lust), sex after the Fall (sinful because of the lust which always attends sex), marriage (which is good in itself and bad only insofar as the lust which attends the sexual act is present), and procreation (which is again good in itself and bad only insofar as the lust which attends the sexual act is present). For Augustine, then, the lust inseparable from the sexual act, not marriage, was the necessary evil. But lustful sex is a very minor "evil" at that—provided sex is used to bring Christian children into the world rather than for gratification of lust. In sum, St. Augustine carefully preserved both his capacity to reckon fully with humanity's disordered sexual appetites and the good of marriage, family, and children. Many today find Augustine's

---

[3] Kamel, "The Beloved Icon," 320.

[4] St. Augustine, "On Marriage and Concupiscence," trans. Peter Holmes and Robert Ernest Wallis, rev. Benjamin B. Warfield, in *Nicene and Post-Nicene Fathers, First Series*, vol. 5, ed. by Philip Schaff (Buffalo, NY: Christian Literature Publishing Co., 1887). Revised and edited for New Advent by Kevin Knight, https://www.newadvent.org/fathers/3001022.htm.

views distasteful, but the Reformers largely adopted them, not least because they believed them to be scriptural.

HEARING SCRIPTURE

Given that the Reformers rooted their teachings on marriage in Scripture, it is important to understand the broad contours of the scriptural narrative concerning marriage and family before looking directly to the Reformers' own teaching. Hermeneutically, the Reformers followed the model of Christ, who, when asked why he did not permit divorce even though the Law of Moses did, replied, "From the beginning it was not so" (Matt. 19:8). Like Christ, the Reformers turned to Genesis.

Prior to the Fall, the goodness of marriage and family is connected to the goodness of the entire created order, and after the Fall, the disorder of marriage and family is likewise connected to the disorder of the creation. Genesis 1–2, as has been commonly noted, features God forming dimensions of creation and then dividing them: day is separated from night, waters above are separated from waters below, the waters below are separated from the land, female is separated from male, and so on. These great asymmetric pairings aren't antagonistic dichotomies—two things fighting against each other—but pairs whose terms are interlocked yet distinct, representing the creative order as one of an interplay between two elements. The cosmic order is rhythmic and beautiful.

The goodness of marriage, as the union of an interlocked yet distinct pair, must be understood in the light of this broader creational order. In marriage, maleness and femaleness establish the primary bonds of our natural relations and the source of our given identities. We have been empowered as male and female to bring forth new images of God and of ourselves, as we see in Genesis 5:1–3. Creating man as male and female is itself a forming and filling act with regard to the human race. "Male and female in the image of God" is the standard unit of humanity, much as the basic unit from which the entire system by which humanity is measured is to be derived. That unit is the germ of social formation, and the engine of social filling. So as regards form, the order of the pattern of humanity is one of disjunction—characterized by two distinct forms—in an inseparable and dynamic relation.

Furthermore, although we tend to frame our discussions of marriage and the relationships between men and women in terms of the binary face-to-face relationship between the sexes, Genesis does not present marriage this way. This is crucial for understanding Protestant teaching on the family. Marriage is presented in Genesis in terms of a wider calling within the world. Marriage was to be the way men and women fill out God's purpose in the world; it is the means by which we fulfill our natural vocations as humans.

The fall into sin, however, disorders this original dispensation. Healthy sexual realities have been marred by the Fall in various and extensive ways. Sin, bodily dysfunction, and psychological disorder undermine the loving one-flesh union that should exist between a husband and wife, often shattering it by divorce, perverting it by oppressive male dominance, or destroying it by myriad other means. In the Fall, the order established by God breaks down.

The Fall was chiefly the fall of the man. He failed in his task of serving and keeping the garden and of upholding the law concerning the tree, allowing the woman to be deceived when it was his duty to teach and to protect her. The woman, for her part, failed in her calling as the helper. In the parallel judgments that follow, both the man and the woman are told that they will experience frustration in the fundamental area of their activity, the man in his labor upon the ground, the woman in her labor and childbearing. Both will be frustrated and dominated by their source: the woman will be dominated by man, and the man will return to the ground. The consequences of the Fall cut to the heart of men and women considered individually and as married: they have become corruptible, subject to their lusts, and doomed to decay.

In the book of Leviticus especially, and in the Pentateuchal code more broadly, the truth of the corruption inherent in fallen flesh is extensively communicated. Bodily emissions, both typical and abnormal, render one unclean (Leviticus 15), as does childbirth (Leviticus 12), the breaking out of the corruption of the flesh in the scale disease described in Leviticus 13–14, or contact with dead bodies (Numbers 19). The fallen flesh is contagiously corrupt, and this corruption is most pronounced wherever the flesh most exerts its natural powers, our sexual functions and faculties being focal points of its activity and communication.

When the Apostle Paul wrote concerning the problem of the "flesh," the term likely functioned to name the vast complex of corruption that, through the purity code, had been partially raised into practical consciousness for him and many of his Jewish hearers. This is why Paul remarks, "If you live according to the flesh, you will die: but if by the Spirit you put to death the deeds of the body you will live" (Rom. 8:13, ESV). The Apostle establishes a parallel between living after the flesh and doing the deeds of the body; to refuse to live after the flesh is to tame the body, to resist the natural tendencies of our corruption.

The connection between "flesh" and human sexuality in Augustine is neither arbitrary nor a relic of a more prudish age; in making this connection, Augustine is articulating a deeply scriptural grammar in his own idiom. Although not infrequently obscured in contemporary translations, the term "flesh" in Scripture often functions as a euphemism for the penis (the Hebrew term being *basar*—see, for example, Exodus 28:42, Ezekiel 23:26, among others). The penis represents not only the generative capacities of all "flesh," but also the nature of flesh in its fallen, corrupt form.

It is in this context that we begin to understand the logic of the covenant sign of circumcision and its connection to marriage and family. Just as humanity must be cleansed of the corrupting influences of the flesh to be fit for God's presence (hence, the reason for the purity codes), so human generative capacities must be made fit for God's service. Put another way, after the Fall, marriage and family life come under the domain of the flesh; therefore, to be made fit once again for divine service, they must be cleansed.

It should come as little surprise then that, in Genesis 17—immediately after promising to be God to Abraham, to make Abraham "fruitful," and to remain faithful to Abraham's "seed"—God institutes circumcision of the male generative organ as the sign of his covenant with Israel. God's people are to prune, tame, and cultivate their generative capacities so that they serve God's purposes. Prior to circumcision, men "are possessed of a blemish before" God, taught the medieval Jewish commentator Rashi.[5] Luther likewise connected the Old Testament sacrament of circumcision to divine judgment. Circumcision is the means by which God displays the spread of corruption from the first parent to all humanity.[6] Calvin sees in circumcision a dual symbolism: in appointing circumcision, God manifested to us that whatever "comes forth from man's seed… is corrupt and needs pruning," thereby to induce us to mortify our flesh, but circumcision also attests the

---

[5] Rabbi Yisrael Herczeg, *Sapirstein Edition Rashi: The Torah with Rashi's Commentary Translated, Annotated and Elucidated*, vol. 1 (Brooklyn, NY: Artscroll/Mesorah Publications, Ltd, 1995), Gen. 17:1–9.

[6] Martin Luther, *Lectures on Genesis: Chapters 15–20* in *Luther's Works*, vol. 3 (St. Louis: Concordia, 2006), Gen. 17:10–11.

blessing given to Abraham.[7] Thus, in demonstrating the need for humanity to cut off the flesh if it is to bear good fruit, circumcision is the sign both of human corruption and of the promise that, once the flesh is cultivated (in the New Covenant, by baptism and the circumcision of the heart), it becomes a great blessing, a gift of God, and even, as attested to Abraham, the means by which God overcomes sin and death.

In its own language, which is not identical to Augustine's but which nevertheless communicates the same truths, Scripture affirms the original goodness of sex, marriage, and family, their subsequent enslavement to corruption, and their ultimate redemption and reconsecration for divine service. Through baptism into and faith in Christ, the seed of Abraham, Christians have crucified the flesh with its lusts, and, provided they make no provision for the flesh, become fitted again for divine service. The Reformers will show us that, like our very bodies, sown in corruption and raised in incorruption, marriage and family life fall under the curse of the flesh but are simultaneously redeemed for service to God.

REFORMING THE FAMILY WITH THE BIBLE AND ST. AUGUSTINE

The Reformers were, like Augustine, dealing with a church that often denigrated marriage as bad and unpleasant and which upheld celibacy in fairly extreme terms. As in many things, however, the Reformers were also heirs to Augustine's views of concupiscence, which gave them a suspicion of the realm of the flesh. The key achievements of the Reformers are therefore to be found in their simultaneous adoption of Augustine's insights with their very positive appraisal of the estate of marriage, rooted in a renewed emphasis upon the redemption of the created order by Christ's triumph over the powers of the world, the flesh, and the devil.

Luther's teachings on marriage have as their backdrop his conflicts against late-medieval monasticism and, simultaneously, his fight against mankind's perennial denigration of marriage and family. In his *Judgment on Monastic Vows*, Luther castigates the understanding of religious vows and monasticism prevalent in the Church in his day, arguing, among other things, that such vows had become attempts to attain justification before God on

---

[7] John Calvin, *Institutes*, IV.XIV.21; John Calvin; *Commentary on Genesis* (Grand Rapids: Baker, 2003), 453-454.

grounds other than faith.[8] But Luther also kept up sustained attacks against the devaluation of the family. For instance, at one point he says, "I have always taught that we should not despise or disdain this walk of life, as the blind world and our false clergy do, but view it in the light of God's Word."[9] For the Reformers, the Scripture—not false clergy and not the world—is more certain than any experience or worldly wisdom, and therefore Christians should allow the Scriptures to teach them what to think about marriage and family. There are four major points of Reformational teaching worth highlighting in this context.

First, marriage and family are divinely established. God created marriage in the beginning, and therefore "it is a divine and blessed walk of life."[10] Indeed, Luther argues that marriage is the first institution, existing before all other human institutions (such as the government) both in time and importance. The means by which children enter the world—the bond of love uniting a man and woman—is pre-political, prior to legal structure, prior to economic transaction. Marriage, therefore, takes precedence over all other natural vocations; it is more to be revered than the offices of bishops and princes and emperors. Luther goes so far as to say that marriage is, for the majority of people, "solemnly commanded by God," since God created humans for it.[11] Although, contrary to many popular conceptions of his position, Luther was forthright that there are "rare exceptions whom God has especially exempted… by a high, supernatural gift" of chastity, his emphasis was on marriage as the normal and, indeed, normative state of human affairs.[12]

Second, marriage is a great good, and the greatest good of marriage is the generation of children in service of God: "The greatest good in married life, that which makes all suffering and labor worthwhile, is that God grants offspring and commands that they be brought up to worship and serve him,"

---

[8] Martin Luther, *Judgment on Monastic Vows*, in *Luther's Works*, ed. James Atikinson, vol. 44, *Christian in Society I* (St. Louis: Fortress Press, 1966), 273.

[9] Martin Luther, *The Large Catechism*, in *The Book of Concord (New Translation): The Confessions of the Evangelical Lutheran Church*, ed. Robert Kolb and Timothy J. Wengert, trans. Charles P. Arand, 2nd ed. (Minneapolis: Fortress Press, 2000), 209.

[10] Luther, *The Large Catechism*, 209.

[11] Luther, *The Large Catechism*, 211.

[12] Luther, *The Large Catechism*, 211.

says Luther.[13] Marriage and the propagation of children are God's chief means of making Christians. The baptized children of Christian parents are the ordinary objects of God's salvation. The glory of marriage in God's sight—its superior status, which places it above all other natural institutions—is a result of its function in God's plan of salvation. Marriage is ordered to the generation and salvation of children. And to God, "there is nothing dearer than the salvation of souls."[14] Marriage finds its purpose beyond itself. It is in virtue of this extrinsic purpose that it constitutes the fundamental institution of natural life while being simultaneously ordered to the ultimate good of man, heavenly life.

Third, the relationship between man and woman is framed by the larger creation and man and woman's shared vocation under God within it. Carefully examined, this assumes and provides meaning to gender distinction. But it also entails the dignity of both spouses' work in the household as well as an elevation of the work of the household itself. The fact of a gender distinction finds its meaning in the divine commission to the human community, in the tasks that lie at the heart of man's (and the family's) vocation. Exercising dominion and filling are not tasks that play to male and female capabilities and callings in an indiscriminate manner, but rather tasks where sexual differentiation can often be particularly pronounced. In the task of exercising dominion and subduing the creation, the man is advantaged by reason of his greater physical strength. On the other hand, the burden of bearing children, of filling the world, chiefly falls upon women. In the task of being fruitful and multiplying and filling the earth, we see a different weighting of the callings but nevertheless an equal dignity afforded to both.

Even after the Fall, this dimension of the status of family life has not changed, and in fact, this primordial vocation takes the mundane, unattractive, and often dangerous work of the household and transfigures it into divine service, a means of worship. Though fraught with pains and dangers, childbearing, Luther proclaimed, is a divine work. Luther even exclaimed that men "should now wish to be [women] for the sake of this very work alone."[15] By the same token, the works necessary to sustain marriage

---

[13] Martin Luther, "The Estate of Marriage," in *The Christian in Society*, vol. 1, in *Luther's Works: American Edition*, vols. 44—47, trans. Jaroslav Pelikan (St. Louis: Concordia Publishing House, 1955), 46.

[14] Luther, "The Estate of Marriage," 46.

[15] Luther, "The Estate of Marriage," 40.

and family life—household chores, changing diapers, and all the rest—are "all adorned with divine approval as with the costliest gold and jewels." Looked at with unbelieving eyes, these tasks are menial, unpleasant, undesirable. But when seen with the eyes of faith, these tasks participate in all the grandeur of the creational order; done in faith, they are our contributions to the originary task with which all mankind is charged; done in faith, they become our dignity and glory.

Such care of the household is for men as well as women. When a father changes diapers, for example, and "someone ridicules him as an effeminate fool… God, with all his angels and creatures, is smiling."[16] Rather than complaining about their lot, parents should confess to God, "I am not worthy to rock the little babe or wash its diapers."[17] We should be confident, Luther teaches us, that in serving our families, we are doing God's will, fulfilling our calling as men and women in God's world.

Fourth, the Reformation contradicted Roman Catholic teaching by permitting divorce on the basis of Scripture. Luther believed that Scripture gave three grounds for divorce. The first ground of divorce, according to Luther, is when the husband or wife is "not equipped for marriage" because of bodily deficiencies (those who are, in Christ's parlance, born eunuchs).[18] The second ground of divorce is adultery, and here Luther appeals to Matthew 19. He argues that Christ permits divorce in such cases, "so that the innocent person may remarry." Crucially, Luther held divorce in such cases to be open to both parties, not just men. The third and final ground of divorce is abandonment, manifested either literally, as when one party refuses to live with the other, or figuratively, when one party "deprives and avoids the other, refusing to fulfill the conjugal duty."[19]

Calvin allowed only one ground of divorce: adultery. Those who seek other reasons to divorce, he writes, "ought justly to be set at naught, because they choose to be wise above the heavenly teacher."[20] Not even one spouse's leprosy—or, in modern terms, one spouse's completely and utterly

---

[16] Luther, "The Estate of Marriage," 40.

[17] Luther, "The Estate of Marriage," 39.

[18] Luther, "The Estate of Marriage," 30.

[19] Luther, "The Estate of Marriage," 33.

[20] John Calvin, *Harmony of the Gospels*, in *Calvin: Commentaries*, trans. and ed. Joseph Haroutunian and Louise Pettibone Smith Library of Christian Classics (Philadelphia: Westminster Press, 1958), 383 (commenting on Matt. 19:9).

debilitating communicable illness—justifies divorce. To those who demur that such illness makes social and sexual intercourse impossible, thereby undermining one of the reasons St. Paul gives for marriage in the first instance, Calvin simply replies that God will give spouses what they need if they obey his command to remain married. Like Luther, however, Calvin does affirm that "the right" of divorce "belongs equally and mutually to both sides, as there is a mutual and equal obligation to fidelity." The wife's right to the husband's body differs in no way from the husband's right to the wife's, for the husband "is not the lord of his body."[21] Thus, divorce may be permitted in the case of adultery.

Although there was some diversity among the Reformers concerning precisely how narrow Scripture's grounds for divorce are, the Reformers speak with one voice in insisting that those who divorce "tear [themselves] in pieces, because such is the force of holy marriage, that the husband and wife become one man."[22]

CONCLUSION

The Reformers upheld the divine institution of marriage and family life, contended that its good consisted first but not only in the generation of children for the purpose of worshiping God, and insisted upon the indissolubility of marriage save on scriptural grounds. Because of their deep commitment to Scripture, few have managed to match the beauty and profundity of the Reformers' teachings on marriage and family life, even as their vision was not without its errors and overstatements.[23]

In tension with this extraordinarily positive vision of marriage, the Reformers also matched St. Augustine's pessimism about human nature left to its own devices. They saw clearly that in the fall of humanity, the order established by God broke down—not completely, but catastrophically. Death and sin entered the world, taking up residence in our flesh as their chief site of operations. As a result, "nobody is without evil lust," Luther tells

---

[21] Calvin, *Harmony of the Evangelists*, 384 (commenting on Matt. 19:9).

[22] Calvin, *Harmony of the Evangelists*, 380 (commenting on Matt. 19:5).

[23] See Matthew Lee Anderson's chapter "Procreation and Children" in this volume for more on this last point.

us.[24] And yet, while "intercourse is never without sin... God excuses it by his grace because the estate of marriage is his work, and he preserves in and through the sin all the good which he has implanted and blessed in marriage."[25] Such is God's power that even from evil he works good. Although the flesh is fatally compromised by sin, God quickens the dead, calling those things which are not into being (Rom. 4:17). In the divine dispensation, the dead flesh brings forth life.

This is the deep insight of the Reformers: marriage and family are disordered by the Fall, but they are also means by which this disorder is overcome. Fraught with pain and danger, filled with work both menial and numbing, marriage and family are, nevertheless, for those to whom they are given, means of salvation.

---

[24] Martin Luther, "Treatise on Good Works" in *The Christian in Society*, vol. 1, in *Luther's Works: American Edition*, vols. 44—47, trans. Jaroslav Pelikan (St. Louis: Concordia Publishing House, 1955), 106.

[25] Luther, "The Estate of Marriage," 49.

VII.

Abortion

STEVEN WEDGEWORTH

PROTESTANTS are currently divided on the question of abortion. The Protestant "mainline" is generally pro-choice, ranging from a spirited defense of a woman's bodily autonomy to a reluctant allowance of abortion in times of perceived necessity. This latter emphasis is usually related to perceived tragic health consequences, though it sometimes includes what is called emotional health. On the other hand, "evangelical" and "fundamentalist" Protestants are generally pro-life, opposing abortion except for cases where the physical life of the mother is endangered. In some cases, even this exception is rejected. Such a disagreement between "pro-choice" and "pro-life" Protestantism, however, is actually a recent development. From Protestantism's inception in the sixteenth century, until the middle of the twentieth, Protestant theologians and moralists maintained a consistent opposition to abortion. This witness was briefly lost, even in some surprising ecclesiastical contexts, until the 1973 *Roe v. Wade* U.S. Supreme Court decision shocked Protestant consciences.

Unfortunately, the newer pro-life arguments offered by Protestant churches and theologians rarely engage with the earlier Protestant tradition. This can leave the impression that the question of abortion is entirely new or that Protestants lack a larger body of moral literature with which they can address it. To help correct that misconception, this essay will demonstrate the older Protestant outlook on the morality of abortion and the status of human life in the womb. While some diversity exists on specific questions, the general consensus is plain: for Protestants, abortion is always a tragedy and, except for cases of medical necessity, a great sin. Most within the tradition are even willing to call it a form of murder.

THE TWENTIETH-CENTURY CONFUSION

Before looking to the older Protestant tradition, it is important to see the extent to which twentieth-century churches, including evangelical representatives, departed from it. One might be tempted to believe that the abortion debate has always featured a predictable "conservative" and "liberal" division, but this is not at all the whole story. In 1968, five years before *Roe v. Wade*, the evangelical magazine *Christianity Today* published an issue dedicated to abortion and contraception.[1] Several of the articles affirmed at least a limited place for abortion, including one written by Bruce Waltke, a respected biblical scholar who has held teaching positions at Dallas Theological Seminary, Regent College, Westminster Theological Seminary, and Reformed Theological Seminary. In his article, Waltke denied that the Old Testament "regards the fetus as a soul."[2] This issue of *Christianity Today* and Waltke's article in particular are widely cited by critics of contemporary evangelicals as evidence of abrupt change due to American political concerns.[3]

---

[1] *Christianity Today* 13 (November 8, 1968).

[2] *Christianity Today* 13, p. 3; Waltke modified his position in a more pro-life direction in 1976. See Bruce Waltke, "Reflections from the Old Testament on Abortion," *The Journal of the Evangelical Theological Society* 19, no. 1 (1976): 3–13.

[3] Jonathan Dudley, "My Take: When Evangelicals Were Pro-Choice," *CNN Belief Blog*, October 30, 2010, https://religion.blogs.cnn.com/2012/10/30/my-take-when-evangelicals-were-pro-choice/; Paul Rosenberg, "When Evangelicals Were Pro-Choice and the NRA Was Pro-Gun Control," *Salon*, July 8, 2018, https://www.salon.com/2018/07/08/when-evangelicals-were-pro-choice-and-the-nra-was-pro-gun-control-a-history-of-hypocrisy/. An additional argument is sometimes made that evangelical political support of abortion was a sort of transactional decision in order to create a broader political coalition with Roman Catholics. See Randall Balmer, *Thy Kingdom Come: How the Religious Right Distorts Faith and Threatens America* (New York: Basic Books, 2007), 5–34; Max Blumenthal, "Agent of Intolerance," *The Nation*, May 16, 2007, https://www.thenation.com/article/archive/agent-intolerance/.

In fact, the story goes deeper than popular magazines. In 1971, the Southern Baptist Convention made a pro-choice resolution on abortion at their annual meeting:

> [W]e call upon Southern Baptists to work for legislation that will allow the possibility of abortion under such conditions as rape, incest, clear evidence of severe fetal deformity, and carefully ascertained evidence of the likelihood of damage to the emotional, mental, and physical health of the mother.[4]

To see the full significance of this statement, note how similar it is to The Episcopal Church's 1967 allowance for abortion:

> …where the decision to terminate has been arrived at with proper safeguards against abuse, and where it has been clearly established that the physical or mental health of the mother is threatened seriously, or where there is substantial reason to believe that the child would be born badly deformed in mind or body, or where the pregnancy has resulted from rape or incest.[5]

Perhaps most surprising of all, the conservative and old-school Orthodox Presbyterian Church studied the issue of abortion in 1970 and 1971, and its committee came back divided. The majority issued a pro-life report, but Paul Wooley, an original faculty member of Westminster Theological Seminary, wrote a minority report denying that the Bible actually addresses abortion. He argued that the majority report was rationalistic and "of Roman Catholic tendency" in its logic. He rejected the argument that a fertilized egg should be treated as a human person, contending that abortion in certain cases could be allowed.[6] Importantly, the following year, the

---

[4] "Resolution on Abortion," Southern Baptist Convention, June 1, 1971, https://www.sbc.net/resource-library/resolutions/resolution-on-abortion-2/. The SBC began to move to a more pro-life position in 1976: "Resolution on Abortion," Southern Baptist Convention, June 1, 1976, https://www.sbc.net/resource-library/resolutions/resolution-on-abortion-3/.

[5] "Journal of the General Convention of the Episcopal Church," The Episcopal Church, September 17, 1967, https://www.episcopalarchives.org/sites/default/files/publications/1967_GC_Journal.pdf, 308.

[6] "Report of the Committee to Study the Matter of Abortion," Orthodox Presbyterian Church, May 24, 1971, https://opc.org/GA/abortion.html.

General Assembly of the OPC returned to the question and essentially rejected the minority report.[7]

Many conservative Protestant ecclesiastical bodies were able to sound an unequivocal rejection of abortion. The Lutheran Church–Missouri Synod,[8] the Reformed Presbyterian Church–Evangelical Synod,[9] and the Presbyterian Church in America[10] all put out pro-life statements in the 1970s. For their parts, both the SBC and OPC quickly came around to the same position. However, even these lacked any serious engagement with the older Protestant tradition. One LCMS report from 1984 mentions the patristic record in a footnote, but it says nothing about Luther or other Lutheran theologians.[11] The others omit the historical record altogether.

In failing to pass along the Reformation witness on abortion and related moral issues, these various churches left readers, and indeed their own church members, with the impression that this witness either does not exist or has fallen out of living memory. They give no clear evidence of a Protestant moral consensus, shared by a common understanding of the Holy Scriptures and the natural law. Thus even today, this witness remains largely unknown.

PRE-PROTESTANT POSITIONS

The Protestant Reformation did not attempt to remake Christianity. Instead, it was a reformation of the various bodies of believers who had possessed the one religion delivered by the apostles and our Lord Jesus Christ. As such, it only sought to change aspects of the tradition which were in error. This

---

[7] "Statement on Abortion," Orthodox Presbyterian Church, May 15, 1972, https://www.opc.org/GA/Abortion_GA39.html.

[8] "Abortion: Theological, Legal, and Medical Aspects," The Lutheran Church Missouri Synod, July 9, 1971, https://files.lcms.org/wl/?id=e7nxDx4aWCrwgvnLzpyE1sHH0DB7BxgoR. For a discussion of abortion debates in the LCMS and a more negative evaluation even of the first anti-abortion declaration from the LCMS, see Peter J. Scaer, "Lutheran Support for the Pro-Life Movement: A Case of Faith Without Works?" *Concordia Theological Quarterly* 77, no. 3–4 (July/October 2013): 229–255.

[9] "Study Committee on Abortion," Reformed Presbyterian Church, Evangelical Synod, May 30, 1975, https://www.pcahistory.org/rgo/rpces/docsynod/007.html.

[10] "Report of the Ad Interim Committee on Abortion," Presbyterian Church in America, June 19, 1978, https://pcahistory.org/pca/studies/2-015.html.

[11] "Abortion in Perspective," The Lutheran Church Missouri Synod, May 1, 1984, https://files.lcms.org/wl/?id=LwM7Yep2wOwuOfDGNqCdUi2G0sCaGFFJ, 34.

meant that the overwhelming majority of Christian moral teaching was received and embraced by Luther, Calvin, and the other Magisterial Reformers. Concerning abortion, they introduced no new position. Indeed, they typically assumed that the answer to the ethical question was already known. But there are some important distinctions about particular issues within the larger debate, especially the timing of ensoulment and how to classify the nature of the sin done in abortion. To understand the full significance of these developments, we should first survey the earlier perspectives on abortion and then see how the Reformation helped develop and even advance a pro-life position.

Ancient Judaism

Scholars debate the extent to which certain Old Testament passages refer directly to abortion, but it is clear that the Old Testament was regularly applied to the case of abortion by at least the time of the first century. A standing body of literature in both the late-antique Jewish community and the early Church Fathers reveals important agreement on the moral gravity involved in ending life in the womb, with a general moral consensus against abortion. But there is also disagreement over the legal status of the unborn human and the due punishments for abortions.

Michael J. Gorman has summarized the first-century Jewish positions in his helpful work, *Abortion and the Early Church: Christian, Jewish, and Pagan Attitudes in the Greco-Roman World*. Gorman explains that there was a basic division between Hellenic or Alexandrian Judaism and Rabbinic or Palestinian Judaism. Both sides of this divide shared a general moral opposition to abortion, though sometimes for differing reasons. But they had important disagreements on the nature of the fetus. As Gorman explains, a major cause of this division had to do with the translation of Exodus 21:22–25. Using the Hebrew text tradition, one reads:

> When men strive together and hit a pregnant woman, so that her children come out, but there is no harm, the one who hit her shall surely be fined, as the woman's husband shall impose on him, and he shall pay as the judges determine. But if there is harm, then you shall pay life for life, eye for eye, tooth for tooth, hand for hand, foot for foot, burn for burn, wound for wound, stripe for stripe.

According to this translation, any reference to the child in the womb is ambiguous at best. It is unclear what is meant by "her children come out." Does this refer to an early but otherwise healthy birth or does it refer to an induced miscarriage? And what is the "harm" being referenced? Moral commentators using the Hebrew text sometimes reached different conclusions.

On the other hand, the Greek translation of Exodus 21:22–25 (which actually appears in earlier manuscripts than those commenting on the Hebrew) has an important difference. Gorman offers the following translation from the Septuagint:

> If two men fight and they strike a woman who is pregnant, and her child comes out while not yet fully formed, the one liable to punishment will be fined; whatever the woman's husband imposes, he will give as is fitting. But if it is fully formed, he will give life for life.[12]

This translation resolves the ambiguities found in the Hebrew. Here the child is clearly in view. Instead of "if there is no harm," it reads "not yet fully formed." This introduces a distinction between a formed and unformed fetus. If the fetus is unformed, then the harm done to it will be punished by a fine. But if the fetus is formed, then the harm must be punished by capital punishment. Thus, for Alexandrian Jews, Exodus 21:22–25 bears direct relevance to the moral status of life in the womb and the prohibition against killing it.

The context seems to suggest that only the formed fetus (and there were debates about what, exactly, "formed" here means) is entitled to the *lex talionis*. Perhaps only the formed fetus is treated as "fully human," at least in the legal context. Even with this distinction in play, however, the Hellenistic Jewish record has more to say.

In his commentary on the Ten Commandments, Philo of Alexandria states that Exodus 21:22–25 refers to an unformed fetus: "if the result of the miscarriage is unshaped and undeveloped, he must be fined both for the outrage and for obstructing the artist Nature in her creative work of bringing into life the fairest of living creatures, man."[13] Even though the unformed

---

[12] Michael J. Gorman, *Abortion and the Early Church: Christian, Jewish, and Pagan Attitudes in the Greco-Roman World* (Eugene, OR: Wipf and Stock, 1998), 35.

[13] Gorman, *Abortion and the Early Church*, 36.

fetus is not deserving of a "life for life" restitution, it is nevertheless human life, a potential "man" that is deserving of respect and protection. Gorman notes that Philo appears to reject the argument that an unformed fetus is merely "part of its future mother" and not to be considered an entity in its own right.[14] As he says later, "the law shows its indignation at such an action; not being guided by the age but by the species of the creature in whom its ordinances are violated."[15] Thus the most basic grounding of the moral concern for Philo is the humanity of the fetus, something which is not determined by its age.

The fuller Hellenistic Jewish position on abortion, then, is that the procedure is always immoral because it involves the killing of human life, though the punishments assigned to it can vary due to the stage of the pregnancy.[16]

For the second Jewish perspective, coming from the Hebrew-speaking communities around Palestine, there were two positions. The majority position did not regard the fetus as a person, at least not legally. Exodus 21:22–25, due to its Hebrew translation, was typically not applied to the question of fetal life. More commonly, the question arose in the case of miscarriages. Here the interest was typically in the nature of ceremonial uncleanness, the issue being whether a miscarriage constituted contact with a dead human person or not. As Gorman shows, the consensus in Palestinian Judaism was that the death of a fetus was not treated as the death of a human person and that neither embryos nor fetuses were given legal standing.[17]

However, there was an important minority position in Palestine that disagreed. It argued that Genesis 9:6 taught that "the blood of man" can exist "within man," and so therefore the child in the womb was a person, even one who was owed the *lex talionis*. This position would then be a more strictly pro-life position than that of Philo.[18] To further complicate matters, even those Palestinian Jews, like Josephus, who generally took the majority view on the legal status of the fetus could still condemn abortion, even stating that

---

[14] Gorman, *Abortion and the Early Church*, 36.

[15] Philo, *The Special Laws*, 3.118, http://www.earlyjewishwritings.com/text/philo/book29.html (emphasis added).

[16] Gorman, *Abortion and the Early Church*, 37.

[17] Gorman, *Abortion and the Early Church*, 40–41.

[18] Gorman, *Abortion and the Early Church*, 44.

it "destroys a soul."[19] David A. Jones argues that the Mishnah contains at least two relevant teachings, that the fetus is not regarded as a man until birth and that the soul is created at conception.[20] It is therefore unjustified to presume that the more permissive legal opinions imply that ancient Jewish writers did not see any moral problem with abortion. The later tradition, at least in Orthodox Judaism, worked its way out in two directions, one entirely restrictive and the other permissive but still morally cautious.[21]

Early Christianity

The Christian church has maintained a robust anti-abortion position from its earliest days. It did not follow any particular school of Judaism in its argumentation, but it did generally use the Septuagint translation of the Old Testament Scriptures. Therefore, the distinction between the unformed and formed fetus appears with some regularity. Various Christian thinkers disagreed over whether the fetus in the womb was always to be regarded as a human person and thus whether all abortions were to be considered murder. But even those who declined to classify abortion as murder still condemned it as immoral, usually as a form of illicit contraception. All early Christians agreed that abortion was immoral and should be punished.

Whether the New Testament discusses abortion is a contested question. There is no clear and direct teaching on the issue, but the Greek term *pharmakeia*, found in Galatians 5:20, Revelation 9:21, and Revelation 18:23, was interpreted by many early Christians as relevant. Most modern translations render the term "witchcraft" or "sorcery," but the earliest commentators took it to refer to a sort of drug or potion which could be

---

[19] Gorman, *Abortion and the Early Church*, 43.

[20] David Albert Jones, *The Soul of the Embryo: An Inquiry into the Status of the Human Embryo in the Christian Tradition* (New York: Continuum, 2004), 110–12.

[21] See Noam Stadlan, "Abortion from the Perspective of Orthodox Judaism," in *Abortion: Global Positions and Practices, Religious and Legal Perspectives*, ed. A. Bagheri (New York: Springer, 2021), 29, 31–32. Stadlan writes, "Even the most permissive maintain that abortion is prohibited except for cause" (29), and "the majority of current published positions, especially by highly esteemed Rabbis favor the position of Rabbi Feinstein" (32). Feinstein taught "that abortion is strictly prohibited except when there is a clear threat to the life of the mother" (31).

used as a poison, including for the specific intention of causing abortions.[22] The first-century Christian document known as the *Didache* speaks of *pharmakeia* in this way.[23] Similar references appear in Clement of Alexandria,[24] as well as later writers like Basil[25] and Jerome.[26] This has caused some commentators to interpret *pharmakeia* as having an immediate relationship to abortion. But it seems more likely that the New Testament verses are using *pharmakeia* in a broader sense. Philo, a contemporary of the New Testament, uses *pharmakeia* to refer simply to the act of poisoning itself.[27] Interpreted this way, the New Testament verses condemn the general use of drugs or potions for malicious ends, and this could be applied to a range of types of poisoning. Still, in the mind of the early Church Fathers, abortion was one such application. Interestingly enough, this connection between poisonings, potions, and abortion continued to be made even into the seventeenth century.[28]

Christian theologians of the first few centuries tended to criticize abortion on a number of grounds. It was frequently connected to sexual immorality.[29] Within marriage, it was criticized in the same way that contraception was condemned.[30] Abortion was also frequently disclaimed as a form of murder.[31] Athenagoras put it bluntly: "we say that those women who use drugs to bring on abortion commit murder."[32] Basil

---

[22] Gorman, *Abortion and the Early Church*, 48; John T. Noonan Jr., "Abortion and the Catholic Church: A Summary History," *Natural Law Forum*, Paper 126 (1967), 90.

[23] *Didache* 2.2; see Gorman, *Abortion and the Early Church*, 49; Noonan, "Abortion and the Catholic Church," 91.

[24] Clement, *Paedagogus*, 2.10.96.

[25] Basil, *Letter*, 188.8.

[26] Jerome, *Letter*, 22.13.

[27] Philo, *The Special Laws*, 3.93–98.

[28] Thomas Watson, *A Body of Practical Divinity* (Aberdeen, 1838), 411.

[29] Noonan, "Abortion and the Catholic Church," 92.

[30] Noonan, "Abortion and the Catholic Church," 95–96; see also chapters five and six in this volume.

[31] Noonan, "Abortion and the Catholic Church," 92–94, 97; Gorman, *Abortion and the Early Church*, 53–56, 60, 66–68, 73.

[32] Athenagoras, *A Plea for the Christians*, 35, trans. B.P. Pratten in *Ante-Nicene Fathers Vol. 2*, ed. Alexander Roberts, James Donaldson, and A. Cleveland Coxe. (Buffalo, NY: Christian Literature Publishing Co., 1885) (hereafter

similarly writes, "Women also who administer drugs to cause abortion, as well as those who take poisons to destroy unborn children, are murderesses."[33]

One significant disagreement had to do with the "form" of the fetus, a question also referred to as ensoulment. This could affect whether abortion was considered "murder" or some other crime. Here, the Christian witness is divided. The majority appear to accept the distinction between the unformed and formed fetus, believing the fetus to have its own soul only after a certain passage of time. Augustine is most commonly counted a representative of this view, though the distinction can also be found in Origen, Tertullian, Jerome,[34] and Gregory of Nyssa.[35]

Augustine mentions the distinction between the unformed and formed child in several places, notably *On Marriage and Concupiscence*,[36] *Questions on Exodus*,[37] and *Enchiridion*.[38] In the first two, Augustine appears to make relatively straightforward statements to the effect that the unformed fetus does not yet have soul and thus its abortion is not considered the killing of a man. He even says, "the fact that the author [of Exodus 21:22] did not want the unborn childbirth to belong to the homicide proves that he thought that it was not man that is carried in the mother's womb."[39] At the same time, Augustine goes on to hedge somewhat, as he says that this is a "great question" that "is not to be hastily decided."[40] Appealing to this qualification, as well as what Augustine had written in *Of the Origin of the Soul*, Noonan says,

---

ANF). Revised and edited for New Advent by Kevin Knight. https://www.newadvent.org/fathers/0205.html

[33] Basil, *Letter*, 188.8.

[34] Gorman, *Abortion and the Early Church*, 57, 59, 69, 70; Noonan, "Abortion and the Catholic Church," 94–95.

[35] David Jones cites Nyssa's *On the Holy Spirit* in Jones, *The Soul of the Embryo*, 116; the Nyssa quote can be found in *The Nicene and Post-Nicene Fathers*, ed. Philip Schaff and Henry Wace (1886—1889), 2/5:320 (hereafter *NPNF*).

[36] Augustine, *On Marriage and Concupiscence*, 1.17.15.

[37] Augustine, *Questions on Exodus*, trans. John Litteral, 21.80, https://sites.google.com/site/aquinasstudybible/home/exodus/questions-on-exodus-by-augustine-of-hippo.

[38] Augustine, *Enchiridion*, 85–86.

[39] Augustine, *Questions on Exodus*, 21.80.

[40] Augustine, *Questions on Exodus*, 21.80.

"Augustine affirmed that, in fact, man did not know when the rational soul was given by God."[41] Augustine did not believe that an unformed fetus should be granted full legal standing. At the same time, he believed that all abortions after formation were murder. But Augustine has more to say about the unformed fetus.

In the *Enchiridion*, he suggests that even unformed fetuses will be resurrected and brought to completion in the new heavens and new earth:

> Now who is there that is not rather disposed to think that unformed abortions perish, like seeds that have never fructified? But who will dare to deny, though he may not dare to affirm, that at the resurrection every defect in the form shall be supplied, and that thus the perfection which time would have brought shall not be wanting, any more than the blemishes which time did bring shall be present.[42]

This is revealing. While Augustine might be willing to make legal concessions because of the fetus's unformed state, the abortion of an unformed fetus still involves the killing of a child of God, one who will be alive at the resurrection. Augustine wanted to be faithful to his understanding of Exodus 21, but he also applied his larger theology of creation and resurrection to explain the fetus's full significance and worth, whether formed or unformed.

Gregory of Nyssa is similar. He too employs the distinction between the unformed and formed fetus, arguing, "while as long as it is in this unformed state, it is something other than a human being."[43] Importantly, he does not apply this to the state of the fetus's soul. To the contrary, Gregory argues that the soul is present in the embryo from the earliest moments, even if it cannot be visibly discerned.[44] Gregory is therefore able to accept the distinction between the unformed and formed fetus without interpreting such a distinction to mean that the soul only enters upon formation. The soul is present from the beginning, even if it cannot yet be discerned. Gregory even goes on to say that this unformed (or not-yet formed) soul is alive: "it is clear to those who have given any attention to the matter, that the thing

---

[41] Noonan, "Abortion and the Catholic Church," 95; see also Jones, *The Soul of the Embryo*, 102.

[42] Augustine, *Enchiridion*, NPNF, 85; see also *City of God*, 22.13.

[43] Nyssa, *On the Holy Spirit*, NPNF, 5:320.

[44] Gregory of Nyssa, *On the Making of Man*, NPNF, 29.4.

which was implanted by separation from the living body for the production of the living being was not a thing dead or inanimate in the laboratory of nature."[45] Like Augustine, Gregory can distinguish legal standing from spiritual identity. The unformed fetus may or may not be a legal entity, but it is to be considered a living soul.

Not all early Christians used the same method of reasoning on this question. An early third-century document commonly attributed to Clement of Alexandria employs an entirely different framework:

> An ancient said that the embryo is a living thing; for that the soul entering into the womb after it has been by cleansing prepared for conception, and introduced by one of the angels who preside over generation, and who knows the time for conception, moves the woman to intercourse; and that, on the seed being deposited, the spirit, which is in the seed, is, so to speak, appropriated, and is thus assumed into conjunction in the process of formation. He cited as a proof to all, how, when the angels give glad tidings to the barren, they introduce souls before conception. And in the Gospel "the babe leapt" as a living thing. And the barren are barren for this reason, that the soul, which unites for the deposit of the seed, is not introduced so as to secure conception and generation.[46]

This excerpt may show a belief in the preexistence of the soul, as the angel is said to "introduce souls before conception." On the other hand, it may only mean that the soul is "alive" in the seed of the father. In either case, the fetus is fully alive and ensouled at conception (if not earlier). While this view could be seen as somewhat unorthodox when compared to later doctrinal consensus, it is important to note how the author connects it to the biblical account of John the Baptist in his mother's womb. Because of New Testament revelation, the fetus was clearly understood to be alive. Some early Christians were willing to extend this backwards to the earliest stages of the embryo.

A final important witness is Basil the Great. He dismissed the entire debate concerning the development of the soul, saying:

---

[45] Gregory of Nyssa, *On the Making of Man*, 29.10.
[46] *Prophetic Eclogues* or *Selections From the Prophetic Scriptures* 8:49, in *The Ante-Nicene Fathers*, ed. Alexander Roberts and James Donaldson (New York: T&T Clark, 1995), 50.

> The woman who purposely destroys her unborn child is guilty of murder. With us there is no nice enquiry as to its being formed or unformed. In this case it is not only the being about to be born who is vindicated, but the woman in her attack upon herself; because in most cases women who make such attempts die. The destruction of the embryo is an additional crime, a second murder, at all events if we regard it as done with intent.[47]

Basil flatly states that all abortions "done with intent" are murders. The distinction between formed and unformed is irrelevant. Perhaps he can say this because he is only concerned with the ecclesiastical punishment. Even though the action, according to Basil, is murder, he goes on to prescribe a ten-year punishment. This was in keeping with the canon of the Council of Ancyra which had softened a prior penalty. Earlier women who had committed abortion were excommunicated for life.[48]

Thus the early Christian church attitude is unified in condemning abortion. There is some contested evidence that it could be allowed in extreme medical situations, to save the life of the mother, but every other instance is strictly condemned.[49] The nature of the condemnations differs between certain writers. For some, early abortions are treated as nearly equivalent to contraception, a sin but not necessarily murder. For others, the stage of development is irrelevant to the discussion, as all abortions are understood to be forms of murder. The punishments for abortions ranged from lifetime excommunication to excommunication for ten years. For some early Christians, the child in the womb developed a soul over a period of time. For others, the soul was understood to be present at conception, if not earlier. Even with this diversity, however, nearly all early Christians stated that the child in the womb, even at the embryonic state, has a spiritual identity worthy of recognition and honor.

Medieval Christianity

As Christendom, at least in the West, moved into the Middle Ages, Christ thinking about abortion and its related questions became more systematic

---

[47] Basil, *Letter*, 188.2.

[48] Gorman, *Abortion and the Early Church*, 64–65.

[49] Tertullian, *De Anima* 25.4–5; Augustine, *Enchiridion* 86. The Jewish position in the Roman empire around this same time permitted abortions in order to save the life of the mother; see Gorman, *Abortion and the Early Church*, 42.

and uniform. The basic argument made previously by Augustine became common orthodoxy and was enshrined in canon law.[50] Abortion was always denounced as a moral evil,[51] but abortions at different stages of fetal development were classified as different kinds of sins deserving of different kinds of penalties.[52] At no point was the morality of abortion questioned, but answers varied concerning what kind of immorality it was. The question of the point at which human life begins was also addressed in more detail, with differing answers.

It is important to note that neither the "code of Justinian" nor English common law granted the unborn fetus legal status as such.[53] This had more to do with differing philosophies of what constitutes a crime and the feasible jurisdictional reach of the civil government than it did with questions of morality, but it does reveal possible disagreements over fetal personhood. [54] What came to be the more dominant perspective was the one associated with Gratian's *Decretals*, the writings of Thomas Aquinas, and later commentators and canonists. At the end of the twelfth century, Gratian asked, "Concerning those who procure an abortion, the question is whether they are to be judged as homicides, or not," answering, "He who procures an abortion before the

---

[50] Noonan, "Abortion and the Catholic Church," 99, 101; see also Wolfgang Müller, *The Criminalization of Abortion in the West: Its Origins in Medieval Law* (New York: Cornell University Press, 2017), 22.

[51] See the argument of Laura Wolk and O. Carter Snead, "Fearfully and Wonderfully Made: The Catholic Church's Position on Abortion," in Bagheri, *Global Positions and Practices*, 53–55, 56.

[52] Noonan, "Abortion and the Catholic Church," 99, 101; Müller, *The Criminalization of Abortion in the West*, 24–25.

[53] Müller, *The Criminalization of Abortion in the West*, 12–14.

[54] Müller writes, "The hazards of miscommunication are far greater than scholarship on medieval crime and abortion has conceded. The absence from the Middle Ages of state-run justice monopolies, the persistent weakness of top-down law enforcement, and the mentioned coexistence of penitential and punitive crimina in the same realm of public order all intimate that current notions may be inadequate for an accurate assessment of criminal phenomena and abortion during the period. Habits of thinking about justice today appear to be incompatible with premodern attitudes…the Latin noun *crimen* covered multiple offenses besides those we consider crimes today and…canonical jurisprudence of the later Middle Ages devised a minimum of three different avenues to remedy them." *The Criminalization of Abortion in the West*, 8–9.

soul is infused into the body is not a homicide."[55] This argument was supported by Peter Lombard, Albert the Great, and Thomas Aquinas.[56] For his part, Thomas seems to have undergone some development. According to Noonan, Thomas had originally argued that abortion was a sin against nature because even the beasts care for their young.[57] But when he discussed the same "sins against nature" later in his *Summa Theologica*, abortion is not mentioned.[58] At another place in the *Summa*, Thomas affirms the "Augustinian" and "Gratian" reading of Exodus 21:22, writing, "if there results the death either of the woman or of the animated fetus, he will not be excused from homicide, especially seeing that death is the natural result of such a blow."[59] John Haldane and Patrick Lee caution against taking this answer to mean that Aquinas was somehow "soft" on abortion,[60] but it nevertheless does show that he was committed to a certain theory of fetal formation and that this theory informed how he thought about the nature of this sin and any potential punishments. For Thomas, the fetus did not have a human soul prior to formation.[61] It was this reason, for Thomas, that abortions prior to the formation of the fetus were not to be considered homicide.

---

[55] Quoted in Müller, *The Criminalization of Abortion in the West*, 24; see also Noonan, 99.

[56] Noonan, "Abortion and the Catholic Church," 101

[57] Noonan, "Abortion and the Catholic Church," 101.

[58] Noonan, "Abortion and the Catholic Church," 101; *Summa Theologica* II–II.154.11–12.

[59] Thomas Aquinas, *Summa Theologiae*, trans. Fathers of the English Dominican Province, https://www.newadvent.org/summa/3064.htm#article8, II.64.8 ad. 2.

[60] John Haldane and Patrick Lee, "Aquinas on Human Ensoulment, Abortion, and the Value of Human Life," *Philosophy* 78, no. 304 (April 2003): 256–260.

[61] Noonan, "Abortion and the Catholic Church," 101–2; Jones, *The Soul of the Embryo*, 120–21. See also Joseph F. Donceel, "Immediate Animation and Delayed Hominization," *Theological Studies* 31 (1970): 76–105. Donceel argues that Thomas was committed to delayed hominization because of his acceptance of Aristotle's theory of the soul. Donceel writes, "Hylomorphism cannot admit that the fertilized ovum, the morula, the blastula, the early embryo, is animated by an intellectual, human soul" (p. 82). He goes on to suggest that this view of the soul has been "endorsed" by the Council of Vienne (p. 88), thus, by his reasoning, giving delayed hominization a strong place in Catholic thought.

Medieval canon law carried on this same distinction between the unformed and formed fetus.[62] Starting at around the thirteenth century, it began to clearly show up in civil law as well as canon law.[63] This became particularly relevant for doctors who might be asked to terminate a pregnancy to save the life of the mother. Opinion varied on this question, with some lawyers and theologians invoking a sort of "self-defense" argument[64] and others allowing therapeutic abortions only in the case of unformed fetuses and never afterwards.[65] Therapeutic abortions would only come to have broader allowance in the sixteenth century.[66]

THE MAGISTERIAL PROTESTANT CONSENSUS

By the onset of the Reformation, the topic of abortion had been discussed in some detail for centuries. The Reformers therefore addressed abortion throughout their work but never felt the burden of settling any significant controversy over the matter. There generally was none. Thus, the material is frequently brief. Still, they do make some important developments, perhaps even modifications, upon earlier thinking. Most important among these are the Reformers' relative lack of interest in, if not total rejection of, the distinction between the unformed and formed fetus, their broad extension of the definition of murder, and their affirmation that the human soul, and therefore the beginning of human life, is present at the moment of conception.

Luther on Abortion

In a discussion of Abraham's second marriage at a very old age, Luther argues strongly for the good of childbirth. Abraham's action, he says, which might strike many as unseemly, is justified on the grounds that he will have more offspring. In this context, Luther then offers a passing condemnation of abortion: "How great, therefore, the wickedness of human nature is! How many girls there are who prevent conception and kill and expel tender fetuses,

---

[62] Müller, *The Criminalization of Abortion in the West*, 33.

[63] Müller, *The Criminalization of Abortion in the West*, 31.

[64] Noonan, "Abortion and the Catholic Church," 107.

[65] Noonan, "Abortion and the Catholic Church," 108–9; Müller, *The Criminalization of Abortion in the West*, 111–12.

[66] Müller, *The Criminalization of Abortion in the West*, 114–15.

although procreation is the work of God!"[67] The way Luther speaks of this is telling. He obviously regards the abortion as a great sin, and he speaks of it as a killing. But he also speaks of it as something that was commonly known. In another place, Luther includes an attempted abortion in the list of gross sins committed by one of his servants:

> She has done me injury in cellar, kitchen, and cupboard, but nobody is to blame for it. Who knows what more she had in mind, for I trusted her completely in my bedrooms and with my children. Finally, she drew a number [of men] to her and became pregnant by one of them. She asked my maid to jump on her body in order to kill the fetus. She got away because of the mercy of my Käthe. Otherwise she would never again have betrayed anybody unless the Elbe had run out of water.[68]

This episode is a rather nasty one, and Luther's manner of speech is likewise nasty. One might also question the veracity of the reporting. Nevertheless, we do see another example of abortion being discussed and Luther's unequivocally negative attitude towards it.

Luther goes so far as to call those who induce miscarriages through negligence "murderers and parricides."[69] This comes up in a complex and occasionally humorous discussion of how fetuses in the womb can be affected by the experiences of the mother. Luther believes that the fetus can be deformed if the pregnant woman is frightened or overly agitated, and he even relays an account, from his own personal memory, of a woman who "gave birth to a dormouse."[70] This occurred because she had been startled by a dormouse with a bell tied around its neck. As ludicrous as this may strike modern readers, the basic concept appears to have been a traditional belief. Commenting on the same Genesis narrative, Calvin writes that, "as it respects physical causes, it is well known, that the sight of objects by the female has

---

[67] Martin Luther, *Luther's Works*, vol. 4, *Lectures on Genesis: Chapters 21–25* (St. Louis: Concordia, 1999), 304.

[68] Quoted in *Luther on Women: A Sourcebook*, ed. and trans. S Karant-Nunn and M. Wiesner-Hanks (Cambridge: Cambridge University Press, 2003), 223; the original source is available in the Weimar edition of *Luther's Works* (Böhlhaus, 1947), 10:520–21.

[69] Martin Luther, *Lectures on Genesis: Chapters 26–30* in *Luther's Works*, vol. 5 (St. Louis: Concordia, 1999), 382.

[70] Luther, *Lectures on Genesis: Chapters 26–30*, 382.

great effect on the form of the foetus."[71] The seventeenth-century embryologist Thomas Fienus wrote an entire treatise on this phenomenon, entitled *De Viribus Imaginationis*.[72] So while Luther's memory might perhaps be somewhat imaginative, the larger general concept was taken quite seriously by philosophers and physicians alike. For our purposes, this is significant because it shows a belief in a certain kind of life for the fetus, and in Luther's case, a belief in the responsibility of others to protect that life. If men were culpably negligent in the care of a pregnant woman, they could become "murderers and parricides" in Luther's estimation.

Luther does write that "physicians say that the fetus begins to live and stir in the fifth month after conception and that during the remaining five months it matures for birth."[73] This could be interpreted as an affirmation of progressive animation. At the same time, Luther does not appeal to this in any of his other discussions, and he is otherwise famously opposed to Aristotelian speculation. There are places in Luther's writings where he appears to affirm traducianism, the theory which states that the human soul is derived from the parents in a similar manner as the body.[74] Indeed, some commentators believe that Luther came to explicitly promote traducianism and that man, both body and soul, began to exist at conception.[75] Luther's comment about when the fetus "begins to live" then is likely only a mention of common medical opinion rather than evidence of a deeper philosophical claim. Luther also makes a passing reference to therapeutic abortions done

---

[71] John Calvin, *Commentaries on the Book of Genesis Vol.2*, trans. John King (Grand Rapids: Baker, 2003), 156.

[72] See Jan Papy, "The Attitude towards Aristotelian Biological Thought in the Louvain Medical Treatises During the Sixteenth and Early Seventeenth Century: The Case of Embryology," in *Aristotle's Animals in the Middle Ages and Renaissance*, ed. C. Steel, G. Guldentops, and P. Beullens (Leuven: Leuven University Press, 1999), 323.

[73] Luther, *Luther's Works*, vol. 3, *Lectures on Genesis: Chapters 15–20* (St. Louis: Concordia, 1999), 206.

[74] Müller, *The Criminalization of Abortion in the West*, 119; Jones, *The Soul of the Embryo*, 143; also Herman Bavinck, *Reformed Dogmatics*, ed. John Bolt (Grand Rapids: Baker Academic, 2004), 2:580. For an explanation on traducianism and its relevance to abortion, see Dennis J. Billy, "Traducianism as Theological Model in the Problem of Ensoulment," *The Irish Theological Quarterly* 55, no. 1 (1989): 18–38; Ted Nelson, "Traducianism? Creationism? What Has an Ancient Debate to Do with the Modern Debate over Abortion?" *Denison Journal of Religion* 13, no. 2 (2014): 1–15.

[75] George Huntston Williams, "Religious Residues and Presuppositions in the American Debate on Abortion," *Theological Studies* 31, no. 1 (1970): 32–34.

to save the life of the mother.[76] This is evidence that such abortions were done in Germany at the time, but it tells us little about Luther's moral evaluation of such a procedure.

Calvin on Abortion

John Calvin gives a more direct judgment on abortion in his commentary on Exodus 21:22, the classic text for Christian thinking on the topic. He writes:

> This passage at first sight is ambiguous, for if the word death only applies to the pregnant woman, it would not have been a capital crime to put an end to the foetus, which would be a great absurdity; for the foetus, though enclosed in the womb of its mother, is already a human being, (homo,) and it is almost a monstrous crime to rob it of the life which it has not yet begun to enjoy. If it seems more horrible to kill a man in his own house than in a field, because a man's house is his place of most secure refuge, it ought surely to be deemed more atrocious to destroy a foetus in the womb before it has come to light. On these grounds I am led to conclude, without hesitation, that the words, "if death should follow," must be applied to the foetus as well as to the mother. Besides, it would be by no means reasonable that a father should sell for a set sum the life of his son or daughter. Wherefore this, in my opinion, is the meaning of the law, that it would be a crime punishable with death, not only when the mother died from the effects of the abortion, but also if the infant should be killed; whether it should die from the wound abortively, or soon after its birth.... We plainly perceive, by the repetition of the lex talionis, that a just proportion is to be observed, and that the amount of punishment is to be equally regulated, whether as to a tooth, or an eye, or life itself, so that the compensation should correspond with the injury done; and therefore (what is first said of the life) is correctly applied also to the several parts, so that he who has plucked out his brother's eye, or cut off his hand, or broken his leg, should lose his own eye, or hand, or leg. In fine, for the purpose of preventing all violence, a compensation is to be paid in proportion to the injury.[77]

---

[76] Martin Luther, *Lectures on Genesis: Chapters 21–25*, 369.

[77] John Calvin, *Commentary on the Harmony of the Law*, vol. 3 (Grand Rapids: Baker Books, 2003), 42.

ABORTION

This commentary is valuable for several reasons. Calvin's opinion on criminally-induced miscarriage is plain enough: it is murder. More than this, however, we see a number of other important features. Calvin uses the Masoretic text rather than the Septuagint. Because of this, he has no need to interact with the question of fetal formation. However, contrary to the Palestinian Jewish tradition, Calvin interprets the "harm" in this text as applying to the fetus as well as the mother. Indeed, he says it would be a "great absurdity" to exclude the life of the fetus from consideration. That Calvin calls the text "ambiguous" indicates his awareness of the history of debate,[78] but he nevertheless confidently sets forth an interpretation that is farther-reaching in scope than the medieval tradition. Both mother and fetus are to be protected, with no regard for the timing of ensoulment or formation. Calvin is even willing to apply the lex talionis to the life of the child in the womb. This is because, in his opinion, the fetus is "already a human being." It is therefore equally owed "a just proportion." Killing the unborn child is murder, morally equivalent to killing any other human being.

Calvin does not share Luther's traducian interests,[79] but he does ascribe life to the embryo from its earliest moments. In his *Sermons on Job*, Calvin writes, "In fact, we see here how Job talks about small children, for when he speaks of aborted children, it is as if he wanted to point out that when God placed a human creature in its mother's womb, there is no soul, but we know that the child is known in its mother's womb, that God breathes into it a soul, and that it is certain a seed of life is present."[80] In another place Calvin makes clear that the soul invigorates and gives motion to the body.[81] In his commentary on Genesis 2:7, Calvin writes, "[Adam's body] was endued with a soul, whence it should receive vital motion."[82] Importantly, Calvin states, "we must hold to the rule that human life in itself is a gift of God so precious and noble that it much deserves to be prized, for we must always remember that God never creates a person without imprinting his image on him."[83] Calvin never uses the distinction between unformed and formed fetuses, and

---

[78] This point is noted by Williams, "American Debate on Abortion," 37.

[79] Calvin dismisses traducianism in the *Institutes* 2.1.7.

[80] John Calvin, *Sermons on Job*, vol. 1, trans. Rob Roy McGregor (Edinburgh: Banner of Truth Trust, 2015), 3:11–1.9

[81] Calvin, *Sermons on Job,* 10:7–15.

[82] Calvin, Commentary on Genesis 2:7, *Commentary on the First Book of Moses*, vol. 1.

[83] Calvin, *Sermons on Job*, 10:18–22.

he consistently speaks of the child in the womb as having a soul and the divine image. Indeed, for Calvin, the body does not grow without the soul, and he rejects the distinction between a sensitive or organic soul and the rational soul.[84] In Calvin's anthropology, man has only one soul, it is what accounts for the life and growth of the body, and it bears the divine image. This is why he can say the fetus "is already a human being," with no further interest in its progressive formation.[85]

The Developing Tradition

As the churches of the Reformation continued to develop, significant divisions arose. The greatest of these was between the Lutheran and Reformed churches. Their principal disagreements were never ethical, however, and while they did often disagree over questions related to the origin of the soul, this was never absolute. The Lutheran churches generally promoted traducianism and the Reformed creationism,[86] but the Reformed tradition always had certain notable exceptions who defended traducianism,[87] and Philip Melanchthon was a creationist and every bit the scholastic as Thomas.[88] Importantly, the disagreement between traducianism and creationism did not have a decisive bearing on the question of abortion. While one might assume traducianism has the stronger claim to ensoulment at conception, many Reformed creationists also taught that the soul was present from the earliest moments of embryonic life. Thus, I will be speaking of a unified Protestant tradition on the moral status of abortion.[89]

---

[84] Calvin, *Institutes* 1.15.6.

[85] Calvin, *Commentary on the Harmony of the Law*, 42.

[86] Heinrich Heppe, *Reformed Dogmatics*, ed. Ernst Bizer (Eugene, OR: Wipf & Stock, 2007), 227; Herman Bavinck, *Reformed Dogmatics*, vol.2. ed. John Bolt, trans. John Vriend (Grand Rapids: Baker Academic, 2004), 580–82.

[87] See Richard Baxter, *Two Disputations of Original Sin* (London: Gibbs, 1675), 108; William G. T. Shedd, *Dogmatic Theology*, 3rd ed., ed. Alan Gomes (Phillipsburg: Presbyterian & Reformed, 2003), 438–82. Shedd also notably cites Jonathan Edwards as a proponent of traducianism. See Shedd, *Dogmatic Theology*, 443.

[88] Williams, "American Debate on Abortion," 35–36; Jones, *The Soul of the Embryo* 143.

[89] In *The Soul of he* Embryo, David A. Jones likewise treats Lutheran and Reformed perspectives on abortion as one, arguing that the theological concept of imputation was the primary means by which both Lutheran and Reformed thinkers located the most fundamental aspect of human identity (141–55). Roland Ziegler, a Lutheran

The seventeenth-century English churchman Andrew Willet (1562—1621) attempted to synthesize key exegetical, doctrinal, and ethical teachings of leading Christian thinkers in his commentary on Genesis and Exodus. Among these were Catholic, Lutheran, and Reformed theologians, as well as patristic and medieval ones. Willet's work contains an extended discussion of Exodus 21:22, the classic text for medieval casuistry regarding fetal life. He notes that Andreas Osiander (1498—1552), a Lutheran, had denied that the death of the infant was addressed by this verse at all. The Roman Catholic Cardinal Cajetan and Genevan Reformed John Calvin, however, both understood the harm as affecting both the mother and child.[90] Willet prefers this second interpretation. He then goes on to ask whether this law applies to all children in the womb, regardless of formation, or if it is limited to the formed fetus. Here he answers with diversity. "Some hold the affirmative," writes Willet, "that if any child whatsoever by this meanes miscarrie, the offender is subject to this law."[91] He cites Gallasius, a French Reformed theologian,[92] who, according to Willet, argued that "who causeth the same to miscarry, may be said to have killed a man."[93] On the opposing side were Cajetan and Augustine, both of whom used the traditional distinction between the unformed and formed fetus to argue that the law in Exodus 21:22 only treated the formed fetus as equivalent to a man.[94] Willet does not clearly endorse either side of this debate, though it might be argued that he favored the latter, since he puts it in the second position and does not then

---

writer, also argues that the "the center of the Christian's existence or being… is not in him, but outside of him," and then goes on to connect this to divine imputation (Ziegler, "Defining Humanity in the Lutheran Confessions," *Concordia Theological Quarterly* 78 (2014): 108). Ziegler goes on to apply this point of anthropology to the questions surrounding abortion and appeals to traducianism as a strong argument against abortion (123). Interestingly enough, Shedd also appeals to traducianism to argue that killing a fetus is "murder in the eyes of God" (Shedd, *Dogmatic Theology*, 471). The parallel arguments in both Lutheran and Reformed writers support my proposal that the two traditions be treated as one on the topic of abortion.

[90] Andrew Willet, *Hexapla in Genesin & Exodum* (London: Haviland, 1633), 401.

[91] Willet, *Hexapla in Genesin & Exodum*, 401.

[92] See Scott Manetsch, *Calvin's Company of Pastors: Pastoral Care and the Emerging Reformed Church, 1536–1609* (Oxford: Oxford University Press, 2013), 40.

[93] Willet, *Hexapla in Genesin & Exodum*, 401.

[94] Willet, *Hexapla in Genesin & Exodum*, 402.

follow it up with a rebuttal. However, it is significant that the person cited for the first position was a Reformed theologian.

William Gouge (1574—1653), in his popular and influential *Of Domestical Duties*, discusses abortion in two respects. There are those who cause a miscarriage through negligence, due to any number of possible causes. These, Gouge says, may be "guilty… at least in the court of conscience before God."[95] But there are also those who willfully abort the child in the womb, "who purposely take things to make away their children in their womb." These, he says, are guilty of "willful murder."[96] James Ussher (1581—1656) classifies negligent miscarriage as an indirect violation of the commandment forbidding killing.[97] Thomas Watson (c.1620—1686), in his *A Body of Practical Divinity*, lists intentional abortion as a form of murder, writing, "many kill the children they go with, by taking such medicines, or strong purges, prove as the death of the child."[98]

Moving closer to the present time, we should notice the significance of Carl Keil (1807—1888) and Franz Delitzsch (1813—1890). Keil and Delitzsch's commentaries on the entire Old Testament, originally published in the late nineteenth century, have become hugely popular. Both men were German Lutherans, but their work has thoroughly spread across the English-speaking Christian world. When they come to Exodus 21:22, they devote a footnote to the history of interpretation. They reject the Septuagint translation, as well as Philo's exegesis of it, stating that the fetal formation distinction is "arbitrary," both logically and grammatically. They also reject the Rabbinic reading which restricted the verse to the mother alone. Instead, they apply the harm to both the mother and the child in the womb. They even apply the law of retribution to both mother and fetus, writing, "the penal sentence in vers. 23, 24… presupposes not death alone, but injury done to particular members."[99] Thus, generations of modern Protestants have understood Exodus 21:22 to apply to both the pregnant mother and the unborn child, with no interest in discerning the possible formation of the

---

[95] William Gouge, *Of Domestical Duties* (London: Haviland, 1622), 506.

[96] Gouge, *Of Domestical Duties*, 506.

[97] James Ussher, *A Body of Divinity* (Port St. Lucie, FL: Solid Ground Christian Books, 2007), 246.

[98] Watson, *A Body of Practical Divinity*, 411.

[99] Carl Friederich Keil and F. Delitzsch, *Commentary on the Old Testament in Ten Volumes* (Grand Rapids: Eerdmans, 1978), 1:134–45.

fetus. The killing of a fetus in the womb, then, was considered manslaughter, at the minimum, and owed retributory justice.

CIVIL LAW

The majority of this essay has been concerned with the history of Christian philosophical, theological, and moral arguments against abortion. It is, however, also important to take notice of the state of the civil laws. Since Protestantism by and large does not have a system of canon law, pastors and theologians have given moral judgments, leaving legal arguments to civil actors and institutions.[100] It is therefore helpful to take notice of the state of some of these laws. The two most important treatments of this are perhaps Joseph Dellapenna's *Dispelling the Myths of Abortion History*[101] and Wolfgang Müller's *The Criminalization of Abortion in the West*. Together, they show that abortion was continuously outlawed prior to the modern era. Müller notes challenges in documenting legal thinking on miscarriages and abortion due to conflicting views of jurisdiction, but he nevertheless demonstrates that abortion was treated as a felony in England by at least the thirteenth century.[102] It was often treated as a capital crime.[103]

Looking backwards, Karl Barth makes this sweeping claim: "The mediaeval period, which in this case extended right up to the end of the eighteenth century, was therefore quite right in its presuppositions when it regarded and punished abortion as murder."[104] Blackstone, on the other hand, notes that there had been some variation, writing, "For if a woman is quick with child, and by a potion, or otherwise, killeth it in her womb; or if any one beat her, whereby the child dieth in her body, and she is delivered of a dead child; this, though not murder, was by the ancient law homicide or

---

[100] Thomas Cranmer had attempted to construct a unified Protestant canon law, but was unable to successfully bring it about. Diarmaid MacCulloch, *Thomas Cranmer: A Life* (New Haven: Yale University Press, 1996), 500–503.

[101] Joseph Dellapenna, *Dispelling the Myths of Abortion History* (Durham, NC: Carolina Academic Press, 2006), 125–565.

[102] Müller, *The Criminalization of Abortion in the West*, 67.

[103] Müller, *The Criminalization of Abortion in the West*, 71.

[104] Karl Barth, *Church Dogmatics*, vol. 3.4, ed. G. W. Bromiley and T. F. Torrance (Peabody, MA: Henrickson, 2010), 416.

manslaughter."[105] Importantly, however, he adds, "But at present it is not looked upon in quite so atrocious a light, though it remains a very heinous misdemeanor."[106] Blackstone is still employing the formation distinction, and thus the law only applied to an ensouled or "quickened" fetus. Such a murder was not fully equivalent to murder, even prior to eighteenth century. Still, it was outlawed as a form of homicide then, and it was a "very heinous misdemeanor" afterwards.

In North America, new techniques and the (at least potentially) more open civil arena saw a new emergence of abortion in the nineteenth century.[107] This in turn provoked a reaction.[108] In 1873, Anthony Comstock promoted a bill which would outlaw abortion at the federal level.[109] That bill became law, and its effects lasted until the middle of the twentieth century.[110] Comstock, it is worth noting, was a descendant of New England Puritanism.[111]

PROTESTANT ANTI-ABORTION THOUGHT IN THE TWENTIETH CENTURY

As one moves into the twentieth century, the Protestant landscape does become greatly divided. Protestant bodies were the first to offer support for abortion, and indeed, abortion became one of several key issues which fractured the older Protestant mainline.[112] It is important, however, to notice how swiftly this development occurred. It was not the product of gradual

---

[105] William Blackstone, *Commentaries on the Laws of England*, Bk. 1, 1st ed. (Oxford: Clarendon Press, 1769), 125.

[106] Blackstone, *Commentaries on the Laws of England*, 125–126.

[107] James C. Mohr, *Abortion in America: The Origins and Evolution of National Policy, 1800–1900* (Oxford: Oxford University Press, 1978), 3–16, 46–85.

[108] Mohr, *Abortion in America*, 146ff.; Frederick Dyer, *The Physicians' Crusade against Abortion*, 2nd ed. (New York: Science History Publications, 2005); Daniel K. Williams, *Defenders of the Unborn: The Pro-Life Movement Before* Roe v. Wade (Oxford: Oxford University Press, 2016), 11.

[109] Alan Carlson, *Godly Seed: American Evangelicals Confront Birth Control, 1873–1973* (London: Taylor & Francis, 2012), 30.

[110] Carlson, *Godly Seed*, 43.

[111] Carlson, *Godly Seed*, 16–18.

[112] See David VanDrunen, "Abortion in the Reformed Christian Tradition," 114–15.

(much less inevitable) progress.[113] Opposition was still strong at the end of the nineteenth century. In 1869, the General Assembly of the Presbyterian Church in the United States of America made this declaration:

> This assembly regards the destruction by parents of their own offspring, before birth, with abhorrence, as a crime against God and against nature; and as the frequency of such murders can no longer be concealed, we hereby warn those who are guilty of this crime that, except they repent, they cannot inherit eternal life.[114]

In the Biblical Repository and Princeton Review, we read these reflective remarks:

> These views need no vindication. They are their own evidence to every unperverted mind. We are pained that a state of things exists which calls for such declarations and warnings on the part of our ecclesiastical bodies. But the proofs of it are abundant and fearful and the action of the Assembly is timely and important.[115]

Indeed, as late as 1920, the Anglican Lambeth Conference condemned even birth control.[116] When the Federal Council of Churches of Christ in America approved birth control in 1931, huge controversy broke out, with the Southern Presbyterian Church leaving the council in response, and several others threatening.[117] Even the landmark 1930 Lambeth Conference, which was the first to countenance some degree of birth control, felt it necessary to state "its abhorrence of the sinful practice of abortion."[118]

---

[113] Carlson, *Godly Seed*, 51–108. J. Douma also notes the abrupt nature of the shift in Protestant opinion: "Within the space of a few years Christian ethicists turned from condemning abortion as murder to defending it." *The Ten Commandments: Manual for the Christian Life*, trans. Kloosterman (Phillipsburg: Prebyterian &Reformed, 1996), 215.

[114] Cited in VanDrunen, "Abortion in the Reformed Christian Tradition," 114. The full minutes of the assembly can be read in *The Biblical Repertory and Princeton Review* 41, no. 3 (1869): 414–16.

[115] "The General Assembly," in *The Biblical Repertory and Princeton Review*, 415.

[116] Carlson, *Godly Seed*, 87.

[117] Carlson, *Godly Seed*, 104–5.

[118] Seventh Lambeth Conference (1930), Resolution 16, https://www.anglicancommunion.org/media/127734/1930.pdf.

Two important anti-abortion voices in the twentieth century can be found in Karl Barth (1886—1968) and Dietrich Bonhoeffer (1906—1945). In his *Church Dogmatics*, Barth condemns abortion, saying,

> [No] pretext can alter the fact that the whole circle of those concerned is in the strict sense engaged in the killing of human life. For the unborn child is from the very first a child. It is still developing and has no independent life. But it is a man and not a thing, nor a mere part of the mother's body...he who destroys germinating life kills a man and thus ventures the monstrous thing of decreeing concerning the life and death of a fellow-man whose life is given by God and therefore, like his own, belongs to Him.[119]

Barth explicitly classifies abortion as murder.[120] Bonhoeffer is equally forceful:

> Destruction in the mother's womb is a violation of the right to live which God has bestowed upon this nascent life. To raise the question whether we are here concerned already with a human being or not is merely to confuse the issue. The simple fact is that God certainly intended to create a human being and that this nascent human being has been deliberately deprived of his life. And that is nothing but murder.[121]

It was entirely normal for Protestant church bodies and theologians to condemn abortion even into the 1950s. This was a continuation of a tradition which reached back into antiquity and one which was fully expressed at the time of the Reformation. While that consensus would eventually break, the break was not a gradual outworking of Protestant principles but rather a violent one that rejected the prior tradition.

CONCLUSION

Protestant Christianity denounced abortion on moral grounds until the latter half of the twentieth century. This was a position which was inherited from prior Christian thought, but it was also strengthened in many ways. The return of traducianism was one cause of strengthened anti-abortion

---

[119] Barth, *Church Dogmatics* 3.4, 415–16.
[120] Barth, *Church Dogmatics* 3.4, 416.
[121] Quoted in Jones, *The Soul of the Embryo*, 147–48.

sentiment, but so also was the theory of immediate creationist ensoulment, a position advocated by none other than John Calvin. These theological perspectives allowed Protestantism to happily accept later scientific discoveries in human biology and embryology. While diversity on the philosophical question of "ensoulment" can be found throughout Protestantism's history, even in the early twentieth century, the distinction between the unformed and formed fetus fell out of use in both exegesis and legal argument. Conception, rather than formation or viability, came to be the primary point of identifying the new human life.

This essay has not looked into exceptional cases wherein abortion could be allowed. This is a contested topic, with even the Presbyterian Church in America's 1978 statement denying that the life of the mother justifies an abortion.[122] However, Protestant thinkers as early as John Selden (1584—1654) did grant this exception. In Selden's case, he made use of both medical knowledge and Rabbinic casuistry.[123] Karl Barth also allowed for abortion if it was medically necessary to save the life of the mother.[124] The PCA amended their statement to allow for this exception in 1980,[125] and such is the majority view among pro-life Protestants today.[126]

The moral and spiritual case against abortion is clear in Protestantism. The legal one, however, is somewhat more challenging. One could not say that Protestantism as a whole, even in its most faithful expressions, has always defended the position that "life begins at conception." Even if it has largely favored such a position, it shared the same layered history as Roman Catholicism on this point. More than philosophy or theological anthropology, the primary argument that Protestants use today is the biological one, what we know now about the union of the sperm and egg. And so here we might say that modern science is necessary to fully inform our theological anthropology. But secular societies, as much as they claim to value the science, tend to hold back from ascribing the full value of human life to moment of conception, preferring to relegate that to the realm of

---

[122] *PCA Digest Positions Papers, 1973–1988*, vol. 2.5, ed. Paul Gilchrist (Presbyterian Church in America, 1993), 23–24.

[123] Jason P. Rosenblatt, *John Selden: Scholar, Statesman, Advocate for Milton's Muse* (Oxford: Oxford University Press, 2021), 46.

[124] Barth, *Church Dogmatics* 3.4, 421.

[125] Gilchrist, *PCA Digest Positions Papers, 1973–1988*, 34.

[126] VanDrunen, "Abortion in the Reformed Christian Tradition," 122.

religious claims—even though, as we have seen, religious claims on their own have not always answered this question in the same way and have indeed been dramatically affected by scientific progress. And so we ask, to what degree does theology need modern science to defend the origins of life, and to what degree does secular law need religious concepts to protect life in the womb?

VIII.

Death and Dying

JOHN WYATT

FOR MOST people and for most periods of history, death and dying have taken place in the home. At the beginning of the twentieth century, less than 15 percent of all deaths occurred in an institution, such as a hospital or nursing home. The overwhelming majority of people died in bed in their own homes with close family, relatives, and friends present at the bedside to witness their final hours and encourage those who were overwhelmed with fear or pain.[1]

But over the last hundred years, death has become increasingly medicalized, and in all technologically developed nations the focus has shifted to the hospital as the locus of dying. In the UK, nearly 50 percent of deaths occur in hospitals, and in some countries the percentage is higher.[2]

When death approaches, or we have a life-threatening illness, we expect to be admitted to the hospital. We expect treatment with the latest techniques and wonder-drugs. It is the medical team who tell us what treatments are available for our condition and the natural assumption is that we will be

---

[1] Philippe Ariès, *The Hour of Our Death* (Oxford: Oxford University Press, 1991).

[2] Joanna B. Broad, et al., "Where Do People Die?" *International Journal of Public Health* 58 (2013): 257–67.

compliant patients in the unceasing battle against death, recipients of whatever therapies are available.

"The body of the dying person became the battlefield where heroic doctors and nurses waged their war against death," wrote Allen Verhey.[3] It's a striking image, illustrating the passivity and depersonalisation that modern medicine can foster. The unique individual, with all the wonder and mystery of his personal story, his loved-ones, his joys and sorrows, has become invisible. Instead, there is a body and an unceasing and ultimately hopeless battle between medical technology and death. If we accept the modern medical narrative of unceasing struggle against disease and death then it seems we are condemning ourselves to die as passive hostages within a ceaseless battle waged by impersonal professionals.

AVERSION AND OBSESSION

Modern attitudes to death have been aptly described as both *aversion* and *obsession*.[4] On the one hand, we practice a culture of death-denial. We avoid reminders of our own mortality and banish the dying to hospitals and intensive care units. We celebrate life and health and maintain the pretense that death occurs to other people. And it is striking how death-denial has also penetrated many Western evangelical churches. Worship services tend to the triumphalistic, upbeat, and celebratory. Death and the prospect of dying remain the final taboo—both inside and outside the Church. The concept of teaching and preparing Christian people to die well can seem strange, depressing, and even inappropriately pessimistic.

But at the same time, medical killing is being promoted, and a number of aging and frightened Silicon Valley billionaires are pouring their wealth into new biotechnology companies dedicated solely to finding technological solutions to overcome aging and death. Our obsessive preoccupation with death leads both to a desire for supporting and normalizing suicide, and at the same time to a desperate technological quest to delay and ultimately banish death from our lives.

---

[3] A. D. Verhey, *The Christian Art of Dying, Learning from Jesus* (Grand Rapids: Eerdmans, 2011), 16.

[4] Vigen Gurion, *Life's Living toward Dying* (Grand Rapids: Eerdmans, 1996), 3.

ASSISTED SUICIDE AND EUTHANASIA

In 2013 Nelson Mandela, the South African statesman, was receiving intensive care in hospital. He was ninety-four years old and had suffered from a range of chronic and distressing medical conditions for years. Newspaper headlines around the world proclaimed, "Fears Grow for Nelson Mandela"; "Family Gathers as Fears Grow for 'Critical' Mandela." One newspaper article reported, "Nelson Mandela spent a second night in critical condition in hospital on Monday night, with his family members, compatriots and well-wishers worldwide fearing that the anti-apartheid icon is about to lose his final struggle."[5]

No doubt that there were countless millions around the world who wished Mandela well, but what were they so fearful about? Was it so fearful a prospect that a frail, ninety-four-year-old man with multiple chronic illnesses might actually die? Was it really terrifying that the "final struggle" of modern technological medicine against disease and death would be lost? There were concerns at the time that Mandela's death might unleash political violence in South Africa, but it is characteristic of our age that an extremely elderly man's dying should be framed in violent terms of the ceaseless struggle of technological medicine against death.

And yet as our culture denies the reality and inevitability of death, it also evinces a strange obsession with the topic. Various forms of legalized medical killing are increasing in many developed countries, and at the time of writing the English and Scottish Parliaments are debating the introduction of laws on "assisted dying"—a carefully crafted euphemism for medically induced suicide.[6] Opinion polls suggest that more than 80 percent of the population are in favour of legalising assisted suicide.

After Mandela's death at age ninety-five and following several years of severe illness, Bishop Desmond Tutu, a lifelong friend and confidant, spoke out. "The manner of Nelson Mandela's prolonged death was an affront. I have spent my life working for dignity for the living. Now I wish to apply my

---

[5] "Fears Grow for Nelson Mandela," *News 24*, June 25, 2013, https://www.news24.com/SouthAfrica/News/Fears-grow-for-Nelson-Mandela-20130625.

[6] Assisted Dying Bill [HL], October 8, 2021, https://lordslibrary.parliament.uk/assisted-dying-bill-hl.

mind to the issue of dignity for the dying."[7] Ironically, Tutu concluded that the only way to avoid the passivity and powerlessness of dying in a medicalized system was to legalise assisted suicide. This way every person would have the option to take control of their own destiny by killing themselves. Bishop Tutu would have been better served by turning to the ancient Christian tradition of faithful dying, which had developed in response to classical pagan stances towards suicide and mercy killing.

GRAECO-ROMAN ATTITUDES TO SUICIDE

Attitudes to suicide within the classical Graeco-Roman period were complex and contested. The Pythagoreans taught that suicide was always wrong because it represented releasing oneself from the guardpost to which one had been assigned by the gods. Plato argued that suicide was generally disgraceful, but there were several situations in which the act of self-destruction could be defended—for instance, if one's mind became morally corrupted and hence one's character could not be salvaged, if the self-killing was compelled by extreme and unavoidable personal misfortune, or if the self-killing resulted from shame at having participated in grossly unjust actions.[8] Both Plato and Aristotle limit their approval of suicide to situations in which there was a betrayal of an individual's social roles and obligations.

The Stoics in contrast supported the concept of a suicide, which was guided by reason and conscience. This was a "virtuous death." Thus, for example, Cato the Younger killed himself after the Pompeian cause was defeated at the Battle of Thapsus. In addition, the Stoic philosophers taught that suicide may be justified if certain "natural advantages," such as physical health, were lacking. So Cicero: "When a man's circumstances contain a preponderance of things in accordance with nature, it is appropriate for him to remain alive; when he possesses or sees in prospect a majority of the contrary things, it is appropriate for him to depart from life."[9] The Roman

---

[7] Desmond Tutu, "A Dignified Death Is Our Right," *The Guardian*, July 12, 2014, https://www.theguardian.com/commentisfree/2014/jul/12/desmond-tutu-in-favour-of-assisted-dying.

[8] Plato, *Laws* IX, 873c–d.

[9] Cicero, *De Finibus* III, 60–61.

Stoic Seneca claimed that since "mere living is not a good, but living well," a wise person "lives as long as he ought, not as long as he can."[10]

EARLY CHRISTIAN ATTITUDES TO SUICIDE

Although suicide might be defended as virtuous and noble by pagan writers, there is no example of a noble or heroic suicide within the biblical narrative. Instead suicide is seen in nearly every case as an act of hopelessness and despair, as seen for example in the tragic deaths of Saul and Judas Iscariot. The only possible example of a heroic suicide might be that of Samson, an ambiguous and complex figure, who pulled down a pagan temple on himself in order to kill the enemies of Yahweh.

Although suicide is not mentioned frequently in the writings of the early Church Fathers, the careful and detailed study of Darrel Amundsen has demonstrated a clear and consistent position of celebrating and defending martyrdom, when it is unavoidably imposed by external events, yet condemning and opposing the deliberate taking of one's own life.[11] The prohibition against suicide was formulated most clearly by Augustine, who famously argued in *City of God* that suicide is morally equivalent to homicide. "It is not without significance, that in no passage of the holy canonical books there can be found either divine precept or permission to take away our own life…. Nay, the law, rightly interpreted, even prohibits suicide, where it says, 'Thou shalt not kill'… The commandment is, 'Thou shall not kill man'; therefore neither another nor yourself, for he who kills himself still kills nothing else than man."[12]

The more innocent one is of a capital offense, argued Augustine, the greater the offense that is caused by killing oneself. "For if it is not lawful to take the law into our own hands, and slay even a guilty person, whose death no public sentence has warranted, then certainly he who kills himself is a

---

[10] Seneca, *Moral Letters to Lucilius*, trans. Richard Gumtree, https://en.wikisource.org/wiki/Moral_letters_to_Lucilius/Letter_70.

[11] Darrel Amundsen, *Medicine Society and Faith in Ancient and Medieval Worlds* (Baltimore: John Hopkins University Press, 1996), 70–126.

[12] Augustine, *City of God*, trans. Marcus Dods (New York: The Modern Library, 1993), Bk. 1:20, 26.

homicide, and so much the guiltier of his own death, as he was more innocent of that offense for which he doomed himself to die."[13]

SUICIDE PREVENTION IN MODERN SOCIETIES

For more than fifteen centuries all cultures informed by Christian beliefs have maintained a consistent opposition to suicide. It's easy to overlook the efforts that we take as a society to persuade people not to destroy their own lives. In the UK and USA every health professional, social worker, policeman, and prison officer receives extensive training on how to detect individuals who are at risk of suicide, how to minimize the risk, and what immediate steps should be taken if the risk of someone ending their life is severe. All health professionals understand that the imminent risk of suicide represents a medical emergency, just as much as a cardiac arrest, and that immediate steps must be taken, including forcibly detaining people in a hospital or other place of safety.

The Samaritans, whose stated vision is that "fewer people should die by suicide," receive 10,000 calls per day in the UK and have over 16,200 trained listening volunteers responded to calls for help. As a society we routinely put even convicted murderers on suicide watch, and we regard suicide in prison as a tragedy which we attempt to avoid. Even the mass medical murderer Harold Shipman was put on a suicide watch for years, and when he did eventually kill himself in Wakefield Prison, an official enquiry was held into whether his suicide could have been avoided.

And yet as the Christian influence within our culture steadily declines, it seems inevitable that societal attitudes to suicide should start to change and the old pagan concept of the virtuous suicide should start to be rehabilitated.

THE NATURAL DEATH MOVEMENT

Elisabeth Kübler-Ross (1926—2004) was a Swiss-born psychiatrist whose 1969 book *On Death and Dying*[14] pioneered what came to be known as the "natural death" or "death awareness" movement. Her book outlined five stages of grief—denial, anger, bargaining, depression, and acceptance—that she argued many people experienced when faced with the reality of their

---

[13] Augustine, *City of God*, Bk. 1:17, 22.

[14] Elizabeth Kübler-Ross, *On Death and Dying* (London: Routledge, 1969).

impending death. In reality there is little empirical evidence in support of the five stages as described by Kübler-Ross, and most experienced doctors and counselors do not employ this framework.

In conscious opposition to the medicalization of dying, the natural death movement insisted that death could not be avoided and must not be denied. Death was part of nature, it was "natural." Several different meanings can be detected in this slogan. One aspect is a focus and celebration of the biological cycles of nature. All living animals have a cycle of birth, life, and death. Spring, summer, autumn, winter. We come into the world, we develop and grow, we flourish, we age, we deteriorate, and ultimately we die. This is the cycle of nature and so death is natural, the ecology of the natural order. We have to die so that others can be born.

But the movement emphasized that there was more to death than the biological reality. In 1975 Kübler-Ross edited a book entitled *Death: The Final Stage of Growth*. "Growing is the human way of living, and death is the final stage in the development of human beings.... We must allow death to provide a context for our lives, for in it lies the meaning of life and the key to our growth."[15]

In this extension of the concept of natural death, dying becomes part of the project of self-realization; far from being the negation of life, dying provides ultimate meaning and becomes the essential key by which we can realize our inherent potential. There are interesting parallels between the ancient Stoic thinking and the modern natural death movement of Elisabeth Kübler-Ross and others. Like the Stoics, the natural death movement advocates the virtues of acceptance, *ataraxia*, and an element of resignation before the unchangeable reality of suffering and death.

Allen Verhey has argued that the death awareness movement which started in the 1960s was a modern retrieval of the nineteenth-century Romantic movement.[16] Just as Romanticism reacted against the Enlightenment's emphasis on instrumental reason and technology as a way to master nature, so the death awareness movement reacted against the medicalization and depersonalization of dying.

But as Verhey and others have argued, the problem with the movement's mantra that "death is natural" is its denial of the *wrongness* of

---

[15] Elizabeth Kübler-Ross, *Death: The Final Stage of Growth* (New York: Simon and Schuster, 2009).

[16] Verhey, *The Christian Art of Dying*.

death. The cycle of nature can bring comfort and consolation, but it is only so much help when I consider my own impending death, or the impending death of a loved-one—an infinitely precious, cherished, and irreplaceable loved-one. Death remains an autobiographical event, an event in someone's story, and it carries, almost inevitably, profoundly destructive elements. Winter moves on to spring, but the person is gone, and the aching arms are empty. So Christian critics have pointed to the fundamentally vacuous nature of the "death is natural" mantra. We need a more profound response that acknowledges the terrible reality, that sees clearly the evil that death represents, and yet looks beyond that evil to the Christian hope that death will one day be destroyed.

DEATH IS AN ENEMY

Authentic Christian thinking has to diverge from the fatalism of the natural death movement. Yes, death is a painful reality of a fallen and broken world which we have to accept. But as Christian believers we cannot join in in the fatalistic acceptance of the cycle of life and death, agreeing that death is as good as life. Death remains an enemy and it is an alien intrusion into reality. Arguably this is where modern medicine gets it right and the natural death movement gets it wrong.

The historical roots of modern healthcare are embedded in a Christian understanding of what it means to be human. The first hospitals were linked to Christian monasteries and were pioneered and led by the Christian church.[17] From the time of the early church, Christian doctors and nurses treated the human body with special wonder and respect because this was the form in which God chose to become flesh. They celebrated the goodness of human life and used their healing arts to overcome disease and suffering wherever possible.

By a refusal to accept death and a ceaseless struggle against disease, modern technological healthcare is continuing to celebrate the goodness of bodily life and bearing unconscious witness in advance to the ultimate destruction of death. The enterprise of modern healthcare is a public statement that death is not natural and that death will not have the last word. But as we saw previously, the noble struggle in favor of life and against death

---

[17] J. S. Wyatt, *Matters of Life and Death: Human Dilemmas in the Lihgt of the Christian Faith* (Downers Grove: IVP, 2009), 141.

can so easily go wrong in the medicalization and over-treatment at the end of life which has become so common.

If there is to be better care of the dying, then doctors and health professionals must recognise the limitations of their technology and their abilities. There are limits to what doctors can and should do in the quest for healing and preservation of life; limits not because of failures in medical technology or professional skill, but rather those that result from the very nature of our humanity, as fragile, dependent beings who are subject to disease, aging, and physical decline.

It may be argued that one of the primary roles of medical professionals in our society is to teach people about the limits that come from our physical nature. This is what Stanley Hauerwas has called "the wisdom of the body." Disease and dying provides an opportunity for learning more about the givenness and limitations of our nature. "Medicine can be viewed as an educational process for both doctor and patient, in which each is both teacher and learner. It is from patients that physicians learn the wisdom of the body. Both physicians and patients must learn that each of them are subject to a prior authority—the authority of the body… medicine represents a way of learning to live with finitude."[18]

ARS MORIENDI

The Europe of the fourteenth and fifteenth centuries was familiar with sudden death. In 1348–49, the Black Death swept across Europe, killing more than a quarter of the entire population, and infectious disease remained a hostile presence in Europe throughout the following centuries, an ever-present reminder of human helplessness in the faces of forces that could not be understood or controlled. War, civil unrest, and famine were continual threats and, for many medieval Christians, one of the greatest fears was that sudden unexpected death might occur without the presence of a trained priest who could hear one's dying confession, administer the last rites, and ensure that the soul was safely ushered into the eternal Kingdom.

It was in this climate that documents known collectively as the *Ars Moriendi*, the "Art of Dying," started to circulate amongst the general population in Pre-Reformation Europe. The anonymous, early-fifteenth-

---

[18] Stanley Hauerwas, *Suffering Presence: Theological Reflections on Medicine, the Mentally Handicapped and the Church* (Notre Dame, IN: University of Notre Dame Press, 1986).

century *Tractatus Artis Bene Moriendi* was the first of the *Ars Moriendi*, and this short tract spread across Europe, translated into many vernacular languages. William Caxton translated the work into English and published it in 1490 as *The Boke of the Crafte of Dying Well*.

It has been estimated that there were at least three hundred different manuscripts of this form produced during the Middle Ages. One of the most remarkable aspects of the *Ars Moriendi* genre is that it was clearly intended not for the priests and "religious," but for the ordinary and largely uneducated masses. These were self-help manuals for ordinary people who faced death without the benefit of a professional expert in how to die well. Instead of passively accepting the ministrations of priests and carers, the dying person was encouraged and exhorted to action, engagement, and preparation for faithful dying. An abridged version of the *Tractatus* was published with a series of striking wood-block prints, described by Allan Verhey as a fifteenth-century equivalent of a Reader's Digest edition, and this proved to be extraordinarily popular.[19]

The *Tractatus Artis Bene Moriendi*, and its early variations and translations, all follow the same six-part structure. They commenced with "A Commendacion of Death," followed by a description of the temptations which confront the dying and advice on how they can be resisted. The third section comprised a short catechism on repentance and the assurance of God's pardon. The fourth considers the example of the dying Christ followed by advice for the dying and for those who care for them to attend to matters of first importance

Finally, there were a series of prayers to be used by those who were accompanying the dying person on their journey. The thought-world of the *Ars Moriendi* resides within the orthodox Catholic understanding of living and dying. Death was not to be improperly hastened, and the pagan practices of suicide or mercy killing were nowhere contemplated. The process of dying was an unavoidable part of the life of every human being and it represented, above all, a vital and critical transition into the next world. As such, the deathbed was the site of a fearsome struggle between the forces of good and evil. The woodcut illustrations showed the dying believer lying on a bed with demons whispering temptations or seeking to seize the person and drag them bodily to Hell. But some of the woodcuts also revealed the Holy Trinity, the

---

[19] Verhey, *The Christian Art of Dying*, 150.

Virgin Mary, and departed saints at the deathbed, to encourage and strengthen the pilgrim on his journey to the next life.

"A COMMENDACION OF DEATH"

The preface to the 1490 English text *The Boke of the Crafte of Dying Well* acknowledges that death is a dreadful and fearful reality; even to "religious and devout persons" death "seems wonderfully hard and right perilous, and also right fearful and horrible."[20] But this is why the author has written his book; "for teaching and comforting of him that be at the point of death."[21] The first chapter cites Aristotle to make the point that death is "most dreadful and fearful."[22] But the "spiritual death of the soul" is much more dreadful and fearful than the death of the body. Psalm 116:15 is quoted: "Precious in the sight of the Lord is the death of his saints," and the author stresses that it is not just saints and martyrs that are cherished by God, but also those who die in a state of true "repentance and contrition."[23]

And the "Commendacion" contains this striking eulogy: "Death is nothing else but a going out of prison and ending of exile, and discharging of a heavy burden that is the body, finishing of all infirmities, escaping of all perils, destroying of all evil things, breaking of all bonds, paying of natural debt returning again into his own country and entering into bliss and joy." As a result death should be welcomed and received as a "well beloved and trusted friend."[24]

The "Commendacion" section contains several quotations from the Roman Stoic Seneca, and there is little doubt that the medieval *Ars* tradition was influenced by the thinking of the ancient Stoics, which was undergoing renewed prominence through the Renaissance movement in Southern Europe. The Stoics saw every event of life as governed by divine reason and therefore anything that occurred, including suffering, dying, and death, should be accepted with equanimity and cheerfulness. Verhey and others

---

[20] *The Book of the Craft of Dying, and Other Early English Tracts Concerning Death*, ed. Francis M.M Comper (London: Longmans, Green, and Co, 1917), 3.

[21] *Book of the Craft of Dying*, 3.

[22] *Book of the Craft of Dying*, 5.

[23] *Book of the Craft of Dying*, 5.

[24] Quoted in William A. Clebsch and Charles R. Jaekle, *Pastoral Care in Historical Perspective* (Lanham, MD: Rowman & Littlefield, 1994), 182.

have pointed to the Stoic influence in the *Ars Moriendi* which had the effect of distorting the historic biblical attitude to death.[25] Both the canonical authors and the Church Fathers had taught that death was an enemy to be resisted, an enemy whose final destruction would result from the death and resurrection of Christ. No biblically informed Christian could agree with the sentiment that death was a "well beloved and trusted friend."

THE TEMPTATIONS OF THE DYING

Within the medieval Roman Catholic thought-world, the deathbed was a site of fearsome spiritual battle because the demons were seeking by subtle and hidden means to capture the soul of the dying believer and drag it to Hell. Under normal conditions a priest could be sought to guide the dying as they suffered the subtle attacks of evil, and to combat the spiritual forces of darkness, so that the soul could be conveyed at the dying breath into Paradise. But if no priest was available, the *Ars Moriendi* would provide vital guidance and assistance through this time of spiritual combat.

The following section focused on five temptations faced by the dying: Doubt, Despair, Impatience, Pride, and Avarice. For each of these there was a corresponding virtue—Faith, Hope, Love, Humility, and Renunciation—that would provide the dying with the spiritual armor to resist every attack of evil.

There is no space here to discuss in any detail the remaining sections of the original medieval documents. Instead we turn to the development and transformation of the *Ars* by English Protestant writers in the sixteenth and seventeenth centuries.

THE ENGLISH *ARS MORIENDI*

William Caxton's English translation *The Boke of the Crafte of Dying Well* was published in 1490. However, in the following two centuries the majority of English works on preparing to die were written not by Roman Catholics, but by Protestants who retained what was valuable of the established tradition and adapted it into a Reformed theological framework. Instead of a concentration on deathbed temptations, they emphasized the fundamentals of Christian belief: the importance of Christ's sacrifice on our behalf, the

---

[25] Verhey, *The Christian Art of Dying*, ch. 7.

forgiveness of sins as a free gift of God's grace through faith, the requirement to live a godly life, and the promise of the resurrection. And the English writers increasingly stressed the importance of preparing for death not as a last-minute climactic struggle, but as a way of living. All of life should be viewed as a preparation for dying well.

A further development in the Protestant reformulation of the *Ars* was a greatly increased devotional emphasis on the importance of the conscience. Although the Roman church recognized the role of the believer's conscience, this role was strictly limited, and most religious activities were prescribed by canon law and ritual. In contrast, the Reformers emphasized the individual's responsibility to apply an awakened conscience to the moral aspects of daily life. Thus, when the believer was encouraged to meditate on the awesome realities of the four Last Things (death, judgment, Hell, and Heaven), godly and virtuous behavior would be enhanced. As Thomas More wrote, "there is not a more meet instrument than the remembrance of the four last things, which as they shall pull out these weeds of fleshly voluptuousness, so shall they… plant in their place not only wholesome virtues but also marvelous spiritual pleasure and gladness."[26]

Of the four Last Things, it was their culmination in the glories of Heaven on which many Protestant writers dwelt at length. It was in Heaven where the magnitude of God's grace towards penitent sinners would be truly revealed, together with the immeasurable wonders that awaited the redeemed.

The *Ars Moriendi* tradition continued to flourish in England into the seventeenth century, with its most eloquent exponent being Jeremy Taylor (1613—1667), "Shakespeare of the Divines," whose twin works *Rules and Exercises of Holy Living and Holy Dying* were widely read and admired for their eloquence and seriousness. In 1729, John Wesley discovered Taylor's works, an encounter he said left him "exceedingly affected" and which contributed to his resolution to adopt a strict observance of spiritual practices. Wesley republished extracts from Taylor's work but this represents effectively the end of the English *Ars* tradition.

A focus on the care of the dying continued in a small number of Catholic institutions such as St. Joseph's Hospice in Hackney, London, but

---

[26] Thomas More, *The Four Last Things* (London: Art & Book Company, 1903), 10 (English modernized).

this remained outside the mainstream of British medicine and church practice.

THE DEVELOPMENT OF MODERN PALLIATIVE CARE

The Protestant Christian ethos of the care of the dying undertook a most remarkable and influential resurgence in the person of Cicely Saunders (1918—2005). She was the extraordinary pioneer of a new way of caring for dying people that influenced specialists across the world, and her remarkable initiative still reverberates today. Initially she trained as a nurse and then as a medical social worker in London in the 1940s. She converted to evangelical Christianity and started attending All Souls, Langham Place, where she was influenced by the newly appointed rector John Stott, one of the most influential evangelical clergymen of the twentieth century.[27]

Saunders was moved by the experience of caring for a dying patient over the last two months of his life and this experience became the touchstone for her own life. She decided to devote herself to the care of dying people, and at the age of thirty-three enrolled as a medical student at St. Thomas' Hospital in London and trained as a doctor. Her robust Christian principles combined with a compassionate nature, an innovative and creative approach to caring, and a steely determination to do the best for her patients.

DEALING WITH "TOTAL PAIN"

One of Saunders's most profound insights was the concept of "total pain."[28] Pain at the end of life was more than just a consequence of biological processes. Saunders identified three other types of pain as well. In addition to physical pain, there was mental or psychological pain, often in the form of anxiety and depression. Often the fear of pain was as bad as the pain itself. There was also social or relational pain: concerns about the effect of the forthcoming death on a spouse or child or the painful consequences of broken and fractured relationships. And finally, there was spiritual or existential pain, feelings of unacknowledged guilt from past events, or a sense

---

[27] Shirley du Boulay, *Cicely Saunders, the Founder of the Modern Hospice Movement* (London: SPCK, 2007), 32.

[28] For an overview of this idea, see Cicely Saunders, Mary Baines, and Robert Dunlop, *Living With Dying: A Guide for Palliative Care*, 3rd ed. (Oxford: Oxford University Press, 1995).

of the meaninglessness of existence. Cicely Saunders and her coworkers developed a form of caring that addressed every aspect of pain and suffering in order to maximize the well-being of the patient over the critical hours and days as death approached. She discovered that if anxiety, loneliness, and spiritual pain were recognized and tackled, then very often the physical pain was much easier to control and alleviate.

Cicely Saunders and the other palliative care pioneers employed the latest pharmacological research evidence on pain-killing medication, together with meticulous observation and documentation from thousands of patients. They showed that it was possible for virtually all physical pain to be abolished or at least substantially reduced, without causing extreme sedation and drowsiness. Their aim was that patients should be alert and able to respond to family, relatives, and carers in the vital last days and hours of life. Psychological pain was tackled with human contact, friendship, music, humor, encouragement of hobbies and interests, as well as professional counseling and support when necessary. Relational pain was approached by supporting and encouraging family members to be present, and encouraging openness and honest communication. And spiritual pain was addressed by placing prayer and worship at the center of the community Cicely Saunders was forming. All patients were invited to partake in simple worship services (often in beds and wheelchairs) in the chapel which was placed symbolically at the center of St. Christopher's, the custom-designed hospice she pioneered in South London.

But above all Saunders and her colleagues emphasized the importance of personal presence, of "being there" for each individual, and avoiding the experience of abandonment. Through a number of intense and personal experiences of caring she learned that "it was possible to live a lifetime in a few weeks; that time is a matter of depth, not length; that in the right atmosphere and with pain controlled so that the patient is free to be herself, the last days can be the richest, they can be a time of reconciliation that makes the dying peaceful and the mourning bearable."[29]

Cicely Saunders and St. Christopher's Hospice in South London became the hub of a movement that has spread out across the world. Many specialists from the USA and elsewhere traveled to St. Christopher's and it became of hub of postgraduate training in specialist care of the dying. The

---

[29] Du Boulay, *Cicely Saunders*, 86.

philosophy and principles of palliative care were established and taught, research into pain relief and symptom control accelerated, and training programs were established. Many other hospices were established across the UK and USA, but increasingly the principles and practices of palliative care were extended into the community, to help people dying at home, and into general hospital practice. What Cicely Saunders had founded was a concept, an approach to the individualized care of the whole person, much more than an institution.

CICELY SAUNDERS AND THE EUTHANASIA DEBATE IN THE UK

It is hardly surprising that Saunders was strongly opposed to the legalization of euthanasia and assisted suicide. In 1969, when an early bill to legalise euthanasia was being debated in the House of Lords, she wrote to the *Times* newspaper, "We, as doctors, are concerned to emphasise that there are few forms of physical distress which cannot be dealt with by good medical and nursing care, that the emotional and spiritual distress of incurable disease requires human understanding and compassion and a readiness to listen and help, rather than a lethal drug."[30]

There is no doubt that the powerful and attractive model of palliative care, which was increasingly spreading across the UK and then across the world, played a vital role in counteracting the legalization of euthanasia in the UK from the 1960s onwards. And yet, despite the progress that has been made, it seems that this highly effective form of caring is still only available for a small minority of people who die in the developed world, let alone around the rest of the world. Only about 10 percent of all deaths in the UK occur in specialist hospices. Outside the UK, expert palliative care is even more uncommon.

High quality palliative care is not technologically sophisticated but it does not come easily or cheaply. It requires a skilled, experienced, and motivated multidisciplinary team available around the clock. It seems scandalous that despite the wealth of expertise that has been built up over the years, so many people still die without proper care.

---

[30] Du Boulay, *Cicely Saunders*, 142.

THE SPIRITUAL CARE OF THE DYING

As we have seen, the modern development in palliative care arose from an authentically Protestant Christian concern for the suffering and abandonment which dying people have regularly faced. Since the 1940s and 1950s, remarkable advances have been made in treating physical and psychological pain at the end of life. But sadly, it is arguably the case that the Protestant churches have not seen similar developments in the spiritual care of the dying. It appears that the pastoral and spiritual concerns of the original *Ars Moriendi* authors have been largely ignored and neglected by modern generations of Christian pastors and workers.

Modern attitudes to death within the Protestant churches often seem to reflect the cultural norms of death-denial. The dying are banished to hospitals and death occurs in impersonal, professionalized settings. We continue to celebrate life and health and maintain the pretense that death is unimportant. Perhaps unsurprisingly, in such a culture, physician-assisted suicide is increasingly seen as merciful, offering a painless transition from life and health to death. The concept of teaching and preparing people to die well, by contrast, and of celebrating the experiences of those in our midst who have died faithfully, seems alien and "medieval." There is urgent need for Christian communities and pastors to reimagine and recreate the ancient practice of *Ars Moriendi* in a form which responds to the concerns of the twenty-first century.

PART THREE:

Property, Wealth, and Poverty

IX.

Work and Labor

JOSEPH MINICH & COLIN REDEMER

INTRODUCTION

IN 2019, attendees in San Francisco showed up to a rave, but the dancing was highly untraditional—even for a rave. Before the attendees stood dancers, but these dancers were not spontaneously moving to the undulating rhythms of the DJ. They were strapped into robot suits. These suits directed their every movement. The dancers may have been professionals, or they may have been corpses. The robotic suits took no notice. While the suits moved to the music there was no telling whether the individual in the suit was skilled at dancing or not. Each robot had been pre-programmed by a coder to move to the particular beat. It was not a rave at all; it was an art exhibit designed to make a sharp point. Boston Dynamics' recent videos of a group of robots "dancing" with one another have further sharpened that point: there may be no need to strap in the human dancer at all.[1]

The artists involved in that robo-dance perform a parody of human life in a rapidly manifesting future. Neither active nor at leisure, they make no decisions. Yet they *move* in all the ways one would expect of a working dancer. Indeed, they are made to move so by a force beyond themselves—whether

---

[1] For an example of this robot dancing:

https://www.youtube.com/watch?v=fn3KWM1kuAw.

through the increasing instrumentalization of their action by systems and persons they neither know nor understand, or (what is its psychological implicate) through an oft-cited sense of being "carried along" even in one's very own activity. Artists are bellwethers of the future. Life imitates art.[2] Imagine such an exoskeleton applied to the average office worker who is needed to perform simple human tasks in partnership with a robotic master. Upon waking up, on a work day, the human steps out of the shower and into a metal suit programmed to go to the office, to type out emails, to move files

---

[2] One frequent mistake in evangelical cultural analysis is to assume that art is downstream of philosophy in a necessary sense. But Picasso was prior to postmodernism. Persons typically engage in their acts before they seek to justify them, whether the sexually libidinous retrospectively "reflecting" on life's promiscuous wooings, or the sage whose wonder is elicited from the act of worship. Just as art anticipates culture, it often anticipates ideas by giving them the first poetic "utterance" that philosophical thought will later formalize (whether honestly in the mode of new insight, or willfully in the mode of sacrificing one seeming truth for the sake of another). In this area, radical leftist thinkers have typically been right to see that the battle for the shaping of a civilization is ultimately to be fought in the domain of culture. It is the shaping of the imagination through stories, through the arts, through film, and even through memes, that "makes the world safe for ideology." For this reason, such a battle cannot be fought in the realm of formal arguments alone. Just as the Bible is largely composed of persuasion through narrative, so do we remain the sorts of creatures who are mostly moved, and even philosophically motivated, in circumstances to which the arts viscerally connect and shape us despite ourselves. Raid a cultured man's soundtrack and watch a plebeian bleed. Of course, for art to be more than a mere lie it always aims for (and is judged by) its relation to the truth. For conservatives who care about the future of civilization, there is a great need to come to grips with the fact that great art, great literature, great film, and even great memes (perhaps the one right victory in the culture wars) are a crucial part of the cultural battle. The entrepreneurs know this, of course, and so a veritable industry of Christian film, Christian music, Christian cultural analysis, and Christian dating advice has filled the evangelical airwaves and mailing lists. And yet the weddedness to a largely American market that is mostly the religious equivalent of the WWE is not the ideal formula for the crafting of great art, any more than the WWE is an ideal formula for masculinity. Rather, what remains to be seen is whether contemporary orthodox Protestant evangelicals will be able to "speak" through the arts in a way that does not capitulate to the market *Zeitgeist*, but rather persuades man honestly through confrontation with the sublime. Another (headier) sentiment has it that the recovery of the arts simply means "being classical." And yet contrary to conservative reduction, it is profoundly necessary that art be contemporaneous with "the now," to subsist at the margins of the already-cultivated garden and the as-yet uncultivated wilderness. Like philosophy, all "great art" once subsisted at this boundary, and whatever will be remembered as "great art" in our own time will retrospectively be seen to have been "edgy" in some fashion or another.

from there to there. Upon returning home the human steps out of the suit. This vision of the future is not so distant as one may at first think. Workforces are being required to track activities and output, trained by data to perform in ever more refined ways. The suit may be invisible but that doesn't make it unreal. This is the human as the extension of the machine; humanity reduced to the contact point in meat space for global technocracy. This represents the ultimate loss of dignity for the worker.

Lest this future seem too grim to be real, in 2016 Amazon filed a patent on a cage for their warehouse workers.[3] We recoil from the image even as we advance. Common sense indicates that such workers are not workers at all.

And this provokes a number of important questions. What is work? What is the right relation of man to his works? Is such a right relation possible in a political community wedded to profit maximization? What is technology and can we have a right relationship to it in our work? And what role, if any, do God, the Church, and the average Christian play in all of this?

For the reader less given to theorizing about such matters there is another, similarly profitable starting point: God sees you in your work. God works beside you. And God is working through you. This is true in your work, whatever it may be, and it is true in ours as we write.

So, let us begin making a way.

WORK AND LABOR IN CREATION

At least three features in Genesis 1 seem relevant to our reflections: that man was created with immediate access to the resources of the world, that his dominion was a co-dominion accomplished with others and their gifts, and that the world of human cultivation is a world of limits. We will look at each in turn.

First, the early chapters of Genesis portray mankind's intimacy with the resources of the world. God begins the project of cultivation and dominion first by creating the earth, but then by planting a garden and commissioning

---

[3] See Isobel Asher Hamilton, "People Are Horrified By an Amazon Patent that Puts Workers in Cages," *Business Insider*, September 11, 2018, https://www.businessinsider.com/amazon-defends-worker-cage-patent-that-was-recently-unearthed-2018-9. See the actual patent here: https://patft.uspto.gov/netacgi/nph-Parser?Sect1=PTO1&Sect2=HITOFF&d=PALL&p=1&u=%2Fnetahtml%2FPTO%2Fsrchnum.htm&r=1&f=G&l=50&s1=9280157.PN.&OS=PN/9280157&RS=PN/9280157.

man to extend it to the whole world. The cultivating God makes a cultivator in his image, and he makes man out of the very earth that man is to cultivate. God blesses this man and gives him the land as a gift.

This primal relation between man and earth precedes and grounds all human systems of exchange and distribution. This is still obvious to us in some sense. While moderns tend to think of the world's resources as accessed through the medium of money (whether given or earned), it is still the case that nobody owns the air, for instance; we promiscuously make use of it without regulation from the political economy.[4] And while it might seem odd to us, there are plenty of forces seeking to monetize even air.[5] It is worth noting, however, that our tacit sense of having a "birthright" to the world's oxygen is precisely the same sentiment that most cultures throughout history extended to all of the world's resources necessary for life. That is to say, for most of human history, the world's resources of land, food, and water were seen as "common" to all members of a community in principle—even if systems of law and jurisprudence governed and distributed access to these to insure the health of the social body and to avoid conflict. This is perfectly consistent with and indeed grounds the robust Christian reflection on private ownership (in both its capacities and limits) as a means of this distribution.[6] This was as true of medieval Europe (before the privatizing impact of "enclosure" laws) as it was of smaller tribal societies. We should ask ourselves whether our modern systems of labor and exchange recognize man's primal birthright, his claim to the resources of this world.

Second, made in the image of God, Adam is a human echo of God's own creative activity. God's creation of the world from nothing and his planting the garden that Adam was to extend echo in mankind's own activities of procreation, naming, ordering, separating, and protecting. And

---

[4] "Political economy" was the original term for discussing economics. This was replaced with the current usage of "economy" and "economics" in the early twentieth century, much to our chagrin. The implication is that economics can be a governing discipline in its own right as opposed to always being understood as having a political character regardless of the mathematical models used or their outcomes. More on this issue will follow.

[5] Though we note here that both the regulation of the air through things such as the Clean Air Act of 1970 and the commodification of "good air" through ever more expensive air filtration systems is well underway, our example will hold of some other common substance even if only at the atomic or astronomic level.

[6] See Eric G. Enlow's chapter on "Private Property" elsewhere in this volume.

just as God is free in his activity—making the world according to the pattern of his eternal wisdom—so man's task of cultivation is quite general, and God permits man to particularize it prudentially. Should Adam begin cultivating the garden in the east or west? What should he name the animals? Should he start digging outside the garden on Monday, or should he seek to understand the qualities of bark? Adam's task of dominion is open and to be performed in wisdom.

Not only is Adam's task open, but from the very beginning, he performs it with another.[7] Eve's gifts are not Adam's. Adam's contribution to creation is not his wife's. This is most obviously displayed in the different roles they take in procreation, but (contemporary sentiments notwithstanding) this difference in vocation cannot be abstracted from the concrete capacities of being a particular kind of body, which indicates a distinctive way of participating in this general calling and task. The way in which Adam and Eve participate in being fruitful and multiplying is obviously different, and so, we should expect, are the ways in which they fill, subdue, and rule. This principle extends to their children and their children's children. Cain and Abel, for instance, performed different tasks for which they were presumably well-suited. Even in the garden, then, we see not only that the task of each person is open, but that their tasks are inflected through their particular natures and competencies.

Furthermore, the New Testament sees the continuity of this pattern in the redeemed humanity of the Church. All are to serve according to their gifts and to inflect these gifts through their gendered natures. Paul's epistles frequently emphasize God's gifting to each a measure of faith and aptitude within the Church, but the external ordering of these gifts runs along the pattern established in creation. This picture of mankind's relationship to the world is confirmed by ordinary experience. We all feel most at home in the human project when we find ourselves actualizing our natures and our particular gifts in ways that extend the reign of God in a maximal way. This is so because the nature of the being that you are is itself the gift God has given to the creation. Our vocation is a being of ourself in the world that we

---

[7] Given the two accounts of creation in Genesis 1 and 2 it may be argued that Adam was created first. But the concept still holds that his work was performed in partnership with God and or with other creatures in that case. Even should a reader insist on disagreeing with us, we would point out that Adam without Eve seems to be incomplete for the short time he is alone, thus returning us to our core point.

must attempt to realize. This is what it means to express your gift. And so, again, we must ask whether modern labor systems recognize and respect each person's aptitudes, or whether some men sacrifice their own for those of another. Indeed, many might find it surprising to note that the general fittingness of aptitude and act, as a goal to be pursued in any civilization, is perhaps a very primal conclusion of natural law and seems to be reflected widely in the *jus gentium*.[8]

Third, another theme in the early chapters of Genesis is the importance of limits. God did not create a monolithic world, but he separated and put boundaries between land, sea, heaven, lights, men, and women, between being and the formless void of nothingness.[9] We begin to see the

---

[8] See *Calling in Today's World: Voices from Eight Faith Perspectives*, ed. Cathleen Cahalan and Douglas Schuurman (Grand Rapids: Eerdmans, 2016). Aristotle wrote of something analogous which, as refracted through Aquinas, has been called the universal destination of goods. Aristotle was exploring whether it is more ideal to have property in common or to have it held privately. It seems that to hold it in common would be ideal as it would foster unity among a people (this thesis was explored by Plato). But as we know, the property managed in common by the hands of many dwindles and the produce common property yields is squabbled over by those who worked to produce it, each one feeling his private pains most acutely. The solution Aristotle puts forward is to argue that property should be held in private but that the use of it should be common. This reduces tension as every owner conducts his business himself, but maintains the goods of community as friendship is developed among those sharing the goods of the ownership of property. The *goods* of the property conduce to the benefit of the whole. Now, the analogy we will draw from this is that the body we each possess is also a kind of property. Indeed, this is why the image of the body recurs in Scripture so frequently. Each of us has our private body but we owe from it a common use in our vocation which is the work I do for my neighbor. Paul writes that we are one body in Christ, each part with its gift doing its work under one head. The gifts that God gives to each one of us are given that we might benefit the whole. In our work everyone's unique mind could be shareable. As Aristotle says it is the legislator whose unique job it is to create in men this benevolent disposition that their property should exist for the common use, so too we have a legislator in God who imbues us by his grace with a disposition to exist for the sake of our fellow men by our possessions and by our acts. Cf. Aquinas, *Summa Theologiae* II–II, q. 66, art. 2; also Aristotle's *Politics* II.5. See also Steven A. Cortright, "The Perennial Catholic Reflection on Property," paper presented at the seminar Property Law and the Catholic Intellectual Tradition, University of St. Thomas, St. Paul, Minnesota, July 18, 2004.

[9] This point about the good of limits is known also by the light of natural reason. Aristotle notes in *Metaphysics*, 994b9–23 that knowledge requires limits. The actual infinitude of a series is incomprehensible. The infinitude of an infinite space is unknowable—we cannot grasp it. We engage in our reality by nature in both our

disintegration of creation back into nothingness when these good boundaries are transgressed. Do modern labor systems maintain proper boundaries between the dominion of one and another? Do we cultivate a sense of *limits* with respect to one another? This is an especially important question in light of the Fall. If one individual is likely to usurp the dominion of another, what is the likelihood of one people or nation dominating another? Even if one people makes better choices, is it their right to seize the dominion of another? If each member of our species has a primal relation to this world, a primal task of dominion over it, and a set of qualities and gifts which have been given to them to carry out this task, then should we not judge societal arrangements by the extent to which they showcase this original arrangement? Is it not possible that our own system, judged by these standards, will be tried and found wanting?

WORK AND LABOR AS FALLEN

One of the perennial temptations of the unwise (and we are all a bit unwise!) is to imagine that we can merely recount the conditions of an ideal body politic and simply become critical about whatever fails to measure up. But this works in civilization no better than it works in marriage. If one cannot be satisfied without Christ for a husband, one can always justify divorce. In point of fact, the task of becoming wise involves a full acknowledgment of how the Fall affects our condition. On the one hand, we can speak of limits as a sort of "structure" of the created order—the boundaries between things. But this theme of limits likewise takes on a historical and moral dimension. We can no more be sane humans while violating the boundaries of the created order than we can be sane humans if we do not wisely "factor in" the limitations of those around us as well as our own limitations. If one will demand Eden and Eden alone, then one can always justify revolution. Rather, perhaps the primary effect of the Fall in human society (and by implication, in labor) is that it must remain, not only in light of finitude but now in light of fallenness, a perennial site of negotiation—of openness to greater maturity. Workers must negotiate with their co-laborers to accomplish the

---

knowing and our acting as if what stands before us is delimited. This perceived limit is real and good as our perceptive ability is good and needs the limit to act. Limits make reality intelligible and our actions meaningful. Modern economists, not being metaphysicians, can be forgiven for forgetting the goods represented by limits.

work before them. So too the lone worker must negotiate within himself, in the process known as deliberation, before he works so as to know the nature of the work. Both of these processes are natural goods intended for our flourishing. In the Fall our "negotiating" sours into contentious rivalry; our deliberation to painful confusion. In our own peculiar historical moment, constitutional republicanism is an attempt to approximate the process by which such negotiation happens on a grand scale, but methods do not achieve anything apart from persons. And it is here that we must confess a tendency of contemporary reflection on labor, that we all tend to be revolutionary killers at heart, willing to murder the neighbor in front of us for the sake of that spectral neighbor I hope arises in the future—and for which I claim my civilizational larceny (in whatever guise) the surrogate. In past ages perhaps such inner evil was more clearly expressed: Ogg clubs Glogg, takes Glogg's things. But the ever more complex ways of hiding the blood of Abel avail us nothing when the ground itself cries out against us.

The New Testament was no stranger to systems of injustice and to unjust labor conditions. It was, thank God, also no stranger to the dignity of man and his vocation on this side of the vale of tears. As pointed out above, the redeemed humanity of the Church already reflects these principles, and is the training ground for the healing of the world—that spiritual *dojo* in which love is trained in order that it may be injected into the bloodstream of the world. And note, a major part of how that happens is as men love the world through their work. Work starts with knowing, and we are such beings as can never know that which we do not first love. It is to the New Testament vision of vocation as radical love that we now turn.

ONLY THE LOVER WORKS

The Church, from the beginning, recognized the primal relation of man to human dominion. On the one hand, Paul is explicit about the superiority of freedom over slavery, implying some understanding of man's fundamental birthright to freedom. But more than this, the place of slaves within the Church is mobile and relativized by a prior relation between each believer and Christ his Lord, a relation which reestablishes man's primal dominion in Christ. Moreover, the New Testament church is organized, as stated above, according to individual gifts and proclivities. God orders the Church and its dominion according to the gifts he has given to men, and the men whom he's given as gifts.

As for limits, it is fascinating to note the degree to which *freedom* with regard to social behavior is an explicit theme in the New Testament. Indeed, it is precisely by relating the *burden* of freedom that 1 Corinthians attempts to curb chaos and encourage the Church to maturity. The motion from chaos to freedom is not accomplished merely by the reinforcement of hierarchies, but largely by people recognizing their limits with respect to one another. If we took 1 Corinthians 13 seriously, imagine how careful we would be to avoid seizing, gossiping about, or transgressing the dominion of another. Paul answers Corinthian squabbling by telling each to die to himself, to put the needs of others first, to lay down his life for the brother. This is another way of saying, "recognize the dominion of your neighbor and limit your own in such recognition."

As it turns out, then, it is in the surprising call to love that the New Testament is the most politically and economically relevant. It motivates us to ask, "What would a society ordered by love look like relative to the world's resources, to the gifts of each individual, and to the recognition of our limits in respect of one another?" Before we answer this, it is worth noting that the New Testament—written in a context of mass social injustice—takes an uncomfortable turn for modern persons. *In the task of loving, we find a human calling from which we cannot be alienated by the deeds of others—a task for which each is individually gifted.* And if true of Roman slaves, it is at least as true of those whose experience of modern economic injustice or illicit coercion forces them into dependencies and relationships (with managers, etc.) that they did not *ultimately* choose for themselves. Choice may be an illusion, or worse. While Paul encourages those who can get their freedom to get it, he encourages those who *cannot* get their freedom to love their masters. Why? It is not to reinforce oppressive hierarchies, but precisely because the Christian slave possess dominion relative to the master! Just as the New Testament encourages wives to exercise dominion through winning unbelieving husbands without a word, so slaves actually participate in the calling behind all callings by witnessing to their masters of another reality. In their death to self, they display his life.[10] Indeed, the New Testament's predominant use of the language of the cultural commission (being fruitful, multiplying, filling, subduing, ruling) has to do with the success of the ministry of the Church.

---

[10] Luther can can talk about how it is godly to fight the Turks on one day, and godly to be their servant on the next. See Gustaf Wingren, *Luther on Vocation* (Eugene, OR: Wipf and Stock, 2004), 34.

We are "filled with the fruit of righteousness" (Phil. 1:11 NIV), or we fill the earth with the knowledge of God (Col. 1:6). Righteousness is the same as justice and fulfilling our vocation—doing the job at hand—is what produces the fruit God asks of us and is the means by which he is made known. In this Plato is in full agreement: justice is to mind *our* business, to do *our* job.[11] This vocation then is not opposed to the temporal dimension of the human project—it is the primal site from which it is accomplished! The resurrection of Christ and his sending of the Spirit are the rain that heals our parched and broken earth, redeeming the human commission, reenergizing the labor of man from its most interior animate principle. his work of creation and of redemption—all of his work is a work of love, and we are called to work in the same spirit.[12]

THE ORIGINS OF MODERN WORK

But to bring our analysis in for a landing relative to our own circumstance, it is crucial that we grasp the larger historical context within which contemporary persons imagine what it means to *work*. For good principles can easily strike a reader in a loose and associational way, with all sorts of applications that are unfitting. So, let us consider our larger historical context for a moment, and then end with some applications to our time.

Once upon a time, nobody "went to work" or "had a job." Until the nineteenth century, the average human existence was a subsistence existence, centered in a household. Men and women lived most of their lives alongside one another, as did parents and children, and work was very immediately related to familial life. This might have been supplemented by bartering, trading, or selling craft goods, farm products, or services in a local market. Crucially, however, work was not primarily tied to acquiring *wages* in order to purchase goods. Rather, work was quite immediately *for* life. This was possible, in part, because previous civilizations typically possessed a thick *commons*, unowned resources that were available for subsistence. Or another way to view the premodern situation is as the monarch or noble or clergy

---

[11] Plato, *The Republic*, 433a–b.

[12] For more specifics on the topic of the specifically Reformed understanding of work, capital accumulation, and theology, we recommend R. H. Tawney, *Religion and the Rise of Capitalism* (New Brunswick, NJ: Transaction Publishers, 1998). Though more needs to be said about the role of ownership, that is beyond the scope of this chapter.

owning more or less all property while honoring the historical and obligatory "use-rights" granted to the people on the land. The progressive evaporation of the commons and the medieval system coincided with the general shift of the human population (especially in the West) toward cities. Survival in cities, of course, depends upon earning wages to acquire goods that used to be more immediate (housing, food, etc.). Modern suburbs are, naturally, an outgrowth of this as anyone living in a modern city can see. What was once the edge of the city is now the city center.[13]

This gradual trend was nascent when the Reformers first started writing about "vocation," and was growing by the time the Puritans reflected theologically upon labor, but it became a definitive feature of the modern world during the long nineteenth century (1789–1921). In that world, "getting a job" was an ordinary feature of life. Most persons are born into a context where access to the resources that make living possible are entirely mediated through access to money. And so people must strategize how they might train themselves to be a competitive product in the "marketplace," such that they can acquire the money necessary to survive. This system has produced the unprecedented reality of the modern socially mobile middle class. It has also, however, fundamentally changed the character of "work." Ivan Illich (1926—2002) points out that "work" is now consciously divided between wage-earning work, and what he calls (in a book of the same title) "shadow work," the enormous amount of human activity around wage-earning that is now cut off from the immediate reward of subsistence, and increasingly becomes coded as a liability.[14] For instance, the work of the housewife is necessary to take care of the man who "leaves the home" in order to acquire the wages to provide for a home in the first place.[15] But the "home" is increasingly a center of consumption rather than production. The

---

[13] This raises concerns we can't here address about the form of life currently adopted by our culture which recognizes no limit. See above where we explore the philosophical and theological import of limit on our reflection.

[14] Ivan Illich, *Shadow Work* (London: Marion Boyars, 1981).

[15] On a more nefarious front which we hint at but do not directly confront above (given that it is a sociological outline) we invite you to consider the rise of commercial surrogacy and the ways biological functionality itself may be commodified and, therefore, when uncompensated be reinterpreted as a liability. For a more thorough introduction to this, see Zineb Riboua, "The Baby Machines: Commercial Surrogacy and Working Wombs," February 22, 2022, https://zinebriboua.substack.com/p/the-baby-machines.

work of the housewife, in a world less heavily dependent on wages, just *was* the work of living, and was done alongside a close-by husband. Children were necessary both to aid with one's subsistence, but also to care for one's self in later life (just as it would likewise be ordinary to care for one's own parents).

But in our era, all of this "costs money" and is coded as a liability that one may elect to refuse or to take up, or, ever more commonly, outsource. Formerly, subsistence often depended on establishing a household. Now, the larger the household, the larger the "liability." In this context, "going to work" is the thing that one does outside the household to sustain the consumption patterns inside a household. It is fair to wonder whether modern households are homes.[16] Illich points out that many languages still do not have an equivalent of the English "work" in the sense of some reified thing that one "goes to" five days a week. He also points out that much of the tension between genders in the twentieth century should be read against the backdrop of *recent* economic innovation rather than any classical gender arrangement.[17]

The benefits of this system, it would seem, come alongside certain risks, tendencies, and inevitabilities. Work and life are increasingly separated, and the nature of "work" is increasingly a matter of market demand rather than immediate necessity and personal aptitude. And while there are gradual compensations for this in our social order (one must keep workers happy, after all), the driving impetus to work is frequently not the common good as such—rather the special interests of some persons over others. And so while labor and dignity are often found together, there remains a whole mass of unskilled laborers who have been quite directly "cultivated" into unskilled existence.[18] Typically, they work in the service or retail industries with no company share and little social mobility. This circumstance complicates any discussion of a Protestant doctrine of vocation. Being a dependent who is basically forced to take up any gig in order to acquire money is not a good

---

[16] For more reflection on the nature of what a home is, see Colin Redemer, "On Homes," *Lamp Magazine*, Issue 02, Assumption 2020, 12–14.

[17] The etymological roots of the word economy hardly need restating. But for those few who are still philologically inclined: οικονομία (economia) is a reference to the Greek οικος (*oikos*) meaning home and νέμω (*nemo*) meaning to distribute or allocate, and is related to terms for money, custom, and law. Let such ancient roots stand like signposts as we work through contemporary problems.

[18] We recommend reading Chris Arnade's *Dignity: Seeking Respect in Back Row America* (New York: Sentinel, 2019).

paradigm case for seeing the relationship between one's labor and the meaning of reality. Rooted in creation, and in God's "placing" his gifts in men to go give to their neighbor, a Christian politics must demur when human political and economic arrangements fundamentally fail to honor the sacred bond between a laborer and the work of his hands (which ideally remain largely free and creative). This does not mean that a doctrine of vocation has nothing to say in such a circumstance. Nevertheless, inasmuch as the doctrine of vocation has ever been transformed into a project for the common good, we witness a concern for the felt ownership of a worker relative to his work. One must not misunderstand this view as sentimental, as though *good* work were always profound and enchanted rather than banal and menial. The latter is part of life, but there is a difference between enduring the banality of one's own affairs versus enduring the banality of another's for wages. This is a crucial distinction. Whatever renders the latter morally plausible as a common trend in our civilization requires the probing of mind and conscience, even if what has rendered it plausible is simple moral atrophy and numbness. And indeed, some thought has already been given to this. The rise of co-ops in recent times is a promising development. In some quarters, there is increasing sentiment that economic life ought to be recentered in the household, and that any labor given to another for wages ought to involve at least some co-share in the fruits of that labor in the form of partial sovereignty (share) over the common product. In short, there are some trends in the direction of self-ownership. Ownership of shares of a company one works for is a step in the right direction, but we remain skeptical that this will fully resolve the problem, particularly for mass workers. More promising still would be to see the always latent politics which underlie economic relations reassert themselves in the revision of national labor laws and a return of mass unionization via new, and Christian, labor unions.

Nevertheless, as Richard Sennett has long argued, there remain alarming trends in (now) post-industrial work life. The reality of "having a job" is *currently* in the process of changing. Most persons born after 1980, for instance, have many jobs throughout their life rather than just one. As the proportion of people working remotely has skyrocketed since the COVID-19 pandemic of 2020, so too has the number of those who decide to join the ranks of the "overemployed."[19] These are people who do not fit neatly into the category we traditionally consider when looking at people with two jobs. Traditionally, we think of the low wage worker struggling to make ends meet, or, more recently, of the young father who takes the second job so his wife can stay at home to watch the kids. This community, rather, considers themselves "awake" to a scam which is being perpetrated on the workers. In response these workers have decided to exploit the system, take multiple full-time jobs, and keep their employers in the dark. These developments evaporate the sense of personal identity (a coherent life-narrative) and community that often attended various blue collar or even life-long corporate jobs a generation ago. But even in the white collar world of skilled labor, there are other forms of increased career dependence. Persons in well-paid positions very often are "switched" from one title to another, and frequently have a redefined position or stake in their company based upon developments far outside their control. And so, just as there is an alarming tendency toward the consolidation of wealth in fewer and fewer hands, so there is an alarming evaporation of self-ownership as it pertains to *the work itself* into fewer and fewer hands. In all of these things, the doctrine of vocation encourages the Christian to endure the effects of the Fall while serving one's neighbor (in common projects) around him, but it also animates the Christian to pursue *the Good* in respect of human labor. Indeed, in response to the phenomenon of the "overemployed" who are "woke" to the "scam" of modern employment, the doctrine of Christian vocation would counsel that they ought not to attempt to do harm in payment for harm—otherwise their soul is at hazard. And the hazard does not come in some abstract form but rather in the concrete. These individuals who are casting off the exploitation of their labor by taking on two jobs are actually replacing one boss for another. And the new one is far more alienating, for it is they themselves who now consider their labor a mere tool to exploit. Before, they may have had some dignity as an oppressed person, but now they are ridiculous caricatures of that which they claim to hate. A soul turned in on itself is horrible to behold. The Christian who finds himself working a bullshit job in a fake economy is no less able to reconceive of his role in terms of a vocation than the farm worker was in ages past.[20] Cultivate the role you're

---

[19] See https://overemployed.com.

[20] On the rise of "bullshit jobs" see David Graeber, *Bullshit Jobs* (New York: Simon & Schuster, 2018).

given unto the Lord and care for those around you. In fact, the role of the Christian in a "bullshit job" couldn't be clearer because the nihilism of modern human life is so near to hand. The vocation is to offer hope to a hopeless workplace. To the extent that the modern economy tears asunder work from the *life* of the worker, the Christian impulse is precisely to keep joined what God (in creation) made together.

THE PRESENT OF MODERN WORK

We are all gig workers now. Working from home presents many problems gig workers have long experienced: the offloading of the cost of "work space" onto the employee, the fragmentation of the workforce away from the camaraderie of the water cooler, the breaking down of the worker's activity to mere data. In practical terms, what can be done?

Contra a certain form of "free market" liberalism, Christians must recognize by natural argumentation that the political comes before and determines economics. We must therefore argue for the pre-economic political relationship. Economics, the management of the home and allocation of goods, always presumes justice as the basis of the allocation of the goods.

If "allocation" of goods is random it is therefore inhumane and not just. In this case it isn't really allocated at all. We don't talk of the "justice" of the hunt wherein we randomly come across game, or the "justice" of the foraging party coming across only poisonous mushrooms. Justice is presumed when we are discussing "home" as well, but to a lesser extent.[21] Fruits that fall off of wild trees aren't "allocated" to us in the way that a certain plot of land may be allocated by an owner. So too the random patch on which I pitch a tent is not a home. Allocation is allocation when determined by a rational mind. This is why the root in *economia* for allocation, νέμω, implying the give and take of a rational actor, is loaned out—given as it were—to the root for custom and law. The echo of this use is still with us in the term "custom," meaning "doing business" or "trade." Now, noticing that allocation is distribution by a rational mind isn't to say there is a once-for-all-time answer to the question of "how much is the just quantity." This is a mistake of Marx. Rather, justice is allocation as determined by a rational mind thinking about justice in the prudential scope of its power in space and time. That's a fancy

---

[21] See Redemer, "On Homes."

way to say that justice is a political consideration. As such, the allocator in the home exists not as a mind-in-a-jar in isolation but rather in a set of relationships with other rational minds who will either be allocated to or will help with the allocation. Therefore, the economic is always downstream from the political, since economics always presumes a pre-economic political relationship. And this political relationship is deliberative by definition and sets the conditions within which the economic activity takes place. Further, political justice is always only justice inside the regime in which one is. Monarchic justice will therefore differ from oligarchic and from democratic justice. The Christian who approaches questions of just distribution must be aware of all of these moving parts in order to respond to his conditions prudently. To put this all in very practical terms, note that when you begin to do business you always arrive in the presence of your partners or customers with a sense of what just trade would be. Then the meeting itself comes before the exchange. Politics is pre-economic.

Interestingly, this is the case even if we consider the temporal development of the family. At some point we can imagine Abraham and his tribe. In essence, it is a roaming family with merely the promise of a political community in the future. In this seemingly pre-political space the word of the father is law. Abraham says, "You get this much, and another gets less." "This is how it is with us," some say with a sigh. But attend to the sigh. It is the sigh of one who feels injustice has been done. Yet injustice can not have been done because the father is law; they know no other way. That sigh is the shadow cast by the rational animal who knows the end of being a rational animal is also a political animal. It is a shadow cast by the political which, while temporally in the future, is still present in the prehistoric family as an end and a good.[22] "The state is by nature clearly prior to the family and to the individual, since the whole is of necessity prior to the part."[23] As the state is the location where the just is determined, so too the political prefigures the economic. Aristotle means that the state is the end—an end as related to humans being political animals. Somehow humans before the state are incomplete. Analogously to the ways happiness is an end of our activity, and happiness logically exists prior to any given activity, the end is always logically prior even when it comes about later in time.

---

[22] To return to an above footnote, it is a limit.
[23] Aristotle, *Politics*, 1253a.

Family is geared toward an end bigger than itself: the political. Families exist in order to form a *polis*, and somehow are not a family without one. As one friend has put it: "We're not meant to do a *Captain Fantastic* and raise our kids as a world entire unto themselves as philosopher kings in the forest."[24]

And this is not what is commonly meant by the "free market." The common meaning is to reverse what we have just observed: that the market should be pre-political, or perhaps trans-political. In this version politics ought to just get in line with whatever the market wants. Desire governs over reason and reason *must* obey. In some sense, this is where we live, and it may turn out that we need to argue against it at the level of the regime. We are not in a monarchy with a single ruler, neither are we truly in a democracy where equality of all reigns over all. We are in some form of oligarchy, but one where the oligarchs desire to honor and promote a life where all make themselves useful to all. This is an oligarchy of usefulness where the most useful will be rewarded the most and the least useful the least. It is no wonder that we consider children, infants, women, old people, all the weak and powerless, the dumb and the crippled *expendable*. This is evil. Monstrous evil! That is not to say there are not other unjust systems of economic organization, but we must discuss where we are.

If one wanted to talk of a "free market," we ought to mean a market where the political organization of humans ought to be unimpeded by economic interests as we determine what a just organization of the economy is. And certainly there are wrong (i.e., unjust) answers to that question. But one of the unjust answers is to say "the economy should be allowed to do whatever it likes." "The economy should be allowed to do whatever it likes" is the same as saying "people should be allowed to do whatever they like." Some people want bad things. Driven by our desire, man has enslaved man. Driven by our desire, we have driven good jobs out of the marketplace. Driven by our desire, we have gigified ourselves and sold our patrimony for a slightly cheaper microwave dinner.

The solution to this is to dig deeper. The refrain on the internet that "I will not live in the pod, I will not eat the bugs" strikes an important chord. We can articulate a desire, as we do in this essay, for work to be meaningful, or even more basically for a return of work as such. To do so will require a reorganization of our economy the likes of which we have not seen in over a

---

[24] This paragraph is paraphrased from, and that quote attributable to, our colleague Rhys Laverty on the Davenant Institute Discord server.

hundred years. This will be a reorganization not done simply by lawyers and lobbyists in Washington, D.C. It will be done by workers themselves who begin to stand up and negotiate for better terms, and who in solidarity with one another elect new politicians who keep the interests of the political community front and center as they enact laws governing the regulation of the economy—the customs of our common home. Strange you may think it to hear us say, but the Church will need some members who work in the unions, or who come alongside and found new unions. For our economic relations to thus be forged anew requires that we recover a sense of Christ as cornerstone of our economic life and as the highest point of the fulfillment of our desires. This is not pie-in-the-sky thinking, or the bugbear "false consciousness." Rather, it is a statement that Christ alone can help us resolve the economic and political problem of each one of us saying "mine" of the same things. The evacuation of the atonement at the heart of our civilization really does cause us to search in vain for alternatives ways of becoming one in the *e pluribus unum* sense.[25] The readiest, and oldest, form of this union is the bloody sacrifice of a scapegoat, but as anyone on Twitter can see, the scapegoats just aren't doing the trick like they used to. A return to Jesus makes solidarity conceivable again.

THE FUTURE OF MODERN WORK

The solidarity we need can only be found in the blood of Jesus: a blood which makes of our many separated bodies one body. If that is our situation, what might we focus on as we face the future? We can gesture toward this both generally and specifically.

Generally, the most immediate implication of what we have said is, not surprisingly, that we must bring our goodwill and peace-of-heart to our neighbors. Together, these allow a certain degree of societal peace to leaven culture, because goodwill necessarily cares about injustice, about stolen dominion, about prevented social action, and feels a limitation relative to the free reign of others. But we must first cultivate and have good-will and peace of heart, and only then can we bless others—even our enemies. It is especially in our most difficult relationships that we most poignantly display the

---

[25] See Joshua Mitchell, *American Awakening: Identity Politics and Other Afflictions of Our Time* (New York: Encounter Books, 2020); and Wilfred McClay, "The Strange Persistence of Guilt," *Hedgehog Review*, Spring 2017, https://hedgehogreview.com/issues/the-post-modern-self/articles/the-strange-persistence-of-guilt.

dominion of God, breaking the cycle of intra-human consumption that so characterizes human affairs. We rule by dying daily.

How an individual links up into a corporate or social project depends very much on one's intellect, aptitude, gifts, circumstances, etc. In principle, to whatever extent we are able to be an agent of healing in this difficult world, we are to be such an agent. But identifying those locations is the task of wisdom. And wisdom lends itself to peaceful hearts and loving souls—not to those who would instrumentalize it in order to seize control of the world for their own comfort. Wisdom is given to those who see that their neighbor has the immediate calling to possess both themselves and their own participation in our common project. With this vision of our fellows in place, we can begin imagining what a common project with them might look like.

Undeniably, we exist in a precarious and precious moment. As we write, inflation is breaking records. We have seen unemployment advance and fall in ways never before recorded. Technology is improving communications and in many sectors efficiency to an extent that it is conceivable for small corporations, mere hundreds of employees, to control global platforms and do the jobs previous generations expected to be done by thousands of people in every hamlet and village on the globe. Further working conditions and the sense of what *work* is have shifted. People, in the COVID-19 pandemic, worked from home *en masse*, or were required to work "at their stations" in the face of uncertain health and safety. National borders are more porous than ever, disrupting work and national development in the countries where immigrants leave, and distorting the labor pool in countries that take in vast numbers of immigrants. Capital itself is crossing borders, seeking exceptions to tax, regulation, and labor law. Labor flows and capital flows are inextricably linked in the search for growth at any expense, allowing economics to dictate politics in an anti-human flywheel that leaves carnage in its wake. It is not just international migration (or the migration of jobs) that changes as capital demands growth and productivity without end; families too atomize from one another and from themselves as the social fabric of given places frays and the country, family, and self dissolve into the undirected, unordered, and unmasked reign of desire. Meanwhile, on the technological horizon, disaster looms: the storm cloud of an automated fever dream world where work is gone forever. The meaning this would have for humanity is very grave. For, indeed, what would we be as humans without work?

We must reclaim a consideration of the rule of politics over economics as a shared work that Christians rightly engage in. As should be clear by now, the work of all Christians extends beyond the remunerated labor which we colloquially gesture towards in response to the question "what do you do for work?" Our real work includes the whole of our active lives while we remain in the body. Everything from cooking dinner to doing the taxes is included. As we close, we should indicate a few things that are thus true about the shape of our shared life together which is, in total, also the result of our work.[26] The Christian is enjoined at the end of our reflection to implement particular policies. For some Christians this will be their particular work, and for others it will be a posture towards which to aspire in the community of deliberation and voting. For the sake of brevity we will indicate three policies. First, the prevention of poverty and misery, especially of pauperization. Second, the opposition of the accumulation of capital as an end. Third, to ensure as much as possible the ability of workers to *deliberate* and *choose*, which is to say—work.

Let us take each in turn. The first of these is the least controversial. Christ tells us to "love the poor" and we know that love involves "giving to the least of these." To this end we see that poverty is a pain Christians are obligated to alleviate to the extent to which we are able. The alleviation of this pain is an act of love done to our Lord. However, we also must maintain the tension of the fact that Christ also said, "The poor you will always have with you," which indicates something *fundamental*. We must never imagine that it is the role of any Christian, or even the role of all Christians together, to *end* poverty. This temptation has never been more vividly presented than in the modern era. Whether this claim comes in the guise of communism or Marxism, or just in the guise of someone insisting that by loving you must eradicate a class of people, we must unmask it for a subtle and insidious form of hatred. To *end* poverty requires *hatred* of the poor. Better the saintly posture that looks at the poor, as God does, and says, "How good that you exist." It is not the case that the Church desires poor people to exist but rather that we, like Mary, say unto God, "Thy will be done." If God has ordained some to be poor for some seasons, yes, even if he has ordained *me* to be poor for some season, or to be middle class, or to be rich, the purpose of this situation must be sought *in him* and not in worldly wisdom. Our calling in all cases is

---

[26] Gillian Rose, *Love's Work: A Reckoning with Life* (New York: Schocken, 1997).

to love, but to bear in mind that Christ asks us *in particular* to love the poor. Therefore, when we deliberate politically we have an obligation to consider the condition of the poor and to find creative ways to offer them special acts of charity in their poverty. It is not for nothing that we remember the actions of Good King Wenceslas as he sees a poor man walking home through the snow in the Christmas season and brings him meat and wine so that he too might celebrate. Our giving to and remembering the poor is thus not about "the alleviation of their material conditions" but rather an act of love done for the glory of God. Creative policies should be worked out to this end at all levels of common life.[27]

Second, and related, Christians must oppose the accumulation of capital as an end. The acquisition of capital as an end is a spiritual sickness and should be recognized as such. As we referred to earlier, private property is a good precisely (and to the extent that) it exists for the common use. So, for example, the acquisition of capital in order to build a restaurant, or order the construction of new dwellings, is a good and ought to, legally, be encouraged. These activities making a profit is a net gain, as everyone in the system of exchange can win: this is real economic value creation. However, the deployment of capital in ways that are clearly extortionary, such as gambling, is rightly illegal. These obvious examples are not alone; however, laying out the law in a total sense outside of a deliberative body which has the authority to author law is unwise. And any such legal body is warned in advance to be wary of the sins of avarice, and of the tyrannical impulse. We often cannot see the common good of some new market or new product until it is realized and we are inside of it. Thus creative and novel expenditures of capital must be allowed so we can remain open to economic development and growth. Policies against capital as an end ought to focus on the acquirer and the care of that person as much as they focus on the community being protected from predatory economic behavior.

Finally, we must work towards policies that enable the workers to deliberate and to choose in their work. Such deliberation and choosing is what is meant at the most fundamental level by the word *work*. The worker,

---

[27] If that means a roast chicken and a bottle of champagne must be delivered to each household on Easter Sunday, then so be it. The obligations of the politically engaged Christian are flexible enough to enable all sorts of solutions, provided we bear in mind this is an act of love indicating the virtue of the political community, not an act done to solve the problem which some person represents.

in his work, is not the antagonist or the opponent to the owner or manager. Rather, they are in dialogue, creatively engaging one another to produce excellence. Christian leaders should thus be open on a fundamental level to teaching their people about the goodness of work and the dignity of work. The collaborative exchange of working together, or loaning out our property to be worked upon by another, is itself the dance of activity in which we are free. Christians should pass laws to recognize the right to form Christian unions so that the principles of our faith can inform our deliberations in our labor.[28] Policies which encourage such deliberation on an individual level (by freeing up oppressive regulation that prevents employment) and policies which allow for organization of group deliberation (such as has been done from time immemorial in guilds and unions) recognize the balanced dance of work and encourage the discovery of vocation in the life of the people.[29] This dance is the opposite of the false dance in which we are trapped in the robot cage.

CONCLUSION

We must at all costs reject the cage, both literal and mental, which threatens to prevent us from working and steal away that bit of our humanity which resides in our partnership with God in bringing about the good, the just, and the true to the extent we are able. Embracing the freedom of the gospel and the hope it offers to all humans to work as agents of God's grace under his promises and pursuing lives of excellence is the only way forward. This is the good news of the gospel which the Church must offer to the world.

---

[28] This may be idiosyncratic for non-American readers for whom faith-based unions are normal (Germany, Canada, etc.). In the United States, federal law outlaws such faith-based unions in spite of the Assembly Clause, Free Exercise Clause, and Free Speech Clause of the Constitution. By outlawing unions which operate on Christian principles we end up in the situation we currently are in, where unions have a much lower vision of man, and of man's work, and are dominated by *ressentiment*.

[29] Legislation increasing private sector unionization ought to be particularly encouraged, as should law requiring stock access or ownership by employees at larger companies.

X.

Private Property

ERIC G. ENLOW

Law makes long spokes of the short stakes of men.
Your rights extend under and above your claim
Without bound; you own land in Heaven and Hell…

Your rights reach down where all owners meet, in Hell's
Pointed exclusive conclave, at earth's center
(Your spun farm's root still on that axis dwells);
And up, through galaxies, a growing sector.

—*William Empson, "Legal Fiction" (1928)*

INTRODUCTION: PROPERTY, HEAVEN, AND HELL

One "legal fiction" of property was, until recently, that the ownership of land extends both upwards and downwards indefinitely, above and beneath the surface.[1] This has not been so always and everywhere; the Romans, for example, whose laws were more shaped by urban contentions over the sky's light and subsurface sewage than the laws governing England's farmlands,

---

[1] Here "legal fiction," like *poesis*, intends something that the law as craftsman has made or modeled, rather than a falsehood or fraud. Strict idealists, prudes in the Platonic mold whether juris- or otherwise, reject all such poetics not strictly conformed to necessary truths.

had a different rule. Nor is it so now in the United States, because the U.S. Supreme Court reduced the long-held property of Americans in this regard quite suddenly in the middle of the twentieth century, taking their common-law rights in the heavens away from them (but not in Hell, for what it's worth), effectively collectivizing what was previously private property in favor of government administration of sky, space, and aviation.[2] But, for many centuries before then, the Anglo-American common-law rule, drawn from a thirteenth-century Accursian maxim, followed by Lord Coke, then Blackstone with some influence from Pufendorf, and, in their train, our American judges, was *cuius est solum, eius est usque ad coelum et ad inferos*, or, "whoever's is the soil, it is his all the way to heaven and all the way to hell."[3]

Writing in 1928 before they were taken away, William Empson (1906—1984), the eminent critic and analyst of ambiguity quoted at the beginning of this chapter, correctly captured the bivalent theo-topological implications of these now lost *ad coelum et ad inferos* rights. (It's worth working through the poem, because the same surprising meanings can be drawn out of any property rule which attempts to systematize the relation between man and

---

[2] *United States v. Causby*, 328 U.S. 256 (1946). There are some interesting political reflections from this little-considered incident of aerial collectivization via redefinition of private property rights. First, although property law has a reputation for timeless continuity, it has actually been subject to numerous radical changes, not just over the millennia but also within the course of decades. For another thing, although this rule of ownership of the heavens appeared very clear for a long time when it had little practical effect, it took on a radically new aspect given technological changes, like the discovery of commercially viable aviation and orbital satellites. The public and commercial exploitation of these would have been obstructed by disaggregated private ownership of the skies. For another, free-marketeers have not worried or complained about this in light of the significant public benefits that arose from reducing the completely unused private property of landowners over the heavens in favor of public and private aviation and space activities that are very important for commerce and security. To give every earth-bound landowner a right to enjoin airlines and satellite passage against aerial trespass based on an ancient right would have granted an "undeserved" windfall to the owner while retarding important technologies and industries. On the other hand, one might consider whether a regime where these heavenly rights had been taken by eminent domain or paid for through a public mandatory licenses scheme would have served the public interest by distributing the profits of the technologies. We are very used to allowing property owners undeserved windfalls and allotting the unexpected to landowners, e.g., when someone discovers oil, a city grows or the government builds a nearby road that elevates property values.

[3] *Bury v. Pope*, 1 Cro. Elizabeth 118, 78 Eng. Rep. 375 (1586).

thing without reference to the basis for their actual connection in the creative, normative, and providential work of God, to make broad claims for man without any sense of or deference to the primary rights of God.) Under the old rule, each property owner's surface claim to apparently individual ownership extends downward, narrowing to a point in Hell where all landowners' rights converge and combine into one common conclave. In Hell, all the *seemingly* individual claims, however broad and exclusive they appeared above, are discovered to be only superficially separate; they come together as one moves downward into a joint ownership of an infinitesimal, infernal estate. They remain separate until suddenly, at the last, they are held in common with all others at their root. All claims of individual ownership of land, though excluding all others on the surface, involve joining with all other owners in a share of Hell.

Correlatively, even the humblest, narrowest, and most crowded of surface claims expands exponentially into the widest imaginable personal estate, growing without limit as one nears God in Heaven and the vision of Him obscures all concern with rival claims. As a matter of nature, Empson's analysis is geometrically true; under the old rule, the surveyor's small surface stakes would literally make of every small land claim, under the "to Heaven and Hell" maxim, not a two- but a three-dimensional gigantic claim of space shaped like a long spoke: a thinning stiletto downwards, but upwards, a broadening plane spreading as conjoined to the infinite arc of Heaven. As a matter of metaphor for all kinds of property, it is an even truer picture of the providential position of property; the laws of men, as they pursue their small surface claims of exclusion or use for a time, nevertheless always grandly show man hung between Heaven and Hell. Just as the fact of self-love must become either selfishness or a living measure of one's love for others (cf. Gal. 5:14), so property must become either a hellish community of those who share only selfishness or a small part of communal life in the heavenly domain for those who take their share in God (and show their great possession in the ways they use their small ones). Property's superficial provision of personal dominion either narrows or expands as we turn from or toward the One who shares all with us. As with man's relation to himself and the law's authorization of self-dominion, the law's authorization of dominion over things is the beginning of an unavoidable problem, which the law cannot solve. As in Empsom's poem, law pedagogically illuminates the difference between a life lived toward Hell or Heaven, but cannot determine man's orientation.

To understand property as a legal or political issue for Christians begins with understanding why it inevitably operates this way to reveal man's desperate position between Heaven and Hell (for those who will see). Whatever form our property laws take as they evolve, an infernal and heavenly connection is established, which cannot be resolved in the property rules themselves if they are to fulfill their necessary legal purpose, to awaken man to his need and salvation in Christ. The resolution occurs only in the way that men act under them toward or away from Christ. Why must property law operate this way? The indomitable, inner, and inherent tendency of any property law, the legal logic required to support objective and certain rules relating persons to things, is to make ownership exclusive and absolute within a defined domain for a distinct and identifiable person. While this is needed for property to serve its social functions, it generates two problems, both related and arising from the separation of person and thing. Both problems impress upon man the significance of his orientation to God, which, alongside practical provision, is property's providential purpose. Better property laws awaken man to this significance better; worse laws obscure it by teaching a variety of false solutions to the problem, ones that do not require man to place a trust in the grace and justice of Heaven.

The first problem is theoretical. Mankind has no non-theological, non-revealed consensus on how persons should be properly related to things in a way that is necessary, natural, or normative.[4] If property is to be based on something more than human will, then it needs an objective connection between the things to be owned and the person owning. It needs a criterion for connecting one to one. No natural fact does this. It may be an unavoidable fact that each person must be somewhere, perhaps also hold on to something, consume something. But it also a fact that another person can crowd, interfere, and displace another. Since property law is called on to

---

[4] In God, according to revelation, the metaphysical condition of real relations with things is satisfied through origin, order, agency, and purpose. Because God has really made, arranged, and directed all things to himself, any other real relation must be through a real relation to him or challenge the underlying metaphysical realities. Man either explains how he takes from God, or faces on the one hand, the opaque and orderless fact of things in themselves, and on the other, God's superior claim: things just being what they are without natural relation to him and in comprehensive relation to God (e.g. Rom. 11:36; Col. 1:16–20).

decide who owns precisely when two men are in factual conflict, these facts cannot resolve the dispute. Law acts when two clutch the same thing at the same time, when one has succeeded contrarily in taking or threatening what another claims. Law acts only when these contrary natural facts overlap. If we await a natural relation between persons and things to resolve disputes, we wait to become bees or ants, distributing goods according to pheromonal hive necessity. However much we admire them, as long as man lacks an absolute biological or psychological compulsion ordering our relation to things as these insects have, we cannot index our acts toward things simply on the basis of our physical sensitivity to external facts. For those who crave a grounding for property in our necessary response to facts about the world, we find that none has yet arrived. Should the law command us to touch and hold nothing until this compulsion or consensus presents itself? Or, should it urge us to clutch and pull until we are in physical control? Or, looking inward, because we think we have reached the right rational conclusions before a consensus of reason has arisen, may we then aggrandize our personal conclusions about things (or will, wish, possession, presence, dependence, or labor with regard to things, depending on your philosophy of property) into a claim of universal right? To avoid chaos as we await rational or cultural consensus, must we defer absolutely to the political and social structure of facts or usages into which we are born, even if it causes us deprivation, death, powerlessness, or burning envy? While we have senses, practices, and feelings toward things, we cannot answer these questions easily in terms of real objective relations outside competing subjectivities.

Things simply do not offer themselves to man, whether individually or corporately, for objective relationship according to any immanent principle in the things themselves. By contrast, a man or group can inwardly intend a one-way relationship to a thing (e.g., through their desire or planning it), but it remains subjective, not a feature of the things themselves which have no wills or intents. Man's intent is outside the nature of the thing. The objective relation certainly cannot be grounded in the nature of those other persons (whom property law is asked to restrain) with conflicting intents, wills, desires, or ability to displace him. But the apparent need of a property law is to resolve disputes among those with competing intents over things. The objective facts of use, contact, nearness, possession, may be admitted, but these show nothing about the real relation between the things and the person claiming ownership. These factual states of affairs can never amount to a normative guide because they do not relate to the nature of the things in themselves nor exclude other persons with overlapping factual relations. For example, many parties may simultaneously desire to use a piece of land or to use it in different dimensions (one farming; one mining; one flying above). Likewise, many parties may simultaneously interact physically with a thing in different dimensions (one holding this part and one that). Possession is equally problematic because it may have been based on what appear to others to be wrongs in personal relation leading to the physical relation with the thing, e.g., killing and seizing, or first occupancy that is wasteful or accidental. Possession may be ambiguous in the sense of displaceable by others with superior power or superior capacity to extract greater value and so denied to be possession.[5]

To look at it another way, things are things precisely because they lack the agential capacity for personal relation according to their own nature. Things are distinguished from other material entities, like people's bodies, because they lack an interior principle capable of relation to other things; things lack the personal will and intent by which law and ethics usually unite persons in unions of right through mutual consent. This makes them at once open to dominion insofar as they are incapable of opposing it, but closed to dominion as not consenting to it. Only God can supply the missing connection between man and things. God's authoritative intent and will for things stands above both all persons and things. But he is still equally present in both and capable of relating them. A man's mind and will does this for his own body but for no other thing. We grant and understand the relation between matter and body through the uniting soul of the man. But, if there is no superior uniting intent and will above man and thing, then any relation between a human agent and thing will stand only on the agency of the individual intending or commanding it. As the relation stands only in the claimant's will and neither in the thing nor the mutual relation between thing and claimant, anyone else can potentially form a rival claim with as good a natural grounding. As even our paradigmatic champion of property rights,

---

[5] In the classic natural law tradition, this same is expressed in the observation that things—like land, sheep, and clothes—are obviously not distributed to people by nature itself. Rather, ownership is claimed in various historical processes, all of which are in some tension with an original state where all things were *res nullius*, i.e., belonged to no one, like the air or sea, or existed in a positive quasi-commons based on everyone's equal right to take. At best, the natural law tradition argues, property is authorized by nature but undetermined in distribution and fundamental form.

the conservative jurist William Blackstone (1723—1780), observed, if the account in Genesis of God's giving dominion and direction to man over things is rejected, we are thrown back only on various airy, conjectural, and disputable philosophies attempting to find an account of a natural relation between man and things or upon legal commands themselves ungrounded in natural relations.[6] God has made us so that the only known natural relation between man and matter is to his own body; beyond that connection, each lacks natural objective relation to any thing.

For these kinds of reasons, though societies are driven by various kinds of facts and necessity to create property law—the physical need of human biology for things to live, the ethical need for things for our various vocations or to express love to family and friends, the political need to resolve disputes over scarce resources that threaten order—there is no broad social consensus or scientific agreement on the best way to gain or distribute these necessaries. There is no agreement on what a good or normative relation of a person to a thing is, i.e., how to justify property by saying what makes it necessary and also good. Given the counter-fires of impoverished need and grasping greed, our lack of understanding leaves public issues of property naturally untethered and easily manipulable.

Driven by necessity (or, as we have faith to say it, the Father's providence), law fills in the gap by proclaiming rules of an absoluteness and certainty wholly disproportionate to the natural understanding and justifications supporting them because no other kind of rules will fulfill their legal purpose.[7] Thus, man is strung up by the first cord between Hell and Heaven; any surface claim to property established by law and politics is either hellish, arbitrary, an enviable and unwarrantable self-assertion, or heavenly,

---

[6] "In the beginning of the world, we are informed by holy writ, the all-bountiful Creator gave to man 'dominion over all the earth, and over the fish of the sea, and over the fowl of the air, and over every living thing that moveth upon the earth.' This is the only true and solid foundation of man's dominion over external things, whatever airy metaphysical notions may have been started by fanciful writers upon this subject." William Blackstone, *Commentaries on the Law of England*, Bk. II, Ch. 1, https://lonang.com/library/reference/blackstone-commentaries-law-england/bla-201/.

[77] With property law, it is often said that a certain rule otherwise inferior in efficiency or fairness is superior to a superior but uncertain rule. The sense of this is that the justice essential for property law requires certainty more than other niceties of fairness.

authoritative, insofar as it is traced to the Father's distribution in history, depending on one's faith. All property regimes lead man either to struggle against others' self-assertion, for those who reject God's providential distribution and look at its natural arbitrariness, or challenge man to rest in God's provision, despite suffering various inequalities and deprivations by the current regime, thankful for what is given.

The second problem is ethical and arises from this disproportion between our available justifications for property and the absoluteness of property's necessary legal claims. If they take their understanding from the law, owners are misled by the certainty and shape of the legal logic required to resolve disputes. Following law's form, they focus more on the necessary narrowing exclusivity of the law of property. Law separates property in particular persons and pronounces a right in them. Thus, each owner pointed to his own, owners are led from their own sincere desire for a good relation to things through God and toward others. They are turned away from the one sure broadening perspective on property. They no longer see the graciousness of God in giving things to man for his vocations and the parallel possibility of imitating God's generosity by being as gracious to others as God has been to us. They are turned by the law, which is misinterpreted as a true normative justification or a guide to how to use things toward the confines of their own right. If the law is not a mere mechanism of God's distribution but reflects a real, natural personal right to dominion over a thing, then one seems right to hold on to one's own without regard for God's will or other's need. If the right is grounded on facts about the thing and man, then why look beyond oneself and the thing?

Once the owner is turned to his property right as a guide to personal action, as an endorsement of the real justice of having for oneself, man finds that property further contracts. First, soon after one focuses on one's own satisfaction (for the law assigns things to owners and the satisfying of owners), satisfaction itself contracts as soon as it exceeds an individual's own absolute needs. The economic law of marginal utility makes each acquisition less satisfying; poverty cherishes one dollar, but wealth, having collected its millions, devalues one more. Subjective satisfaction in property is also diminished by covetous comparison with the possession of others. Man delights in simple sufficiency until he sees the greater possession of others. Unless it satisfies the immediate needs of poverty or is received as a surplus to be distributed, gifted, and shared in imitation of God, property diminishes continually, narrowing into the shared infinitesimal conclave of its root.

The logic of property law was not intended to guide use of property, only to open the possibility of use by establishing clear rules for who can use and what they can use. When a person looks to the law to guide good use or as an endorsement of an actual right to exclusive possession, his outlook tends against all the most appealing accounts of what real relations between persons and things should be. Somewhat plausibly, as Locke would have it, a person can be related to a thing if he mixes his labor with it. But property titles would be uncertain if they were tied to factual competitions over whose labor was mixed or whose most mixed in this or that thing. Who mixes their labor more, the one who hires a worker to plow a field or the one who does the plowing or the solider who spilled his blood defending the field? On such questions, an ordered system of rights cannot stand. In any case, no legal system has been proposed that attempts to shape property rights according to the normative justifications of Locke's theory. Property law always absolutizes away from conditions of use or mere possession. Thus, the owner who accepts the Lockean theory but follows his broader objective property rights will find his own justification for ownership condemning him. Or, perhaps, a person can make a real relation with a thing because human personality to realize itself must work in the world beyond the mind; it is a condition of human freedom and rationality to act in the world, have that act recognized, and recognize others' acts. As Kant would argue, the world is presented to the mind and will in ways that require us to recognize our own and others' interactions with it as normative for us all. But, then the whole shape of property law would be drawn from the nebulous shape of preexisting limits on the will according to the conditions of the will's universalization in collective freedom. Whatever that might entail, it is insufficient for the needs of defining rules of property law. The subtleties of these conditions of universalization, again, would not provide law with the bold and assured guidance necessary to make a practical system work; at least, no judge has ever been found who decides cases by looking at the shapes in such amorphous clouds. Or, perhaps, as Aristotle would have it, property is to be preferred because it allows ethical development of individuals. But, again, no law of property has ever hinged on debatable questions of who is being ethically developed by their property and who is not. Indeed, the possibility of this ethical development through use of property seems to be that the individual is responsible for making his own judgments of use of property, not having them forced upon him.

In sum, those who would turn to the most widely offered justifications of property are most likely to find any actual legal system condemned by the principles that justify it. Law necessarily focuses on the practical conditions and needs of exclusivity more than on the structures which might dignify relations between persons and things. Productive use, labor, freedom, virtue might justify but not create the conditions of certainty. The kinds of principles that are most likely to justify property in terms of the dignity and objective substantiality of the relations between persons and things are the least likely to supply usable norms. Those who turn to justifying principles in order to support ownership are most likely to find any practical system condemned by the principles that attract them. On the other hand, those who turn away from the proposed justifying principles of property law and focus on the law receive clear and precise encouragement. The owner is torn between viewing his property narrowly as the law describes it but without appealing moral sanction, or viewing his property according to justifying principles that violate the structures of the law. Those who follow the actual realized principles of law find themselves drawn to a baser and narrower understanding; those who follow appealing justifications find the actual structures of property law in confusion. All this arises because property law, to be practical and functional, operates on different principles than the ones by which men find themselves morally edified in their relations to things.

Thus, man in his property claims is again suspended between Heaven and Hell. Christians should understand property properly in this inherent tension between the political-legal principles needed to make property certain and the principles that could dignify and justify persons' exclusive relations to things. To return to Empson, depending on one's orientation, the certainty and exclusivity of human ownership draws some owners (most?) to a common ownership in the tiniest Hell shared with those who share this downward focus on the surface of the law; some (a few?) who have an upward sense from the surface to the broader cosmic spectacle, to where their greatest property lies, toward an ever-expanding and personal share of God. These latter do not *have* as much as *receive* with a joy that provides occasion for further sharing as God has shared with them (cf. 1 Cor:7:29-31).

Part of the goodness of the divine gift of property law (and because all legal rights of any kind are expressible in property terms, as they are all "had," we might say part of the goodness of the divine gift of law itself) is that it reveals man's position poised between Hell and Heaven, as his own constitution connects soil and spirit, in a crisis demanding resolution. The "legal fiction" of property, and really every kind of right, necessarily makes of them something that can be taken in an evil or virtuous way, as a share in either Heaven and Hell. What the law makes of things for persons by defining rights into a logical system of exclusivity is always a representation of the human situation itself, and it is one that helps us understand that we relate to things either to our suffocation as we draw in amongst ourselves or our glorification as we exist in and reach out toward God. Property is part of the way that the great divine law of righteousness is known, the one by which all men know that they deserve death (Rom. 1:32), and all men are taught of their need for God's grace.

CHRISTIANS AND THE RELATION OF PERSONS TO THINGS

Though beginning with its spiritual dimensions, we do not mean to deny that property law is about persons' relations to things. The difficulties of expressing the grounds and propriety of this relation in atheistic or naturalistic terms, without reference to the normative will and work of God in providing things to persons and nations, is not a reason for Christians to deny this critical aspect of property.[8] One of the great nominalist sophistries of our times is to reduce property to a legal relation between people, to abstract persons away from things as if property related only one person to other persons. (Because property law commands people, they contend that ownership is not a connection between me and my property, only a right to command others in respect of property.) But we know that man can have a relation to a place and possession without others, at least other men, because

---

[8] The same analysis could be applied to the international "property" law by which nations relate to national territories. As recent genetic discoveries illuminating prehistory reveal clearly that no people is autochthonic, the justification for national connection to land is completely disproportionate to international law's absolute assertions of national rights in land. The relation of land to nation, rather, forces the wise nation (and the wise individual who has property in a people's territory) to consider their dependence on God and His providence: Acts 17:26–27: "From one man he made every nation of men, that they should inhabit the whole earth; and he determined the times set for them and the exact places where they should live. God did this so that men would seek him and perhaps reach out for him and find him, though he is not far from each one of us."

the representation of the Adamic situation begins with this position and we ourselves experience relation to things (without relation to persons) as undeniable facts longing for recognition. When my watch is stolen, it is not my right to command the thief which I want back; it is my watch. What is the origin of this modern and reductionist tendency? If property only involves relations between men, then the duties of receiving all things from God are taken away. Practical atheism in our accounts of property liberate man from duties to God and the greater duties to other men, which God has commanded. Then, also, the political dimensions for government control would be greatly expanded because any kind of property in any thing would actually be a dominion over another person. All property would be immediately reducible to simple power relations and hierarchies among people. That was the motivation for this view among the progressive pragmatists of the early twentieth century in America, not to mention their cousin Marxists. It is still the dominant legal view of property today in the American legal academy: all talk of property really disguises an assertion of control over persons. The idea that property is only power over people, not provision for persons' relations to things, is forwarded to attack property, to put it in immediate conflict with freedom and political equality; on this view, all discussion of property in things is really a blind, a camouflaging of some will to power over others.

But some Christians have also taken this view. Why? Perhaps, worthily, to focus attention on the way property rights affected the poor. The idea may be that it would be better for the poor if we deny that property involves relations between persons and things. (To the contrary, the strong rules of property inalienability in Israel ensured basic wealth for the people. The case of Naboth in 1 Kings 21 illustrates why the poor need strong relations to things more than the powerful; those rich in power have no need for rules of property to control and oppress others.) But, among Christians as we struggle to understand our place, there may also be a gnostic, spiritualist, Albigensian, "super apostolic" pleasure that comes in the denial of personal relations to things and much more in the destruction of private legal rights in things that seem to run contrary to the brotherly sharing arising from love.[9] Christian leaders focused on the ethical needs of the Church (i.e., how property should

---

[9] Col 2:23: "Such regulations indeed have an appearance of wisdom, with their self-imposed worship, their false humility and their harsh treatment of the body, but they lack any value in restraining sensual indulgence" (NIV).

be used among Christians) might also confuse this with the legal and political questions of the state (i.e., what are the conditions for establishing property so that things may be used within political situation). Christians who want to establish voluntary community of goods need property, even if to be able to direct things to a Christian community. It just feels more "spiritual" to distinguish ourselves from our bodies and the things that bodies feed upon, clothe themselves with, inhabit and locate themselves within. Perhaps, one might speculate, a view of humans stripped of their relations to things, like people stripped of their clothes, would better allow us to see people and treat people as they are, equally nude. Without tailoring and uniforms, man would be forced to deal with man as God sees him and there would be a more equal justice. There might be a feeling that a reduction of property law to relations between people is somehow more angelic, spiritual, or righteous. This has its secular parallel in the argument of Plato and the Stoics versus Aristotle about whether material things are necessary for an individual's virtuous life.[10] The more idealistic and more will- or mind-focused ethicist wants to reject any proper need for the spiritually autonomous to own and have anything outside his own soul or his virtue.

As Plato wanted to deny property to his super-ethical guardians in the perfect republic, some Christians want to deny property to all. But this is contrary to the truth for Christians. One valid aim of property law, taken as a part of an overall just legal system, is to provide things for people to take and have, just as God originally provided man with general dominion over creation, a place on the land and then clothes. Dispossession, placelessness, the inutility of what is had, is an objective curse.[11] By contrast, the gift of land is a real symbol of the highest spiritual blessings. For example, in Psalm 37:11 and Matthew 5:5, in the Old and the New Covenants, truly receiving land is shown to be a real blessing, sufficient at least to be a figure for our right relationship with God.

An important antidote to this anti-property attitude is considering that God himself is an owner. As we learn about the value and possibility of the human body in Christ's incarnation, so the possibility of a real spirituality of property and ownership, a reality and virtue in the connection of persons to things, is contained in the revelation of God as an owner (cf. Rom. 11:35-

---

[10] Aristotle, *Politics*, Bk. II, Ch. 3.

[11] For example, consider Cain in Genesis 4:11–12.

36). Just as a false spirituality of hatred for the body conflicts with God's incarnation, so a false spirituality against ownership of things conflicts with his ownership (so, too, greed in ownership conflicts with God's generosity.) Sometimes, however, God's ownership of things is put forward as a basis for state ownership of things or for the collectivized ownership of things by the people corporately, as if collectivization were more consistent with God's ownership. But, if God's ownership is in conflict with individual, private ownership, then it is in equal conflict with the state or people's corporate ownership. God's ownership and incarnation is not an invitation to abolish the property or the body, but an anticipation of our right relationships to our bodies and to our property.

Acknowledging God's ownership is not an abolition of property, but the beginning of the puzzle of how to own as God does. Part of the way that property functions providentially is through the opaqueness of its justification and the questions we have about any system of distribution of goods. How can we relate to things as God does? It is far clearer to us that we can, must, and will relate to things than how it is right or how it is possible. The Decalogue tells us that we should not steal or covet other's property, but does not set forth a system for determining who owns what. We can read the Decalogue's obscurity on the correct system of property law, its silence on how property should be distributed or determined, as consistent with its injunctions against stealing or coveting others property, in this light. Property rights will always come about by the force of God's providential work in necessity and history and as part of the work of his image bearers; it must be respected as part of the providential work of God in history, and like governments, not understood or reduced to a comprehensible or engineered artifact of man's devising for his purposes alone.

PROPERTY AND POLITICS

Property—in the broad sense of the laws relating persons to things—needs to be situated in the context of politics. Property is so fundamental to polity that almost any political debate can be reformulated as a debate about property. As nation after nation discovered in the twentieth century, any major change to property law, whatever else remains constant, amounts to a political revolution, threatening incalculable costs to life and unpredictable effects on social order. Understanding the closeness of property and polity enables us to be both wiser and more restrained in our political analysis and rhetoric. Radical changes to property are radical changes in political constitution. Politics focused on radical change to property laws are like discussions of radical changes to overthrow one ruler and replace him with another. Christian duties of submission to rulers are related to the Decalogue's duties not to steal and not to covet things; in both cases, the Christian is called to trust in the providence of the present and the actual, even if, only *in extremis*, there are exceptions where revolution and redistribution can be justified. Just as the Christian duty of submission to rulers spans aristocratic, oligarchic, and democratic constitutions, so too, we are called not to steal or covet in many different and conflicting systems of property.

Beyond this relation between property and political constitution and the ways that both relate to God, the central Christian truth about property relevant to politics is limited and already self-evident. If one speaks in honest and plain terms about property in itself, one says little of controversy or even interest to politicians or the politically engaged. The central truth: the preservation and protection of property is a proper, positive, and essential end of government. Why is this self-evident? Because "property" simply refers to the dimension of any social order whereby persons are related by law to things. In your politics, is there to be a rule or principle settling who can acquire, retain, have, use, sell, or control this car, that sandwich, my shirt, your land? Then, your politics supports property. Anarchism aside, there is no political debate that the law needs to relate persons to things in these kinds of ways.[12] And, why must all political regimes establish systems of property and preserve them as a function of their continued political existence? Because relations to things—things like food; clothing; shelter; medicine; places of public worship, assembly, and business; the physical means of making the same; tools and production equipment; the markers of social status; the tools of pleasure, edification, and self-expression—all are essential

---

[12] It is very difficult to keep a thing from being owned or had by someone. All things, according to the needs of the governmental order and law, will have to be assigned a rights holder to resolve disputes when they arise. If we say that it is illegal for one private person to own another, then the "ownership" of the person must seem to vest either in the person himself or the government because the power to dispose of the person will vest somewhere. If in self-ownership, then it would seem that regulations of suicide, prostitution, or organ sales becomes untenable. If in the government, then the power over life and death and control of the body rests in the government.

constituents of social order. Take away the lawful and reliable relation of people to things (like water, food, and shelter), and you immediately have death, breakdown, and riot. Less immediately, but just as surely, take away ordered relations to the physical artifacts of the mechanical arts, the cultural arts, status, education, expression, and you cannot imagine a functioning society. No society without bread in men's mouths; no bread without plows in farmers' hands; no plows without hammers in smiths' hands; no smithies without builders, architects, and engineers; none of these without men regularly able to take, use, and control things. Not being immaterial beings, without ordered relations of persons to things, men do not have any kind of social order. No matter how varied the proper and permissible ways of practically ordering persons to things may be, some system of property is necessary to achieve any kind of social order.[13] Opposition to property as such is just anarchism.[14]

Communists, socialists, and capitalists, the Left and the Right, don't disagree about whether the law should relate persons to things by rules of law establishing rights and wrongs. They do disagree about the political importance of equality, liberty, individuality, and material prosperity, or how to maximize them, but not about property itself. Both have parallel temptations to avoid the necessary spiritual dilemma represented by property by claiming that the important issues of property can be resolved without representing man in his perilous responsibility before God. Classical liberalism, for example, does so by claiming that the structure of property is dictated by nature, somehow outside politics, and that ownership can be just

---

[13] Granted, it is sometimes more useful to seek a desired social order by laying down how persons should relate to persons. But the laws would be endlessly long if, for example, in seeking to provide for people to have places to live, it did so only by speaking of persons' relation to persons without relating them to things. Rather than provide a description of all the personal relations that are necessary for a place to be mine to live in in terms of relations between people, it is easier for the law simply to recognize one relation between me and my house. If ordering persons in relation to the physical world is thus a required part of all practical governments, then in any feasible legal-political order, there will be a place for property law. Anyone who can see that it is necessary, perhaps not logically but practically, for social order to be defined, established, or commanded in terms of persons' relations to things, will agree that the establishment of property is a proper end of government, even if they desire the government to own all.

[14] Thus it was Pierre-Joseph Proudhon (1809—1865), the famous originator of the phrase "property is theft," also first styled himself an "anarchist."

in itself, rather than a field of responsibility and obedience to God. Socialists, in a parallel way, by claiming that the ownership of property by the state is justified by the nature of human society, and that such collective ownership, while actually only a transference of dominion from one individual agent to another corporate one, will allow man to avoid the practical perils of human sin, rather than delivering man into an equally perilous situation of political inequality.

The disagreements of the Left and Right often pose as fairly technical disagreements in political philosophy. But these disagreements reveal the bewildering nature of any attempt to derive property arrangements from nature or the nature of society because they disagree about the key distinctives of the whole range of social action: the "who, what, when, where, and why" of property. One who would try to find a way through these debates must come with a full account of the whole nature of social action.

Who should own? The government, private persons, some mixture? (There is no avoiding this choice; when the government exercises the same corporate control over a thing as an individual private person, the government "has" and "owns" it just as much as a private individual person with the same control.)[15] Perhaps, contrary to what is true today, most private property should not be owned directly by artificial persons (i.e., joint stock corporations or government agencies), but natural corporations, like families, which have no legal recognition as corporate legal owners and suffer from rules of dissolution through no-fault divorce that would cripple business corporations. In many countries, foreigners are not allowed to own land or controlling interests in corporations; perhaps, property rights in some things should be limited to those who share political allegiance. Answering these kinds of questions determines the character of a political economy.

What things should be owned by the various governmental or private persons? This also is subject to great debate. Maybe, the government should own all the means of production and private persons only non-productive, consumable property? Perhaps, we shouldn't allow persons to own inventions, i.e., patents over novel substances or processes? It's settled that other people can't be owned and sold (although if the state controls all

---

[15] But there are a variety of options within these two: natural persons other than individuals like families, clans, and tribes, or artificial persons like business corporations, trusts, and mixed government-private agencies like a corporation which the government requires to be owned by workers.

relations to things then it is unclear in what sense the men entangled in these things are not themselves "owned"), but what about selling genes, placentas, cadavers, blood, or extra kidneys; renting wombs for surrogacy; or signing over one's services for a limited indenture or apprenticeship? Maybe, as in the economy of the Middle Ages, money should not be owned, at least not to the extent of allowing sale or rent for profit, but only used? Maybe, as the U.S. Supreme Court held, people should be considered to have property in vital government grants like welfare and housing benefits?[16]

When or how long should things be owned? Forever if vested in a perpetual person like a family or government, forever through control of inheritance and succession, or perhaps only for a life or a more limited term?

Where can things be owned? Can one remotely own things like land or buildings without living therein, e.g., an absentee landlord, or without at least having residence in the same state or country?

Why or for what purposes can things be owned? This last question can be thought of in two ways. First, when we decide that something is property, for what purposes do we relate the person to the thing? What powers do we give the person over the thing? The now classic list of the standard incidents of ownership by A. M. Honoré (1921—2019) included the following purposes of property:

> …to possess: to have exclusive physical control of a thing;
> …to use: to have an exclusive and open-ended capacity to personally use the thing;
> …to manage: to be able to decide who is allowed to use the thing and how they may do so;
> …to the income: to the fruits, rents and profits arising from one's possession, use and management of the thing;
> …to the capital: to consume, waste or destroy the thing, or parts of it;
> …to security: to have immunity from others being able to take ownership of (expropriating) the thing;
> …[to] transmissibility: to transfer the entitlements of ownership to another person (that is, to alienate or sell the thing);

---

[16] *Goldberg v. Kelly*, 397 U.S. 254 (1970).

The incident of absence of term: to be entitled to the endurance of the entitlement over time.[17]

When put all together, these rights create the standard idea of property in the liberal tradition, summarized by Blackstone as "that sole and despotic dominion which one man claims and exercises over the external things of the world, in total exclusion of the right of any other individual in the universe."[18]

The biblically informed reader will note that the property rights of biblical law seem quite different from a sole and despotic dominion. Reflecting on the equity of the Mosaic law of property gives us some idea of the possible validity and practicality of regimes of property very different from our own. They force us away from shibboleths of socialism and classical liberalism. Against the idea that property necessarily vests in "one man," as Blackstone states, or the socialist state, biblical ownership of land rests with the tribe, clan, and family against the rights of the individual alone or the organs of national government (cf. Num. 26:55, 36:8). Rules allowing the vesting of property rights in families survived quite a long time into the modern era. There is no universal and necessary reason to suppose that individuals, certainly not business corporations, need to be predominating persons owning property to realize the ends of justice. Indeed, until the late nineteenth century, corporations were legally incapable of owning other corporations, rendering impossible the economic structure of modern life. The prohibition arose from concerns with precisely the kind of concentrated economic power that the modern rule allows.

Most of the absolute dominion over things that Honoré and Blackstone describe is also partially restricted in the biblical regime of property nor does it vest in the state. So, rather than establishing absolute rights of exclusive control, Moses's law allowed for entry into the land of others and allowed

---

[17] A. M. Honoré, "Ownership," in *Oxford Essays in Jurisprudence*, ed. A. Guest (London: Oxford University Press, 1961), 107–47. More subtly, the list also included duties as incidents: *The prohibition on harmful use*: requiring that the thing may not be used in ways that cause harm to others; *Liability to execution*: allowing that the ownership of the thing may be dissolved or transferred in case of debt or insolvency; and, *Residuary character*: ensuring that after everyone else's entitlements to the thing finish (when a lease runs out, for example), the ownership returns to vest in the owner.

[18] Blackstone, *Commentaries on the Laws of England*, Bk. II, Ch. 1.

limited appropriations from other's land.[19] Similarly, in the common law before the nineteenth century and in many countries still today, land was not trespassed merely by entry upon it; trespass was found only if there was some damage to the land and free passage over others' unenclosed land was a common right (a right still protected in many countries).[20] Again, rather than property giving an exclusive right to use a thing or to its income, Mosaic property law limits the owner's use. For example, it recognized God's ownership of the first fruits of the land (Ex. 23:19), and it required lending and loaning to the poor without charge, interest, or return (Ex. 22:25; Lev, 25:35; Deut. 15:7). Rather than allow an absolute right of use, consumption, profit, or exclusion, the property law of Moses requires that, every seventh year, the land be rested and the poor and wild animals have access to its uncultivated produce and, every year, that a tenth of the produce of the land be given to the ministers of religion, the Levites, and the poor (Ex. 23:10; Deut. 14:22). At all times, including the harvest, the poor have the right of gleaning, to take in a limited manner the produce of the land (Lev. 19:9; Deut. 23:24, 24:19). Also, the owner is not allowed to sell food to the poor for a profit nor to charge interest to the poor on loans (Lev. 25:35-37). Compared to Honoré's absolute right to alienate, biblical law restricted the absolute or permanent right to sell land, allowing only leases of land for the period between jubilees, when land is returned to the original owner, and always subject to a right of redemption.[21]

In all these ways, biblical law clearly differs from modern U.S. property law over the first "why" of property law. Why do we relate persons to things, to do what with them? Do the powers assigned to owners in the Mosaic law

---

[19] For example, Deut. 23:24–25: "If you enter your neighbor's vineyard, you may eat all the grapes you want, but do not put any in your basket. If you enter your neighbor's grainfield, you may pick kernels with your hands, but you must not put a sickle to his standing grain" (NIV).

[20] The importance of doctrines holding that property may be used in limited ways by nonowners is obvious in modern intellectual property law. Although exceptions are quite limited in patent law, e.g., in the case of experimental or prior commercial use, they are quite broad in trademark and copyright fair use, without which comparative advertising or a scholarly article critiquing a novel would be prohibited. These exceptions to the owner of intellectual property's rights of exclusive use are very well established and present an analogy to the biblical law and grounds for considering other ways property law could allow limited use of property without damaging the other aims of property law.

[21] Lev. 25:23.

correspond to those in the standard liberal conception described by Honoré? No, it assigns markedly different rights to property, to different persons, for different times. It foresees and forecloses the tendency of property owners to absolutize their claims into Blackstone's "sole despotic dominion." Modern law, for practical reasons, does this also (and did so in Blackstone's day, as he clearly recognized). We recognize many limitations on the use and control of property through property and income taxation, and nuisance, zoning, regulatory, and eminent domain rules. But Mosaic law denies that property is an absolute individualistic dominion for a different reason: it limits property rights in respect of God and for the imitation of God.

This shows the second issue in the "why" of property, not by what powers over them do we connect persons to things, but what is the purpose of property. The purpose of Mosaic property law is to respect God's ownership and distributions. The basic Mosaic restraint on alienation of land, the ability to sell land permanently, the right to create a market in land, is respect for God's right: "The land must not be sold permanently because the land is mine and you are but my aliens and tenants" (Lev. 25:23 NIV). Land is distributed by God and held subject to the terms of that distribution. The basic Mosaic restraint on use of land, the requirement of leaving things for the gleaning by the poor, arises because the Israelites were commanded to "remember that [they] were slaves in Egypt" whom the Lord redeemed; as the Lord redeemed them, they are to redeem others (Deut. 24:22). This is, of course, parallel with the duty expressed in the Decalogue to rest on the Sabbath day from extracting value from property because the Israelites should "remember that you were slaves in Egypt and the Lord your God brought you out of there" (Deut. 5:15). The duty to share property and not to charge the poor interest is justified similarly: "do not take interest of any kind from him, but fear your God, so that your countryman may continue to live among you" (Lev. 23:35). Moderns in limiting property rights do so without reference to the rights and dispensations of God. American law for a variety of noble and ignoble, political and practical reasons restrains property rights. But we do it without reference to something higher than our own practical and political interests. For this reason, modern political debate about property tends to oscillate between an incapacity to justify any limit on individual property (classical liberalism) and an assertion of a right to reorder it in any way the political body desires (pragmatism, communism, and socialism). Our "why" of property swings between conceptions of property grounded in absolute individual right and conceptions only grounded in practical political utility. The miserable state of modern political thinking about property arises from the paltry grounds we can offer for it once we eject God and his providence from the picture.

CONCLUSION: PROPERTY, PRACTICAL POLICIES, AND PROVIDENCE

In Empsom's vision, law makes much of the small claims of men to things and land. As a matter of necessity, it draws men into contact with Heaven and Hell. What practical lessons does this grand vision of property offer us? First, the most important goal for Christian as such is to recover the role of God in our accounts and arguments over property. Every ideology that Christianity resists attempts to resolve the puzzle of property (and politics) in a way that eliminates reliance on God's providence (as it eliminates the source of man's value in the image of God). Because the kinds of questions discussed above (the who, what, when, where, why of property) are so complex, because they have been given so many opposed answers and so many seem to be justifiable in some part, any given system is open to substantial question and revision. In the end, everyone has to admit that the institution of a property regime, distributing things to owners and assigning precise rules for what ownership entails, does not occur by any static rule of nature but through choices.

As discussed above, we lack an innate or natural hook between persons and things that could otherwise justify property in static nature. This results in a great difficulty in justifying property rights. There is a spiritual significance or providence to the disproportion between the practical need to establish property rules and the unclear and disputed justifications that could guide such an establishment. The practical upshot of this for Christians is not to adopt any political ideology or policy, but to remain skeptical of the various political forces that assert technical solutions to a problem that will remain fundamentally spiritual. Classical liberalism and Marxism, in their different ways, each seek to reframe property in a way that offers a way out of its inherent spiritual agony. This is not an argument for instituting the Mosaic law of property, but the Mosaic law of property, with its essential differences from the proposals of modern ideologies whether of the classical liberals or socialists, reminds us that the modern ideologies are not grounded on necessities of universal or natural justice as they claim. Mosaic law is not required for Christians, but it is a paradigm of justice, one just way for a certain people to unite practical need and right before God. All contemporary accounts seeking to justify property without God should be rejected; they all simply amount to governments and owners reshuffling property under different names in order to obscure the fact of their indebtedness to God. Christians should understand that man's only right relation to the things of the world is to receive them as gifts of God's creation and providence. The Mosaic law shows us one way this can be done in a property law.

Property emerges and evolves historically through political processes. What we think of these historical and political processes determines a great deal of what we think of property. Every system of property must explain why the existing system, given that it could have been quite different, should continue to be respected.

The Christian has both a high and low view of politics. On the one hand, he believes that God's providence is displayed in political leaders; on the other, that their authority over us is grounded in their role as God's servants. This difference has great consequences for property. A belief in providence similarly both builds up and humbles the claims of owners. Those who view the political leader as a servant of God receive property within the political process as if receiving it from God. This raises our view of property. The owner claims title from God, albeit indirectly, and takes his property rights with the greatest authority; a person who takes property from him rebels against God's disposition. On the other hand, the property owner who receives from God has a diminished sense of dominion; the one who understands that he receives all property from God also understands his immediate moral responsibility to use property only for the purposes for which God has given it. Rejection of divine providence over political systems and over the distribution of property emboldens radical changes in property and constitutional law. But it requires those who advocate for radical change to ground their claims on human claims of right. It leaves man free to throw down governments and redistribute property, to decide on matters of right according to his own autonomous right. But the winners of this process, whether the capitalist or the socialist manager, also take without the responsibilities to God that come with receiving from God's hand. The Christian should stand against both kinds of political radicalism, not out of defense of the status quo, but in recognition of divine power and meaning in history.

Only the society that recognizes God's acts of grace in providing property and political authority has a possible middle path between absolutization of political office or property and anarchy. For the faithful society, both property and political constitution rest not only on their practicality, which is always shifting, but a practice of discerning and proclaiming the authoritative work of God in history. Neither political regimes nor property regimes offer us convincing grounds to justify themselves adequately to support the practical certainties required in law and politics. Actions inevitably go beyond what is directed on the boldest and most detailed theories of property and politics. There is no geometric reasoning, no *a priori* science of law and politics. Many things are done in consequence of which rights are acquired under some color of legal authority; territories are conquered, constitutions written, offices and properties granted, justly and unjustly. Once God's providential control over history, nations, and individuals is denied, it is precisely these acquired rights that are most difficult to justify. Why should this nation have this land or this person that estate? A society that denies God's role in distribution will vainly seek another principle to justify them, other than their own power and will.

Christians, then, should support property analogously to the manner in which they support government, relying on God's providence and not man's wisdom, submitting for the Lord's sake to these analogous institutions rather than for the sake of whatever cultural or philosophical account is given of their legitimacy (cf. 1 Pt. 2:13). Most importantly, when we are owners, this will allow each Christian to recall the real spiritual situation of the owner and to consider their ownership a matter of grace, shared from Heaven, rather than as self-centered "right," shared with other owners only in self-regard. Also, if we accept property on the basis of God's providential distribution, we will avoid the weakness of atheistic philosophical accounts of property that seek a basis of right outside God's acts in creation and administration of the world. Because the alternative justifications of property are so weak, Christians should be the strongest supporters of property in general.

As a matter of public policy, Christians should be open to practical modification of contemporary property regimes by ordinary political means, though resistant to ideological arguments that attempt to seal these in stone or radically transform them according to some system. If Christians look skeptically at atheistic accounts of property, which attempt to derive the details of property law from ideological or philosophical principles, they will increase their openness to practical proposals to improve property law. Those who have a strong ideology of property, whether based in Marxism, classical liberalism, or some other determining system, tend to regard property rules as necessarily fixed in great detail. Christians should support property law as they find it in the same way that they support political regimes as they find them: open to their orderly modification but closed to radical proposals attacking the polity itself or based on an ideology that pretends to a unique solution to the puzzles of property.

Given the purposes of property law in the Mosaic law—both the very different set of powers it gives to owners than we do today and the very different reasons in relation to God for which they are given—Christians should be very open to the justice of property law systems different than those instituted today in the United States. It is certainly necessary to consider that the principles of Mosaic law were shaped to the needs of the specific place and people in Israel, but most modern ideologies of property offered in the United States are very difficult to accommodate to the general equity or principles of justice found in the divine law. If a proposed ideology of property, whether Marxist or classical liberal, seems to rule out the Mosaic property regime as a matter of equity and justice, rather than in relation to practical differences in situation, then either the modern ideology has been misunderstood or it teaches a different sense of justice. (For example, if a modern ideology of universal justice seems to requires either that productive property be owned by the state or that private ownership must be in individuals, then it is in conflict the equity of the Mosaic law.) Given the difference in founding principles, all atheistic accounts of property law will vary from the Mosaic law because God's law respects God's rights and ownership. There is no good reason to believe that our contemporary system of property law with its myriad contingent, questionable choices is grounded on some universal basis of justice. [22] On the other hand, however much we work to improve property law, we should never expect that the fundamental problem of property will be resolved into some harmonious Marxist utopia or a well-oiled classical liberal machine. Law will always make something greater of property than a mere practical provision. As in Empsom's vision,

---

[22] Examples or such questionable choices would be how corporations can be owners but not families; or the fact that people cannot be owned, but their wombs can be rented and the resulting children bound to the paying parents.

property will always remain a place of showing the tension between Heaven and Hell, and this is its greatest providential purpose.

XI.

Taxation and Welfare

ALLEN CALHOUN

THE ROAD FROM REFORMATION TO WELFARE

CONFLICTING narratives drive the political conversations in the United States and Europe surrounding welfare, social services, and distributive taxation. In a 2021 interview, for instance, tax historian Joseph J. Thorndike and tax policy expert Goldburn P. Maynard, Jr., discussed the puzzling disconnect between widespread enthusiasm among American voters for taxing the rich on the one hand and the unpopularity of the federal estate tax on the other.[1] They concluded that *stories*, not facts, determine American voter sentiment and that voter sentiment, in turn, affects tax policy—less so than it affects other political issues but probably more so than in Europe.

In the United States, Democrats have successfully told the story that the rich do not pay enough tax. They have done so at a time when the wealth gap is an increasingly moralized issue, especially as the role of economic inequality in perpetuating racial inequality has become more evident. At the same time, well-funded conservative groups have succeeded in narrating the story that

---

[1] Goldburn P. Maynard, Jr., interview by David D. Steward and Joseph J. Thorndike, *TaxNotes*, November 9, 2021, https://www.taxnotes.com/opinions/interview-wealth-inequality-and-taxes-us/2021/11/09/7cl8w.

the estate tax and capital gains realization at death threaten to undermine the promise of the American dream.

No story about such highly moralized territory as welfare, social services, and distributive taxation will ever rest on completely neutral facts. But because these are ethically laden topics, one story *must* be told—that of the theological origins of welfare and tax policies. This essay tells an abridged, post-Reformation, and Eurocentric version of that story. Western Europe is the most useful "laboratory" for testing hypotheses about the eventual outcomes of Reformation-era social theology. Europe is where Protestant doctrines can be traced to the "implicit religion" of contemporary welfare systems in traditionally Protestant countries.

Sociological Discourse

Sociological connections between Protestant theology and attitudes toward economic systems, like Max Weber's argument in *The Protestant Ethic and the Spirit of Capitalism*, have been available for more than a century. The last three decades, however, have seen an awakening of scholarly interest in the ways Christianity has in particular shaped the welfare states of Western Europe. The "power resource theory" of welfare-state development assumed in the 1970s that the working classes' socialist organizations drove the "social democratization" of capitalism.[2] The theory underwent revision in the 1980s in the face of evidence that both social democracy and Roman Catholicism also promoted welfare-state development.[3]

Even the modified account, concluding that the continental welfare regime was "a manifestation of Catholic social doctrine," could not explain the variation in the types of welfare states.[4] In 2009, Kees van Kersbergen and Philip Manow revised the sociological approach to give greater attention to the hitherto neglected role of *Protestant* social teachings. Sigrun Kahl has supplemented the Van Kersbergen-Manow approach by showing that the different types of European welfare states emerged "through the

---

[2] Philip Manow and Kees van Kersbergen, "Religion and the Western Welfare State—The Theoretical Context," in *Religion, Class Coalitions, and Welfare States*, ed. Kees van Kersbergen and Philip Manow (Cambridge: Cambridge University Press, 2009), 1.

[3] Manow and van Kersbergen, "Religion and the Western Welfare State," 1.

[4] Manow and van Kersbergen, "Religion and the Western Welfare State," 10.

institutionalization of religious doctrines into countries' poor relief systems, and the secularization of these institutions."[5]

Because Reformation traditions follow different trajectories in their approach to welfare, it makes sense to look at the three primary strands—Lutheranism, Calvinism, and Anglicanism—separately. But what will become clear is that while Protestants often had slightly different emphases, they were ultimately in accord on these issues. In other words, there is a clear "family resemblance" among Protestant approaches.

LUTHERAN SOCIAL TEACHING: THE "LITURGY AFTER THE LITURGY"

Retrieval of Social Teaching

The turn in sociological research to the historical force of "implicit religion" has rescued Lutheranism from what was, at best, a supporting role in Max Weber's theory. Weber argued that Protestants saw themselves standing before God without mediation by priest or sacraments and, therefore, sought evidence of their salvation in their worldly callings.[6] The resulting "worldly asceticism" was most evident among Protestants whom Weber called "Calvinists." Lutheranism was not seen as having the same connection to capitalism as "Calvinism."[7]

In light of current widespread criticism of the Weber thesis, however, Lutheranism's marginalization was probably a blessing in disguise. A Lutheran genealogy of modernity has been free to emerge in the last three decades without the preliminary need to deconstruct Weberian assumptions. A substantial body of scholarly work on the Lutheran roots of contemporary government assistance is taking shape, partly because one group of Lutheran countries in particular—the Nordic nations—are seen as model welfare states.

This section provides a brief overview of the history of government welfare and social services in historically Lutheran countries, describes

---

[5] Sigrun Kahl, "Religious Doctrines and Poor Relief: A Different Causal Pathway," in *Religion, Class Coalitions, and Welfare States*, ed. van Kersbergen and Manow, 267.

[6] Max Weber, *The Protestant Ethic and the Spirit of Capitalism*, trans. Talcott Parsons (Mineola, NY: Dover Publications, Inc., 2003).

[7] Robert H. Nelson, *Lutheranism and the Nordic Spirit of Social Democracy: A Different Protestant Ethic* (Aarhus: Aarhus University Press, 2017), 20.

characteristics of the "implicit religion" of Nordic welfare states in particular, and then suggests ways in which a distinctively Lutheran theology shaped welfare, social services, and taxation in those states.

Development of Government Assistance in Historically Lutheran Countries

On the eve of the Reformation, "the church's sanctification and idealization of poverty" had turned poverty into a crisis.[8] Almsgiving, which had served as the medieval system of poor relief, functioned as a symbiotic relationship in which the wealthy assisted the needy through charity, thereby atoning for their own sins and receiving blessing from the intercessions of the poor.[9] By the early sixteenth century, it had become apparent that the medieval system was not adequate to meet the needs of the poor. Luther believed that the papacy was partly responsible for poverty in Germany through its collection of annates (technically, the papacy's right to claim the first year's profits of a benefice).[10] He was convinced that the doctrine of the priesthood of all believers implied that the German rulers possessed as much divinely bestowed authority to govern as the pope did.[11] And, reacting simultaneously against the medieval symbiosis and the emerging profit economy, Luther eschewed "all syntheses of self-love and neighbor-love" because "self-interest is always wrong."[12]

Heeding Luther's exhortations to provide for the needs of the poor through social assistance, Lutheran towns began establishing "common

---

[8] Carter Lindberg, "Luther's Struggle with Social-Ethical Issues," in *The Cambridge Companion to Martin Luther*, ed. Donald K. McKim (Cambridge: Cambridge University Press, 2003), 171.

[9] Lindberg, "Luther's Struggle," 171.

[10] Nelson, *Lutheranism and the Nordic Spirit*, 72.

[11] Martin Luther, "Temporal Authority: To What Extent Should It Be Obeyed," in *Luther's Works* (hereafter *LW*) (American Edition), ed. Jaroslav Pelikan and Helmut T. Lehmann, 55 vols. (Philadelphia: Muehlenberg Press and Fortress Press, and St. Louis: Concordia, 1955–86), 45:100; "An Open Letter to the Christian Nobility of the German Nation concerning the Reform of the Christian Estate," *LW* 44:54. See also Allen Calhoun, *Tax Law, Religion, and Justice: An Exploration of Theological Reflections on Taxation* (Abingdon, UK: Routledge, 2021), 182; Nelson, *Lutheranism and the Nordic Spirit*, 73.

[12] Sean Doherty, *Theology and Economic Ethics: Martin Luther and Arthur Rich in Dialogue* (Oxford: Oxford University Press, 2014), 67.

chests." Luther's own town, Wittenberg, published an ordinance in 1522 directing the use, under the supervision of the town council, of property confiscated from the town's cloisters for loans and outright contributions to orphans and those who had fallen into poverty through age, sickness, or misfortune.[13] The Wittenberg ordinance inspired similar legislation in Nuremberg, which was "the first attempt by an imperial city in Germany to establish an obligatory, secular welfare state system."[14] Nuremberg's measures, in turn, may have served as the blueprint for Strasbourg's poor-relief legislation, linking Lutheran and Reformed social-assistance models.[15]

In Lutheran territory, the famous ordinance of the parish of Leisnig provided for the funding of the village's common chest through ongoing taxation. Luther took a personal interest in ordinances in the Lutheran cities in Saxony, and his own pastor in Wittenberg, Johannes Bugenhagen (1485–1558), wrote and edited numerous church ordinances for Lutheran cities in the north. Bugenhagen's Hamburg ordinance of 1529 became a model for church orders in northern Germany and Scandinavia.[16]

In addition to common chests (later, the "poor tax"), early Lutheran systems of poor relief were characterized by "eligibility determinations." The civil authorities determined which of the poor would receive "outdoor relief" (i.e., monetary allowances), and which would receive "indoor relief" (i.e., support in kind in an institution such as a workhouse or hospital).[17]

German poor relief began moving from the local to the regional level in the late 1520s. The three leading states of the Reformation—Saxony, Hesse, and Württemberg—had systems of social assistance in place by 1550, and by the end of the century Lutheran princes throughout Germany treated poor relief as falling under their police power. In 1794, the Prussian state assumed responsibility for poor relief.[18]

At the end of the nineteenth century, 6.7 percent of the population of (Lutheran) Berlin was receiving outdoor relief, and in (Lutheran) Frankfurt am Main and Stuttgart the percentages were 6 percent and 6.5 percent

---

[13] Calhoun, *Tax Law, Religion, and Justice*, 164–65; Carter Lindberg, *Beyond Charity: Reformation Initiatives for the Poor* (Minneapolis: Fortress Press, 1993), 119–20, 201.

[14] Lindberg, *Beyond Charity*, 135.

[15] Lindberg, *Beyond Charity*, 137.

[16] Lindberg, *Beyond Charity*, 139.

[17] Kahl, "Religious Doctrines and Poor Relief," 272.

[18] Kahl, "Religious Doctrines and Poor Relief," 273–74.

respectively. The percentages in (Catholic) Cologne and Munich were 3.8 percent and 1.2 percent, respectively. Poor relief in Catholic regions remained primarily the purview of individual charity.[19]

The move from local to national social assistance occurred later in Scandinavia, where poor-relief systems were "built *with* the collaboration and *within* the framework of existing church institutions."[20] The kings of Denmark and Sweden contributed funds for outdoor relief but insisted that poor relief remain primarily the responsibility of municipalities. The Danish state did not become directly involved in social assistance until enactment of the Danish Poor Law of 1708.[21]

While Germany may provide helpful comparisons of early modern Protestant and Catholic poor-relief systems, the Nordic countries represent a purer "laboratory" for examining the genealogy of Lutheran welfare states. Their populations were overwhelmingly Lutheran and their level of collaboration between Church and state almost theocratic.[22] The next subsection describes the unique characteristics of modern Nordic welfare states, which sociologists of religion have recently identified as a sort of "implicit" Lutheranism.

The "Implicit Religion" of the Nordic Welfare States

Even compared to other nations with robust social-assistance systems, the Nordic countries share a lower level of income inequality and lower relative poverty among vulnerable groups.[23] The Scandinavian "participation rate" is the highest in the world, at around 80 percent, meaning that the taxes incurred and state support lost by a person moving from outside the labor force into the labor force total on average 80 percent of the income she will

---

[19] Kahl, "Religious Doctrines and Poor Relief," 274.

[20] Kahl, "Religious Doctrines and Poor Relief," 272.

[21] Kahl, "Religious Doctrines and Poor Relief," 273.

[22] See Roger Jensen, "The Formation and Identity of the Church as a Present Challenge in Norway," in *Exploring a Heritage: Evangelical Lutheran Churches in the North*, ed. Anne-Louise Erikkson, Goran Gunner, and Niclas Blader, Church of Sweden Research Series 5 (Eugene, OR: Pickwick Publications, 2012).

[23] Nelson, *Lutheranism and the Nordic Spirit*, 174.

earn in her new job. In comparison, the participation rate in the United States is 33 percent.[24]

Robert H. Nelson concludes that religion historically has been the most effective instrument in the Nordic countries for overcoming the "free rider" problem that besets welfare systems in other parts of the world. Nelson notes especially one Nordic peculiarity: although gender equality is comparatively high in the public sectors of Nordic countries, very few women occupy executive positions in private companies.[25] Nordic women appear willing to make personal sacrifices to serve in the public sector but do not regard private-sector profit-making in the same "Godly" light.[26]

Moreover, as John Witte writes, "the rise of the modern welfare state over the past century is in no small measure a new institutional expression of the Lutheran ideal of the magistrate as the father of the family called to care for all his political children."[27] A 2009 study by the Center for the Study of Religion and Society at Uppsala University found that the Lutheran countries "were the first to develop systems of welfare and social insurance" at the end of the nineteenth century because Lutherans saw no threat to the Church from the emergence of a strong government apparatus of poor relief.[28]

A corresponding deference to the state's expertise characterizes the Nordic countries. "Technical administration" became an important political emphasis in Sweden and Norway after World War II, in Denmark in the late 1950s, and in Finland in the early 1960s.[29]

In summary, two trajectories in Lutheran history shaped Nordic social democracy: a trust in the economic and social expertise of the state's bureaucracy, and a sense that the interests of Church and state were similar, if not identical. The following subsection demonstrates that these features

---

[24] Nelson, *Lutheranism and the Nordic Spirit*, 27.

[25] Nelson, *Lutheranism and the Nordic Spirit*, 27–28.

[26] Nelson, *Lutheranism and the Nordic Spirit*, 23, 27–28, 32, 99–100, 104, 111, 120, 278.

[27] John Witte, Jr., "From Gospel to Law: The Lutheran Reformation and Its Impact on Legal Culture," in *Protestantism After 500 Years*, ed. Thomas Albert Howard and Mark A. Noll (New York: Oxford University Press, 2016), 69.

[28] "Welfare and Religion in a European Perspective: A Comparative Study of the Role of Churches as Agents of Welfare with the Social Economy," in *Welfare and Religion in 21st Century Europe*, ed. Anders Backstrom, Grace Davie, Ninna Edgardh, and Per Pettersson, 2 vols. (Burlington, VT: Ashgate, 2009).

[29] Nelson, *Lutheranism and the Nordic Spirit*, 219, 222–23, 226, 230–43.

are not historical accidents, but rather natural outgrowths of Luther's theology.

Luther's Regularization of Poor Relief

By removing any salvific value from the relationship between rich and poor, Luther cleared the way for poverty to be seen as a problem to be addressed rather than an essential component of the plan of salvation. Sean Doherty writes that "Luther ferociously exposed the way in which the debased forms of pre-Reformation piety reinforced the conditions of the poor by treating poverty and almsgiving as meritorious" and that he worked to replace those conditions with an arrangement that "sought a structural and durable solution to the *causes* of poverty as well as alleviating particular cases of hardship."[30]

That answer, however, raises another question: why was Luther concerned about the needs of the poor to such an extent in the first place? Deep theological currents were in play, namely Luther's stress on the doctrine of the *communicatio idiomatum* ("communication of properties") and the redistributive structure of his Eucharistic theology.

According to Luther, the "happy exchange" between Christ and the believer mirrors the exchange between the two natures of Christ.[31] The believer's soul, Luther wrote, is united with Christ "as a bride is united with her bridegroom" and "everything they have they hold in common, the good as well as the evil."[32] In this exchange, Christ distributes the prerogative of priesthood, thereby conferring on the initial distributee the role of *distributor*.[33]

Luther saw this dynamic at work in the Eucharist, writing:

> But in times past this sacrament was so properly used, and the people were taught to understand this fellowship so well, that they even gathered food and material goods in the church, and

---

[30] Sean Doherty, *Theology and Economic Ethics: Martin Luther and Arthur Rich in Dialogue* (Oxford: Oxford University Press, 2014), 201–2.

[31] Martin Wendte, "Mystical Foundations of Politics? Luther on God's Presence and the Place of Human Beings," *Studies in Christian Ethics* (2018), journals.sagepub.com/doi/10.1177/0953946818792628.

[32] Martin Luther, "The Freedom of a Christian" in *Luther's Works*, ed. Jaroslav Pelikan, Helmut T. Lehmann, and Christopher Boyd Brown (St. Louis: Concordia Publishing House, 1955-), 31:351.

[33] Luther, "The Freedom of a Christian," *LW* 31:355.

there—as St. Paul writes in I Corinthians 11—distributed among those who were in need.[34]

Martin Wendte writes that for Luther the Lord's Supper erased the distinction between "the sacred and profane spheres," i.e., it served as Luther's paradigm of how "God and God's Word are always working for humankind in a materially mediated way."[35] To be sure, Christ's distribution of spiritual benefits in the *sacrament* is a means of salvation, but the distribution of material goods to the poor in the *sign* aspect of the practice is also a means of grace, though not in a salvific sense. The two distributions are formally parallel, so that Luther considered it a travesty that, in the *sign* as well as *sacrament* of the Lord's Supper, possessions were no longer "given, with thanksgiving to God and with his blessing, to the needy who ought to be receiving them."[36]

Carter Lindberg has written that Luther's social ethics "is aptly described as 'the liturgy after the liturgy.'"[37] Luther did not see virtue as the goal of life in an Aristotelian or modern sense. Rather, salvation was for him "the presupposition of life."[38] Faith allows the believer, liberated from anxiety and self-interest, to turn her attention to the needs of her neighbor.[39] The divine distribution that begins in the sacrament spills over into the rest of life. For that reason, the poor are to be cared for. But all distribution on the pattern of the Lord's Supper must be devoid of spiritual pride and self-seeking. Therefore, the civil authorities should administer poor relief.

REFORMED SOCIAL TEACHING: PROVIDENCE AND PRECEPT
Max Weber's Long Shadow

Scholars often say that Calvinism has opposed state-administered poor relief because of its spirit of "individualism and voluntarism."[40] It is difficult, however, for those who take this position to explain why "most of the leading

---

[34] Martin Luther, "The Blessed Sacrament of the Holy and True Body of Christ, and the Brotherhoods," *LW* 35:52, 57.

[35] Wendte, "Mystical Foundations of Politics."

[36] Luther, "A Treatise on the New Testamen, that is, the Holy Mass," *LW* 35:96.

[37] Lindberg, "Luther's Struggle with Social-Ethical Issues," 166.

[38] Lindberg, "Luther's Struggle with Social-Ethical Issues," 166.

[39] Calhoun, *Tax Law, Religion, and Justice*, 172–73.

[40] Kahl, "Religious Doctrines and Poor Relief," 283.

figures in English poor law reforms were Puritans,"[41] why labor laws in the Calvinist Netherlands and Switzerland appeared relatively early,[42] and why Calvinist and Puritan countries, though late to adopt national social insurance systems, were the first to adopt national social assistance schemes.[43] Looking at the thought of Calvin and the later Dutch Calvinist Abraham Kuyper (1837—1920) shows that Calvinist social theology undeniably does stress the importance of work, but not because of a commitment to individualism.

Golgotha's Mystery: The Source of Solidarity

Kuyper was deeply concerned about the appropriate Christian response to poverty, the dangers of wealth, and relations among the social classes. He identified sin as the source of economic inequality, but he also thought of the dawning awareness of sin as the force that activates the process of *undoing* inequality. He wrote that the wellspring of human solidarity is the Lord's Supper, when "you feel for the poor man as for a member of the body and you feel for your hired servants and maids as for the children of men, human beings like yourself."[44] "Divine compassion," he added, "sympathy, suffering *with* us and *for* us—that was the mystery of Golgotha."[45]

Calvin had argued that the human predisposition to compassion for the poor precedes the divine commandment to relieve the needs of the poor,[46]

---

[41] Kahl, "Religious Doctrines and Poor Relief," 286.

[42] Kersbergen, "Religion and the Welfare State in the Netherlands," 120.

[43] Kahl, "Religious Doctrines and Poor Relief," 284. National social insurance systems are contributory common funds—like Medicaid, Medicare, and Social Security in the United States—that protect against future risks to individuals. National social assistance systems are government-financed cash or in-kind benefits.

[44] Abraham Kuyper, "The Social Question and the Christian Religion" (1891), in Abraham Kuyper, *On Business and Economics*, ed. Peter S. Heslam (Bellingham, WA: Lexham Press, 2021), 227.

[45] Kuyper, "The Social Question and the Christian Religion," 227.

[46] John Calvin, *Commentaries on the Four Last Books of Moses, Arranged in the Form of a Harmony* (Edinburgh: Calvin Translation Society, 1854), 3:127; John Calvin, *Mosis reliqui libri quatuor in formam harmoniae, digesti a Ioanne Calvino: cum eiusdem commentariis*, vol. 24, *Ioannis Calvini opera quae supersunt omnia* (hereafter *CO*), ed. Edouard Cunitz, Johann-Wilhelm Baum, and Eduard Wilhelm Eugen (Braunschweig: C. A. Schwetschke, 1882), 680.

and Kuyper agreed.[47] In Calvin's thinking, this primal instinct binds rich and poor together in social solidarity reminiscent of the symbiotic relationship that Luther rejected. Calvin retained a symbiosis, but without salvific effect.[48] The rich serve as God's agents, distributing goods, while the poor are God's representatives, gathering God's goods.[49] Solidarity is not an incidental consequence of social action; it turns out to be the goal of that action.[50]

Rebuking Dutch conservatives for their misuse of Jesus's words in Matthew 26:11—"You always have the poor with you"—Kuyper drew a sharp distinction between parts of Scripture that tell us "how things will always be" and those that say "how things must be." God's will and God's command are "utterly different," Calvin himself wrote, noting that "God requires of us only what he commands."[51] God permits economic inequality on the one hand but equips humans with the impulse to solve it and, in fact, commands them to do so.[52]

Kuyper would have preferred for the task facing Christians between the "already" and the "not yet" to fall to private initiative, especially the Church. In his extensive work on pension schemes, he described the provision of security for retired workers as an "abnormal task" of the state, necessary because of specific circumstances.[53] He based his position on the stance that Calvinism took on the issue of poor relief when it "reinstated the diaconate" to assume that function.[54]

Calvin's hope during his first stay in Geneva that the Church there would remain "relatively autonomous" was only intensified by his collaboration in Strasbourg with Martin Bucer, who was the first of the

---

[47] Kuyper, "Commentary on Lord's Day 42 of the Heidelberg Catechism," in *On Business and Economics*, 40.

[48] See André Biéler, *Calvin's Economic and Social Thought*, ed. Edward Dommen, trans. James Greig (Geneva: World Alliance of Reformed Churches, 2005), 285.

[49] Calvin, *Sermons sur l'Harmonie des Trois Evangelistes*, CO 46:551 (on Mt. 3:9f.). The translation is from Biéler, *Calvin's Economic and Social Thought*, 277.

[50] See Calhoun, *Tax Law, Religion, and Justice*, 208–10.

[51] John Calvin, *Institutes of the Christian Religion*, trans. Ford Lewis Battles, ed. John T. McNeill (Philadelphia: The Westminster Press, 1960), 1.17.5, 1.18.4.

[52] See Calhoun, *Tax Law, Religion, and Justice*, 216–18.

[53] Kuyper, "Draft Pension Scheme for Wage Earners," in *On Business and Economics*, 242.

[54] Kuyper, "Draft Pension Scheme for Wage Earners," 248.

Reformers to hold that there should be a church office for the care of the poor.[55] The *Ecclesiastical Ordinances* that Calvin drafted for Geneva after his return in 1541 distinguished four church offices—pastors, elders, doctors, and deacons—and treated poor relief as "spiritual work" by entrusting it to the deacons.[56]

Calvin disfavored government administration of poor relief, but a development is apparent throughout the course of his revisions to the *Institutes*. In the 1536 edition, civil government's appointed task had been "to form our social behavior to civil righteousness," but in the 1559 edition Calvin envisioned an overlap of functions.[57] The civil administration and the Church's government ruled some things "in common."[58] Among the things ruled in common by Geneva's Consistory was intervention on behalf of the poor.[59]

Making Society into a Community

Calvin's Geneva became "one of the first attempts to establish a welfare state in modern Europe without the need for begging;"[60] "Calvinist/Reformed Protestant countries introduced social assistance before Lutheran countries;"[61] and in 1909 Kuyper took credit on behalf of the ARP for being the first party to confront the social question comprehensively.[62]

---

[55] Matthew J. Tuininga, *Calvin's Political Theology and the Public Engagement of the Church: Christ's Two Kingdoms* (Cambridge: Cambridge University Press, 2017), 58–66. For a treatment of Bucer's ideas about welfare reform, see Bradford Littlejohn, "Against the Infinite Stimulus of Greed: Martin Bucer's Reformation of Welfare," in *A Protestant Christendom? The World the Reformation Made*, ed. Onsi A. Kamel (Landrum, SC: Davenant Press, 2021), 112–25.

[56] Tuininga, *Calvin's Political Theology*, 225, 227. See Calvin, *Institutes* 4.3.9.

[57] Calvin, *Institutes* 4.20.9 (1559).

[58] Tuininga, *Calvin's Political Theology*, 314, quoting Calvin, *Praelectionum in Ieremiam prophetam pars altera cap. VIII–XXXI, CO* 38:220 (on Jer. 19:1–3).

[59] Tuininga, *Calvin's Political Theology*, 70, 74.

[60] Tomlin, "The Reformation and the Future of Europe," in *The Protestant Reformation of the Church and the World*, ed. John Witte, Jr. and Amy Wheeler (Louisville: Westminster John Knox Press, 2018), 199. See Martin Bucer, *De Regno Christi*.

[61] Kahl, "Religious Doctrines and Poor Relief," 283. "Social assistance" is distinguished here from "social insurance."

[62] Kuyper, "The Social Question" (1909), in *On Business and Economics*, 293.

Kuyper felt obliged toward the end of his life to answer the accusation that his party had first placed all its hopes on "private initiative" but later switched "to state socialism."[63] He admitted that he had initially "expected more from private initiative than could be attained" but refuted the charge that he had fundamentally changed his mind.[64] Government assistance had always been in the foreground, he wrote, because only the government can put in place the "orderly conditions" in which a solution to the social question can emerge.[65] Forces more powerful and more insidious than the government had also "intervened" in social life. From his vantage point in 1917, the only chance that social life had for developing "freely" was for the government to place it "under the regulation and protection of the law."[66]

Labor and pensions were foremost among Kuyper's preoccupations within the broader social question, because as a Calvinist he considered wealth-creation an integral part of the divinely commanded dynamic needed to bind rich and poor together in social solidarity. Work was never an end in itself for Kuyper. He wrote: "Once you have put in your best efforts so as to have enough for yourself and your family, you are to go back to work and carry on in order to earn more—so that you can help those who are in need."[67]

Kuyper wrote a series of articles during his second term as a member of Parliament outlining a "comprehensive, mandatory pension plan." Pensions would be available for the elderly, widows, and orphans.[68] The "Draft Pension Scheme for Wage Earners" of 1895 articulates reasons for "government involvement in pensions."[69]

First, government legislation mandating pensions was necessary because "Reformed theology failed to work out the fundamental idea behind the diaconate." The diaconate was supposed to care for *all* of the poor members of society. Confining its aid to churchgoers, Kuyper wrote, violates the biblical teaching that "God makes his sun to rise on the evil and the good,

---

[63] Kuyper, "The Social Question" (1917), 328.
[64] Kuyper, "The Social Question" (1917), 328.
[65] Kuyper, "The Social Question" (1917), 329.
[66] Kuyper, "The Social Question" (1917), 345.
[67] Kuyper, "Commentary on Lord's Day 42 of the Heidelberg Catechism," 76.
[68] Jordan J. Ballor and Melvin Flikkema, "Text Introduction to 'Draft Pension Scheme for Wage Earners,'" in *On Business and Economics*, 233.
[69] Kuyper, "Draft Pension Scheme for Wage Earners," 245.

and sends rain on the just and the unjust."[70] State assistance, he concluded, has "a double advantage: when the funds dry up it can coerce contributions through taxation."[71]

Kuyper spoke for Protestant social theology generally when he suggested that voluntary philanthropy is often an occasion for sin. Human beings end up pleased, he said, with their own generosity. They also unintentionally humiliate the poor.[72] And, along with humiliation comes oppression. Freedom to live "unhindered" in "relationships that belong to your nature"[73] had disappeared after the French Revolution, destroyed by an "antisocial system of limitless competition."[74] Kuyper argued that private efforts to spring the mass of workers from the trap of capitalism had led to "socialism"—which had come to characterize the agenda of the trade unions. "Clearly, only the government can help," he concluded.[75]

Dismissing the "chameleonic concept of 'the common good,'" Kuyper insisted that "clever jurists" and theorists keep their hands off the pension scheme. The scheme "should arise from life itself."[76] As Kuyper's flexibility suggests, Reformed social teaching is not driven by a polarity between the individual and collective unit. It submits to the dictates of providence—however surprising and fluid they may be. Calvinism remains shy about reducing the sovereign action of God to natural principles. Kuyper represented Calvin faithfully by responding to the disjunction between the way things are on the one hand and God's commands on the other.

ANGLICAN SOCIAL TEACHING: A COVENANT WITH THE NATION
Two Difficulties

The task of teasing out a coherent Anglican social teaching (AST) is more difficult than the comparable Lutheran and Reformed tasks because pluralism within the Anglican tradition means that "no single, internally

---

[70] Kuyper, "Draft Pension Scheme for Wage Earners," 248.
[71] Kuyper, "Draft Pension Scheme for Wage Earners," 249–50.
[72] Kuyper, "Draft Pension Scheme for Wage Earners," 249.
[73] Kuyper, "Draft Pension Scheme for Wage Earners," 235.
[74] Kuyper, "Draft Pension Scheme for Wage Earners," 235.
[75] Kuyper, "Draft Pension Scheme for Wage Earners," 236.
[76] Kuyper, "Draft Pension Scheme for Wage Earners," 244.

coherent and sufficient" AST is available.⁷⁷ And, like all Christian traditions, Anglicanism has seen religion relegated to the private sphere. These difficulties are heightened for Anglicans. AST originating in the Church of England often sounds as if it still spoke with moral authority, but the present lack of common reference points and shared vocabulary makes it hard for people to hear what the church is trying to say.⁷⁸

Despite the resulting crisis in AST, the intellectual and spiritual resources of the various Anglican traditions provide building blocks for a renewed AST. The following subsection traces the rise, fall, rise, fall, and perhaps rise again of that large, diverse body of social teaching.

Development of the Church of England's Role in Government Welfare

From Richard Hooker to Rowan Williams, the Anglican tradition has been receptive to sources of authority supplemental to Scripture on the structure of a godly society.⁷⁹ The tradition of the English Reformers presents a picture, like that of Reformed social teaching, in which Church and state were independent yet interdependent. Hugh Latimer, in a 1549 sermon preached before King Edward VI, proclaimed, "The king correcteth transgressors with the temporal sword; yea, and the preacher also, if he be an offender. But the preacher cannot correct the king, if he be a transgressor of God's Word, with the temporal sword; but he must correct and reprove him with the spiritual sword."⁸⁰

Reformation-era poor relief in England was more secularized and centralized than in the Netherlands, if less so than in the Lutheran states. In 1572, English municipalities were required to establish "poor rates," with the

---

⁷⁷ Malcolm Brown, "The Case for Anglican Social Theology Today," in *Anglican Social Theology*, ed. Malcolm Brown (London: Church House Publishing, 2014), 26.

⁷⁸ Malcolm Brown, "Anglican Social Theology Tomorrow," in *Anglican Social Theology*, 185.

⁷⁹ See Will Adam, "Natural Law in the Anglican Tradition," in *Christianity and Natural Law: An Introduction*, ed. Norman Doe, in *Law and Christianity*, ed. John Witte, Jr. (Cambridge: Cambridge University Press, 2017).

⁸⁰ Hugh Latimer, "Seven Sermons Preached Before King Edward VI, 1549: Sermon the First," in *Sermons by Hugh Latimer* (Cambrdige: Cambridge University Press, 1844), 86.

result that poor relief was legislated at the national level but funded at the local level.[81]

William Temple (1881—1944), writing in 1941, noted that the Church of England had retreated after the Restoration from its Reformation-era claim to "moral control." But the established church is "bound to 'interfere,'" Temple said, "because it is by vocation the agent of God's purpose, outside the scope of which no human interest or activity can fall."[82] After John Wesley's (1703—1791) revival brought "the Church back into politics," the path from abolition of the slave trade to prison reform to the Factory Acts was one of increasing interest on the part of the Church in "the structure of society."[83]

The flowering of AST began in the middle of the nineteenth century when F. D. Maurice (1805—1872) and Charles Kingsley (1819—1875) launched the Christian Social Movement, "which subjected the whole order of society to criticism in the light of Christian beliefs about God and man."[84] With the emergence of the social movement came the Church of England's emphasis on "incarnational theology." Maurice believed "a united and just society" would only be possible if its members recognized "Christ as brother" and their resulting "interrelatedness as God's children."[85] Brooke Foss Westcott, Bishop of Durham from 1890 until his death in 1901, followed Duns Scotus in holding that the incarnation of the Son of God was not contingent on the fall of humankind, but was intended from the beginning of God's plan for creation "as the fullest expression of the Father's love and as the crowning glory of humanity."[86] Paul Avis (b. 1947) describes Henry Scott Holland, Regius Professor Divinity in the University of Oxford from 1910 to 1918, as a "quintessential representative of the incarnational, immanentist theology" of the late-nineteenth-century "Anglican liberal catholics," who considered "the Church, the ministry and the sacraments" to

---

[81] Kahl, "Religious Doctrines and Poor Relief," 278.

[82] William Temple, *Christianity and Social Order* (London: Shepheard-Walwyn, 1976), 38.

[83] Temple, *Christianity and Social Order*, 31.

[84] Temple, *Christianity and Social Order*, 31.

[85] Alison Milbank, "Maurice as a Resource for the Church Today," in *Theology Reforming Society*, ed. Stephen Spencer (London: SCM Press, 2017), 30.

[86] Paul Avis, "Anglican Social Thought Encounters Modernity: Brooke Foss Westcott, Henry Scott Holland and Charles Gore," in *Theology Reforming Society*, 56.

be "the key channels of grace because they were the continuous historical expressions of the Incarnation."[87]

From Maurice's articulation in 1849 and 1850 of the principle of "cooperation"—the organization of society around human fellowship implied in the gospel rather than around competition and private property[88]—to Westcott's successful mediation in a "bitter and protracted Durham coal strike"—achieved by "bringing the parties together in his palace and making it clear that they would not leave until they had agreed terms[89]—the incarnational, immanentist Anglican thinkers and activists were deeply focused on social issues. They were not, however, particularly political, and they were not "socialists" as that term later came to be understood. The "Christian Socialism" allegedly inaugurated in the mid-nineteenth century was merely a useful description for what Maurice, Kingsley, and others were already doing.[90] Maurice was relatively conservative in his political opinions.[91] Westcott avoided identifying as a socialist, despite his appreciation for its ethical ideal. He understood Christian Socialism "as a matter of inward disposition."[92] And Holland distinguished between economic and moral socialism, the latter a matter of the conscience and ultimately—in Paul Avis's words—"unthreatening."[93]

An emphasis on "mediating institutions" permeated the Anglican social tradition that began with Maurice. Resembling the doctrine of subsidiarity that flourished later in Catholic Social Teaching, the Anglican stress on mediating institutions between individual and nation also paralleled Kuyper's doctrine of "sphere sovereignty."[94] It was part of the genius of William Temple, wartime Archbishop of Canterbury, to articulate intermediate social *principles* as well.

---

[87] Avis, "Anglican Social Thought Encounters Modernity," 66.

[88] Jeremy Morris, "F. D. Maurice and the Myth of Christian Socialist Origins," in *Theology Reforming Society*, 6–7.

[89] Avis, "Anglican Social Thought Encounters Modernity," 52.

[90] Morris, "F. D. Maurice and the Myth of Christian Socialist Origins," 4, 16.

[91] Morris, "F. D. Maurice and the Myth of Christian Socialist Origins," 10.

[92] Avis, "Anglican Social Thought Encounters Modernity," 64, 77.

[93] Avis, "Anglican Social Thought Encounters Modernity," 69–70.

[94] William Temple gave a nod to "Dutch social philosophy," which he said had "more than any other laid stress upon the State as the Community of communities," in developing his own doctrine of subsidiarity. Temple, *Christianity and Social Order*, 72.

The "Temple Tradition"

Temple inherited "a strong sacramental ecclesial social collectivism" from the Maurice-Gore tradition, as well as an ontology from the natural law tradition "in which association is integral to human development."[95] At the same time, both the faith and expertise of individual Christians were essential to Temple's vision. The combination of these qualities produced a social theology "in which the church acts upon individuals who use their influence in civil life to enact political solutions."[96]

The early Temple believed that the incarnation made sense of the world "by making its meaning intelligible."[97] By 1939, however, he saw instead "a fearful tension between the doctrine of the love of God and the actual facts of daily experience."[98] Trying to honor both the Roman Catholic tradition that there is a natural order emanating from God and the continental Protestant tradition that we are delivered from "natural disorder,"[99] Temple nevertheless continued to lean more toward the Catholic emphasis.

At the same time, however, he adopted a chastened social theology "content with a less grandiose superstructure" than found in Catholic Social Teaching.[100] He considered "regulative" principles—e.g., freedom, fellowship, and service—of a high order, with little immediate application.[101]

The fame of the Temple tradition lies in its use of "middle axioms," which stand "between general principles and actual legislation":[102]

> 1. Every child should find itself a member of a family housed with decency and dignity....
>
> 2. Every child should have the opportunity of an education....

---

[95] Matthew Bullimore, "Public Theology or Ecclesial Theology," in *Theology Reforming Society*, 156.
[96] Bullimore, "Public Theology or Ecclesial Theology," 156.
[97] Alan M. Suggate, "The Temple Tradition," in *Anglican Social Theology*, 55.
[98] Suggate, "The Temple Tradition," 55.
[99] Suggate, "The Temple Tradition," 63.
[100] Ronald Preston, introduction to the 1976 edition of *Christianity and Social Order*.
[101] Temple, *Christianity and Social Order*, 78–80.
[102] Stephen Spencer, "William Temple and the 'Temple Tradition,'" in *Theology Reforming Society*, 100.

3. Every citizen should be secure in possession of such income as will enable him to maintain a home....

4. Every citizen should have a voice in the conduct of the business or industry which is carried on by means of his labour....

5. Every citizen should have sufficient daily leisure, with two days of rest in seven....

6. Every citizen should have assured liberty in the forms of freedom of worship, of speech, of assembly....[103]

These axioms flow from higher-order principles: the family as the primary social unit; the sanctity of personality; and the principle of fellowship.[104] Those three principles derive from even higher-order derivative principles—freedom, social fellowship, and service—which flow, at last, from God and God's purpose and the dignity, tragedy, and destiny of humankind.[105]

Temple outlined a method by which the Church can have an impact on society: (a) announce Christian principles; (b) point out where the existing social order conflicts with those principles; and (c) pass on to individual Christian citizens, "acting in their civic capacity," the task of reshaping the existing order to conform more closely to the principles.[106]

Armed with a bridge between theology and legislation, Temple was the ecclesiastical architect of post-war Britain's welfare state.[107] He used the term "welfare state," not as a description of conditions that a government can or should bring about, "but as a rationale for the state itself."[108]

Like Reformed social teaching, AST views society in relational, not economic, terms. Temple argued that, in the "region of causes and effects, economic science is autonomous," but that in the realm of natural law science must only be regarded as a means to human life. Even a system good at

---

[103] Temple, *Christianity and Social Order*, 96–97.

[104] Temple, *Christianity and Social Order*, 85–95.

[105] Temple, *Christianity and Social Order*, 58–77.

[106] Temple, *Christianity and Social Order*, 58.

[107] John Hughes, "After Temple? The Recent Renewal of Anglican Social Thought," in *Anglican Social Theology*, 97.

[108] Malcolm Brown, "Anglican Social Theology: Today and Tomorrow," in *Theology Reforming Society*, 137.

raising the general standard of living may still be condemned on moral grounds if "it is the source of wrong personal relationships."[109]

Unemployment was for Temple "the most hideous of our social ills"; it causes those without work to fall "out of the common life."[110] The familiar refrains of Protestant Social Teaching ring clear in *Christianity and Social Order*: social exclusion breeds "moral isolation"; pay is no remedy because "it is part of the principle of personality that we should live for one another."[111] Work is important above all other social conditions because without it a person's very humanity is sapped.[112] Help given in charity is "blood-money."[113]

But the ability to reach consensus decayed, and middle axioms became unworkable. It has fallen to Rowan Williams (b. 1950) and others to rebuild AST.

Rowan Williams: "Making Sense"

Williams, who was Archbishop of Canterbury from 2002 to 2012, argues that the welfare state in today's "radically pluralist" societies serves a purpose far from any arrangement Temple could have imagined. Society has responded to pluralism by withdrawing from judgment and seeking instead "a pragmatic minimum of peaceful coexistence between groups."[114] Using "economic adjustments" like "palliative welfare benefits," states avoid having to answer questions about their own legitimacy. But the "administrative state," paradoxically, takes measures to ensure its survival that end up causing "permanent large-scale unemployment," eroding public healthcare and education, and fostering the creation of an "underclass."[115]

Building on a wedge that the later Temple had introduced between (a) "making sense" of the world by showing that the world already makes sense and (b) "making sense" by transforming it from *nonsense* into *sense*, Williams

---

[109] Temple, *Christianity and Social Order*, 81–82.

[110] Temple, *Christianity and Social Order*, 33.

[111] Temple, *Christianity and Social Order*, 34–35.

[112] Temple, *Christianity and Social Order*, 33.

[113] Temple, *Christianity and Social Order*, 36.

[114] Rowan Williams, "The Judgement of the World," in *Christian Theology* (Oxford: Blackwell Publishers Ltd., 2000), 34–37.

[115] Williams, "The Judgement of the World," 34.

argues that human "belonging" in the world is not self-explanatory.[116] In the same vein, the Anglican ethicist Oliver O'Donovan (b. 1945) argues that the existence of a universal moral order is an ontological claim, not necessarily an epistemological one. Alan Suggate writes: "Neither [what is good for nature nor what is good for humanity] is simply given to us in nature or in our genes; it has to be worked at as a responsible task."[117]

Neglect of that task, as Temple anticipated and Williams bemoaned, leads to parallel worlds: the real economic world and virtual economic worlds. The real economic world would ask us to invest in the "demanding process of producing goods that contribute to human well-being." But, instead, we pursue "a market consumer society, giving free rein to our desires by aiming for maximal choice and minimal risk."[118] The task of the Church, for Williams, is a eucharistic "unveiling." "The material world remains itself," Suggate writes, but "becomes sacramental." The Church's sacraments themselves are "first-fruits" of the process of giving material things meaning by communicating divine generosity through them.[119]

At the same time, however, Williams himself cautions that the Church must preserve some of the discontinuity between Heaven and earth. He writes that, although incarnational theology proved a powerful resource for Anglicans, it can too easily slip into "ideology" by uniting what needs to be kept apart to some degree.[120]

IDENTIFYING A PROTESTANT SOCIAL TEACHING OF WELFARE AND GOVERNMENT ASSISTANCE

Distinctive Protestant Features

Although no such thing as a single formal body of Protestant Social Teaching (PST) can be placed alongside Catholic Social Teaching (CST), a sufficient number of recurring themes run through the various expressions of

---

[116] William Temple, "What Christians Stand for in the Secular World," in *T&T Clark Reader in Political Theology*, ed. Elizabeth Phillips, Anna Rowlands, and Amy Daughton (London: T&T Clark, 2021), 231.

[117] See Suggate, "The Temple Tradition," 69.

[118] Suggate, "The Temple Tradition," 69–70.

[119] Suggate, "The Temple Tradition," 72.

[120] Rowan Williams, "Beginnning with the Incarnation," in *On Christian Theology*, 85.

Protestant ideas of government welfare to make possible the identification of common denominators.

PST, first, betrays nervousness about individual charity and defers to the *state* as the provider of assistance and to the government-assistance policies of individual nation-states. Lutheran, Reformed, and Catholic social teaching are all in some sense culturally relative. The church in Norway did not speak for the Lutherans of Germany, nor did Kuyper opine on Switzerland's social policies or Temple on those of the United States. This relativism precludes PST from articulating meta-principles as readily as CST does. Temple's primary considerations came the closest to doing so, but he acknowledged the indeterminacy of foundational "pillars."

With its stronger statist and nationalist emphases, PST stresses the expertise of civil authorities. This tendency has been particularly clear in Lutheranism, but it is evident as well in Kuyper's habit of lecturing Dutch economic liberals from his position as a theologian and, as a politician, rebuking conservatives for their economic naivete. This feature also surfaces in the Anglican tradition of placing state and Church face-to-face as separate equals with (limited) jurisdiction over each other.

By deferring to the state and its laws, PST risks conflating the moral order of the universe with a given system of positive law. But, as Bradley Lewis points out, CST often suffers the same fate by confusing the two meanings of "common good," i.e., "the end or final cause of political association" and "the whole order of the universe and its ultimate end in God."[121]

An eschatological reserve that nevertheless generates an active response characterizes PST. Social teaching in the Protestant traditions does not offer as strong a teleological emphasis as CST does. PST has shown itself quicker than its Catholic counterpart to regard poverty and inequality as needs to be addressed; but, perhaps paradoxically, PST is reluctant to hope for a resolution of those needs in this life. The combination of deference to individual nations (with all of their inadequacies) and their laws, an unglamorous view of poverty, and a willingness to accept half-measures allows PST to work within the confines of social structures and policies rather

---

[121] V. Bradley Lewis, "Catholic Social Teaching on the Common Good," in *Catholic Social Teaching: A Volume of Scholarly Essays*, ed. Gerard V. Bradley and E. Christian Brugger (Cambridge: Cambridge University Press, 2019), 235.

than stepping outside of them to evaluate them from a panoptic viewpoint. This feature is both a strength and a weakness.

Building on the Distinctives

The historical distinctives of PST suggest directions in which a more integrated Protestant social theology of government welfare can be constructed.

First, lacking the "theological foundationalism" of CST, a coherent PST can offer guidance at a relatively detailed level.[122] Without a set endpoint, as in the universal destination of goods, PST stands more open to the unpredictable and potentially disruptive intrusion of the gospel into human systems.

The quasi-sacramental currents in PST arise from the political nature of the eucharist rather than from the sacramental nature of material deprivation. A constructive PST will articulate a chastened version of "the preferential option of the poor" that understands poverty as first and foremost a problem to be addressed rather than as a means for the wealthy to save themselves by charitable giving.

PST will also attend at least as much to inequality between rich and poor as it does to absolute poverty. It will seek to redraw the contours of its society to resemble in some small but unmistakable way the radical equality among people proclaimed in the gospel of Christ.

In the final analysis, however, PST is likely to be more reluctant than CST to apply Christian "principles" to politics and economics. One of the more extreme examples of this reticence is found in Karl Barth's thinking:

> Barth is allergic to the idea of application, the idea that God's work must somehow be applied in order for it to be rendered concrete. For Barth, God's action possesses a concreteness in itself; it need not be further concretized via principles, for it *is* concrete and possesses its own inner clarity and perspicuity.[123]

---

[122] Anna Rowlands, "Fraternal Traditions: Anglican Social Theology and Catholic Social Teaching in a British Context," in *Anglican Social Theology*, 142.

[123] Christopher R. J. Holmes, "Karl Barth on the Economy: In Dialogue with Kathryn Tanner," in *Commanding Grace: Studies in Karl Barth's Ethics*, ed. Daniel L. Migliore (Grand Rapids: Eerdmans, 2010), 203 (italics in original).

While perhaps not as allergic to the application of principles as Barth's theology was, most Protestant visions of government welfare, social services, and taxation will tend to be more *ad hoc* than their Catholic counterparts. PST in general is often criticized for offering a less coherent body of social teaching than CST. The criticism may be misdirected. PST may simply be imbued with a sharper sense of the persistent mismatch between Heaven and earth.

XII.

Environmental Care

JAKE MEADOR

> Woe, woe, woe! Woe for my brothers and sisters! Woe for the holy trees! The woods are laid waste. The axe is loosed against us. We are being felled. Great trees are falling, falling, falling. Justice, Lord King! Come to our aid. Protect your people. They are felling us in Lantern Waste. Forty great trunks of my brothers and sisters are already on the ground.
>
> —*C. S. Lewis*[1]

IN SETTING out a Magisterial Protestant approach to issues of environmental care, we face a problem. This problem is somewhat unique relative to the other subjects of this volume. Problems of taxation, for example, were known to both biblical authors and the primary magisterial sources. So too just war, poverty, the duties of the magistrate, and so on.

On issues of environmental care, however, a unique problem seems to assert itself. The primary impetus for our renewed attentiveness to ecology is the changes brought about by industrial technology and its descendants, all of which have had the unhappy effect of distancing us from the land and

---

[1] C. S. Lewis, *The Last Battle* (New York: Collier Books, 1956), 16–17.

from other creatures, and doing severe violence to the world itself. These technologies would have been unfathomable not only to the biblical authors, nearly all of whom lived in agrarian settings, but also to the urbanites that sit near the headwaters of the magisterial tradition.

In many cases, this has led Christians (and non-Christians, for that matter) to despair of finding help on these questions from older theological sources and even from Scripture itself. This is, however, an unnecessary and wrongheaded move. It begins with a simple and not uncommon mistake: it asks the wrong question. The question we should be asking is not, "Can the Bible and the magisterial tradition help us address contemporary environmental questions?" To pose the problem in this way puts the cart before the horse.

Rather, we can ask broader and better questions of the older sources. First, how should we imagine humanity's relationship to land and animals? Second, how should human beings understand their relationship to their tools? These are questions that the Reformers can help us to answer, for they are perennial questions concerning human life in God's world. In answering these questions, we will also begin to develop a Magisterial Protestant approach to environmental care.

THE BIBLICAL RECORD

To begin our account of a Reformed ecology, we must start with Scripture and, in particular, with the creation account. The first thing we must note is that while God makes man in his image, he also makes him as a contingent being, which sets him quite apart from God. The structure of the creation week, crowned as it is by God resting as the King delighting over his realm on the Sabbath day, suggests that mankind's vocation in the world is to be a steward. The earth belongs to God, the Psalmist tells us (Ps. 24:1). But he gives it to mankind in what you might call a conditional sense. The earth supports our living in it and we steward, protect, and elevate the earth through attentive care and submission to God's law. So, the understanding of the creation account, and of the Old Testament more generally, is that mankind does not "own" the earth or rule over it in an absolute sense. Rather, man stewards the world under the lordship of God. Lingering behind this is also a danger: what is entrusted to man can be taken away as well.

Indeed, the pattern set out in the creation account is echoed elsewhere in Scripture. In Deuteronomy we see God giving to his people a land intended for their sustenance and care. But still the land does not belong to *them*, but to *God*. And in Deuteronomy the danger that is implicit in the creation week is made explicit: what God gives, God can take away. Old Testament scholar Sandra Richter makes the point well, writing that,

> Throughout the book of Deuteronomy, Israel is reminded that the land of Canaan is a gift. It is the land which Yahweh "swore to Abraham, Isaac, and Jacob, to them and to their descendants after them" (Deut 1:8). In the language of ancient international diplomacy, the land of Canaan is a land grant. And, of course, land grants could be recalled. Thus, although the offspring of Abraham are invited to abide on the land with joy and productivity, the book of Deuteronomy is eminently clear that the land will never be truly theirs. Rather, as the curse sections of Deut. 28 and the transitional materials of chaps. 29–34 detail, Yahweh retains the right to reclaim his land; to uproot his people "from their land in anger and fury and in great wrath, and to cast them into another land as it is this day" (Deut 29:28). As it was in the garden, so it is in the land of Israel: God owns the land, and it is humanity's privilege to live on it. Thus, both the land and its produce and even its animal inhabitants do not actually belong to Israel but to their suzerain lord, Yahweh.[2]

A second and related point follows from this first point about mankind's contingency. One of the chief temptations humanity will always feel is a desire to get out from under the authority of God, falsely experiencing his benevolent care as a kind of overbearing tyranny. We will seek to become like God, to become self-sustaining, no longer needing his care to live well in the world. Rather than stewardship, we desire autonomy.

As we consider the biblical account, note the specific temptation presented to Eve in Genesis 3 by the Serpent. He tempts her by suggesting that this desire is actually obtainable; she *could* be like God. Specifically, he tempts her with a form of knowledge that is not Eve's naturally but is reserved for God. He tempts her by suggesting to her that her created existence given to her by God is lacking something, that there is an absence she experiences that is not natural to her state, but is rather unjust and oppressive. And so Eve takes and eats and gives to Adam and he does the

---

[2] Sandra Richter, "Environmental Law in Deuteronomy," *Bulletin for Biblical Research* 20, no. 3 (2010): 358.

same. And so the world falls into shadow because humanity sought to be like God.

This story continues in Genesis 11, where we see humanity once again seeking to reach unto the heavens and become gods. It is not a coincidence that a poem about the Tower of Babel narrative supplied the title for C. S. Lewis's novel *That Hideous Strength*. For Lewis, the hideous strength is humanity's attempt to become like god through their own means. At the Swiss L'Abri Francis and Edith Schaeffer (1912—1984, 1914—2013) used to have a small Bible verse posted in one of the rooms, coming from the prophet Isaiah. It reads, "Behold, all ye that kindle a fire, that compass yourselves about with sparks: walk in the light of your fire, and in the sparks that ye have kindled. This shall ye have of mine hand; ye shall lie down in sorrow" (Isa. 50:11 KJV). The Tower of Babel is a story of mankind walking by the light of his own sparks. God, in his mercy, would not allow him to do so for long. Instead, God came down and confused mankind's languages, thwarting our futile attempt to become like him.

From these texts, we observe that one of the foremost temptations that people face is a desire to transcend our own bodies, our own earth, and to lay hold of something like divinity for ourselves, to make ourselves gods.

As we continue in the Old Testament, we see that this human lusting to be like God does great damage not only to ourselves, but also to the natural world. In his book *Far as the Curse is Found*, Michael Williams argues that there is an environmental element to the flood narrative of Genesis 6–9. The flood is a kind of purging of nature's assailants that, amongst other things, has the effect of preserving the natural world from the rapaciousness of human beings.

> God must protect the creation from the creature called to be his image bearer, his moral reflection within the creation. Though the creature, who was called to rule on God's behalf, employs his giftedness for that commission against God and God's cause, God steps in and declares that he will preserve the created order in spite of man.[3]

Later in the prophets, Isaiah 24:4-5 (ESV) says,

---

[3] Michael Williams, *Far as the Curse is Found* (Phillipsburg, NJ: P&R Publishing, 2005), 91.

> The earth mourns and withers; the world languishes and withers; the highest people of the earth languish. The earth lies defiled under its inhabitants; for they have transgressed the laws, violated the statutes, broken the everlasting covenant.

Then in Jeremiah 2:7, the prophet recounts God's faithfulness to Israel and how Israel responded:

> I brought you into a plentiful land to enjoy its fruits and its good things. But when you came in, you defiled my land and made my heritage an abomination.

The story throughout the Old Testament is that God gives the gift of land to humanity with the intention that the land would nourish and sustain them and they, in turn, would care for and protect the land. But when God's people fail in that calling, God can and will take the land away. The loss of land is a common form of divine judgment throughout the Old Testament.

This basic story continues in the New Testament, as Paul reminds his readers in Romans 8 that the creation groans due to the weight of humanity's sin. From all this we might observe that human sin often manifests itself in ecological decay.

God gave the world to humanity to steward and tend, so when humanity fails in that calling, the world suffers. There is a kind of feedback loop between human sin and environmental decline. We might also note, in passing, that this truly *is* a loop. At its worst, environmental decline often means things like famine, and famine creates conditions in which it is far more difficult to be good for the simple reason that one becomes narrowly focused on survival. Under such conditions, one becomes willing to do any number of horrifying things simply to stay alive. So what we are describing is really a vicious cycle initiated by humanity's rebellion, set loose on the world, and which now compounds itself across time as mankind sinks deeper into sin and the earth's sufferings multiply as a result.

Finally, we might consider the end of creation as described later in the New Testament. Though often misread as a text describing the future obliteration of the earth, 2 Peter 3 is better read as describing a kind of recapitulation of the flood at the end of all things, when the world is purified, the dross being purged away and the good left behind. This reading of Peter's text is supported by the account offered at the end of Revelation when the author describes a "new" heavens descending to the earth. The Greek word translated "new" in English generally means "renewed or restored," rather than "newly made." The word used in Revelation 21 is in fact the same word used by Paul in 2 Corinthians 5 to describe the "new" creation that each of us becomes when born again. But the newness Paul has in view there is not that we become new human beings that did not previously exist, but rather a renewal and restoration of already existing people to their intended end. Thus the biblical picture of last things suggests to us not the destruction of this world, as some suggest, but rather the renewal of the world in a way that mirrors the renewal of human persons, both of which are accomplished through a work of divine grace.

This, then, is the biblical story of the physical creation: human beings, as contingent creatures, must live in the world, must derive their life from the world. But due to sin, it is now hard for us to do that and, indeed, in trying to sustain our life in the world, we often do great harm to the world. In the worst situations, people willfully and indiscriminately destroy God's creation, and so creation groans, longing for Christ's return when it will be purged of its pains and restored.

How can the Reformed tradition help us to read and understand this teaching? Two particular avenues come immediately to mind.

SIMPLE PIETY

One of the core concerns of the Reformation from its earliest days was a restoration of the simple piety of the Gospels over and against the arcane complexities too common in the late medieval church. In this way, Reformers like Martin Bucer (1491—1551) and his friends in the Strasbourg Reformation were the true heirs of Erasmus, the great medieval humanist and moralist.

In our current moment, one of the chief challenges of environmental care has to do with the lack of agency many people feel as they confront these questions. While it is true, in one sense, that the problems before us are too large to be solved by individual action alone but will require broad, state-level action, it is also true that the consensus that births such action arises from individuals desiring some good together. How do you help individuals come to desire such things together, particularly when real action to curb our current environmental decay will be costly and require changes in how we live?

People learn to desire the good of the earth and to accept required sacrifice when they rediscover the joys that come from a real sense of agency as it relates to their life in the world and the care of their given places in it. Thus, there is not a competition between the broad level responses our crisis demands of us and the smaller lines of work that individual people might adopt as a means of caring for the world. The two rise and fall together. Given that, a recovery of ordinary piety as it relates to the land can be a great good. Were we to return to a simple desire to care for what is ours with intelligence and affection, we would have a healthier planet. And if you care about plain, homespun virtue and simple Christian faithfulness, the magisterial tradition has much to offer.

Consider these words from Martin Bucer, written while he was still a relatively young man at the beginning of his career in *Instructions in Christian Love*, which was published in 1523. Note how care for the physical creation is present at the very beginning of the Reformation, at a time when Calvin was still a Parisian teenager:

> With the loss of the knowledge of God we have lost also the knowledge of creatures. As we no longer wish to live to serve God, his creatures were rightly taken away from our service. If we ignore the creator, it is fair that we are deprived also of the created. We have followed Satan and despised God. Hence our whole mind has been perverted to the point that it can no longer be useful to anyone, but rather has become so universally harmful that we have deserved for ourselves eternal condemnation. Thus the whole creation, which should have been used only to the praise and glory of its creator and for the preservation and profit of men, has been disgraced, profaned, and depraved by our diabolic misuse and self-seeking.[4]

In saying this, Bucer is simply making the same point Richter made above. Mankind's "ownership" of the world is not absolute, but conditional. And when we choose to treat the world with carelessness and cruelty, God intervenes and withdraws it from us. Bucer goes so far as to suggest that there is something Satanic about environmental destruction: "dark, satanic mills" indeed. Bucer would have us recognize that a suffering planet is a form of divine judgment against men who have misused and mistreated God's world.

This is not an idle question for Bucer, either. Given where he was born, it is probable that his father's line of work was building the barrels that the famous wine of the Selestat region would be stored in before being sold.

---

[4] Martin Bucer, *Instructions in Christian Love* (Eugene: OR, Wipf & Stock), 27.

Simply to live, Bucer's family depended upon a certain degree of attentiveness not only to the growing of trees and working with wood, but also the care and maintaining of grape vines and the production of wine. Without an attentiveness to the natural world and a sustainable relationship to it, Bucer's life would have been impossible.

Note also the practical way Bucer approaches the question, a signature of his which marks him as Erasmus's true heir. He is not particularly interested in complex ritual as it relates to the Christian life. He's interested in ordinary Christian love offered in response to God's grace and in service to one's neighbor. At times, this leads to an almost utilitarian note in his thinking that might be off-putting to some contemporary environmentalists who object to the idea of "using" the earth. But Bucer does not mean it in an exploitative way. He means something closer to Wendell Berry's candid, if theologically overstated, observation in "The Gift of Good Land," that,

> To live, we must daily break the body and shed the blood of Creation. When we do this knowingly, lovingly, skillfully, reverently, it is a sacrament. When we do it ignorantly, greedily, clumsily, destructively, it is a desecration. In such desecration we condemn ourselves to spiritual and moral loneliness, and others to want.[5]

We all must "use" the creation, then. But we must use it with knowledge, love, skill, and reverence. This is something any of us can do. You do not need to be on a governance committee working on environmental legislation to do this. You do not need to work for an NGO to do this. You do not need to own a large company or extensive tracts of land to do this. You simply must care enough to learn and to try and to fail and to improve.

To take one example, learning to eat seasonally according to the rhythms of your home place will often mean purchasing locally grown food, which usually means buying from the sorts of small, local farmers whose operations are more conducive to the health of the soil than are the large monoculture farms that dominate American agribusiness. Barbara Kingsolver's book *Animal, Vegetable, Miracle* is a remarkable and compelling portrait of the delight and agency one discovers when simply choosing to live according to the natural limits of the land which governed mankind's relationship to the earth for nearly all of human history.

---

[5] Wendell Berry, *The Gift of Good Land* (Berkeley: Counterpoint Press, 1981), 281.

Likewise, there is a certain joy to be had in learning to root oneself more literally to a small place by simply reducing the amount of travel one does via private automobile. Though this is easier to do in some phases of life than in others (as a family of six with young children, my wife and I find this much more difficult to do than I did while a single twenty-something, fresh out of college), there are always ways of trying to adopt a geographically smaller life, thereby reducing our dependence on fossil fuels and the fickleness of global markets. Become a regular at your neighborhood coffee shop or grocery store if you are fortunate enough to have one. Learn to use the trails in your city; give yourself enough time to get somewhere such that you can walk there rather than drive. Walking is one of the best ways to get to know a place, to understand what holds it together, what it values, and so on. Thinking Christianly, we might say that walking is one of the best ways of learning how to love one's neighbor by learning about the places that one shares with one's neighbor. This is all to say nothing of the many other obvious ways we can learn to use the earth skillfully for the love of neighbor as Bucer exhorts us to. Gardening, planting trees, buying a community supported agriculture (CSA) share or a subscription to a local farm, and simply cultivating a greater knowledge of plants and local wildlife are all wonderful ways of learning to be emplaced, as we might call it, and, in that process, learning how to skillfully use the earth.

To be clear, my point here is not that this particular line of thought is uniquely available to Reformed Christians and not to others. Rome, the Radicals, and Orthodoxy can all offer means of accentuating the goodness of ordinary, quiet piety and relating that to the land. My point so far is merely that one needn't *leave* the Reformed faith to find this value.

The second consideration, however, is a bit different. It has become something of a truism in contemporary theological debate to link Protestantism to a host of evils that all tend toward a deadening of the imagination and a solidifying of reality. If the world no longer strikes us as beautiful or enchanted, many argue, you can blame it on Protestantism. But actually this gets the matter almost entirely backwards. If we wish to preserve a high view of the natural world, if we even wish to see it as being in some sense "sacramental" (a tricky word to use, given the importance of keeping this sense of "sacramentality" distinct from the actual sacraments of baptism and the eucharist), then it is actually the magisterial tradition that can lead us to such a vision.

To make the case, we'll start with debunking the common slur against Protestants before attempting a deeper plumbing of the Protestant imagination. The argument made for the "disenchanting" effects of Protestantism, when it is made at all, usually turns on eucharistic theology and, specifically, the possibility that Christ is truly present in the elements. The argument goes that because the Reformers rejected the real presence, they were implicitly rejecting the idea that the physical can also be something more than mere matter. In losing the real presence, they lost enchantment altogether.

Here's what is striking about that argument: taken on their own terms as stated at the time of the Reformation, it is actually the *Roman* doctrine that obliterates nature, arguing that via transubstantiation the bread and wine are obliterated and become the body and blood of Christ. This is how the Council of Trent describes it:

> If any one saith, that, in the sacred and holy sacrament of the Eucharist, the substance of the bread and wine remains conjointly with the body and blood of our Lord Jesus Christ, and denieth that wonderful and singular conversion of the whole substance of the bread into the Body, and of the whole substance of the wine into the Blood... let him be anathema.[6]

Put briefly: grace obliterates nature.

In contrast, the Reformers held that the elements remained truly bread and wine and, *nonetheless*, Christ himself was present in them in his divinity, dining with his people, giving them food for their spiritual journey, and even offering a foreshadowing of the feast at the end of all things described in John's Revelation.

It is actually magisterial sacramentology that offers the best grounding for a beautiful, ontologically dense creation, for it is the magisterial account of the eucharist that offers by far the best account of how bread and wine can *actually be* bread and wine while also being more than *just* bread and wine. The Roman tradition does not offer this, nor does the Radical tradition, which genuinely *does* hollow out the elements in the way some Catholic critics claim the magisterial tradition does.

---

[6] Council of Trent, Thirteenth Session, Canon II, accessed July 8, 2022, http://www.traditionalcatholic.net/Tradition/Council/Trent/Thirteenth_Session,_Canons.html

But this thick Protestant imagination of nature is not constrained to questions of sacramental life. It is rooted in Eucharistic theology, to be sure, but the implications of it are pervasive. Consider how John Calvin, often wrongly portrayed as a dour-faced crank, speaks of the natural world in his extensive writings:

> In every part of the world in heaven and on earth he has written and engraved the glory of his power, goodness, wisdom, and eternity. Truly as St. Paul said the Lord never left himself without a witness, even to those to whom he has sent no knowledge of his word. For all creatures, even from the firmament to the center of the earth, could be witnesses and messengers of his glory to all people. For the little singing birds sang of God; the animals acclaimed him; the elements feared and the mountains resounded with him; the rivers and springs threw glances toward him; the flowers and the grasses smiled. So that in truth there was no need to seek him afar, seeing that everyone could find God within himself, inasmuch as we are all sustained and preserved by his virtue abiding in us.[7]

What Calvin's thought suggests for us is that not only do we owe a certain sort of debt to the earth to care for and nurture it as the conditions of our existence as the stewards of God's rule, but also that the earth itself speaks to us of God. Thus to do violence to the earth is to deprive ourselves of one of the ordinary means by which God is able to speak to us. The little singing birds cannot sing of God to us if we destroy their habitats. The rivers and springs will not throw glances toward him if they are dried out. The flowers will not smile if they are not planted and watered.

Christians are, first and foremost, people who say *Credo*: "I believe." We believe in God the Father, Almighty, Maker of Heaven and Earth. To make this declaration is not simply to say that we believe that God exists as we might say we believe that, say, Bigfoot exists. It is, rather, to say that we *trust* this God, that we believe that he is good and that he is good *for us*. And we know this because he speaks to us and we hear his voice, as sheep hear and respond to the voice of the shepherd. (Incidentally, many of the common images Scripture gives us for understanding God are rendered functionally meaningless in an entirely urbanized, "developed," industrialized world that

---

[7] François Wendel, *Calvin: The Origins and Development of His Religious Thought*, trans. Philip Mairet (New York: Harper & Row, 1963), 161.

has obliterated nature.) If Christians are people who trust God because they hear his voice, then we should desire to hear his voice in all the places it can be found. It rings to us most clearly in Scripture, of course, and Scripture is the authoritative revelatory norm that norms all other sources of revelation. But in saying this we are saying that there are *other* forms of revelation. And if we are children of the magisterial tradition, then we should say with Calvin that those sources include singing birds and animals and mountains and rivers and flowers. And we should desire to hear their voice. Yet if our nation and many of the world's other nations do not change their course, that voice will continue to be muted and in many places will be lost altogether.

Environmental apocalypse is one of the signs C. S. Lewis uses in his fiction to denote a coming apocalypse. He uses it in *That Hideous Strength* where one of the first signs of the N.I.C.E.'s relentless evil is the tearing down of Bragdon Wood. He also uses it in *The Last Battle* where Shift the Ape announces his villainy to us by, amongst other things, demanding an international diet and imported foods, refusing to live off the food his own land freely offers him. And as the evil continues, the beloved trees of Lantern Waste are felled. The scene describing that tragedy provides the epigraph for this chapter. If we are people who care about justice, who care about neighbor, then we must care about our brothers and sisters in the creation. If we allow their voice to become even more alien to us, it may be the case that God's voice will also soon land strangely on our ear, if it lands at all.

MORE FROM DAVENANT PRESS

RICHARD HOOKER MODERNIZATION PROJECT
Radicalism: When Reform Becomes Revolution
Divine Law and Human Nature
The Word of God and the Words of Man
In Defense of Reformed Catholic Worship
A Learned Discourse on Justification

INTRODUCTION TO PROTESTANT THEOLOGY
Reformation Theology: A Reader of Primary Sources with Introductions
Grace Worth Fighting For: Recapturing the Vision of God's Grace in the Canons of Dordt

VERMIGLI'S *COMMON PLACES*
On Original Sin (Vol. 1)
On Free Will and the Law (Vol. 2)

LIBRARY OF EARLY ENGLISH PROTESTANTISM
The Laws of Ecclesiastical Polity: In Modern English, Vol. 1 (Preface–Book IV)
James Ussher and a Reformed Episcopal Church: Sermons and Treatises on Ecclesiology
The Apology of the Church of England
Jurisdiction Regal, Episcopal, Papal

DAVENANT GUIDES
Jesus and Pacifism: An Exegetical and Historical Investigation
The Two Kingdoms: A Guide for the Perplexed
Natural Law: A Brief Introduction and Biblical Defense
Natural Theology: A Biblical and Historical Introduction and Defense

DAVENANT RETRIEVALS
A Protestant Christendom? The World the Reformation Made
People of the Promise: A Mere Protestant Ecclesiology
Philosophy and the Christian: The Quest for Wisdom in the Light of Christ
The Lord is One: Reclaiming Divine Simplicity
A Protestant Christendom? The World the Reformation Made

CONVIVIUM PROCEEDINGS
For the Healing of the Nations: Essays on Creation, Redemption, and Neo-Calvinism
For Law and for Liberty: Essays on the Legacy of Protestant Political Thought
Beyond Calvin: Essays on the Diversity of the Reformed Tradition
God of Our Fathers: Classical Theism for the Contemporary Church
Reforming the Catholic Tradition: The Whole Word for the Whole Church
Reforming Classical Education: Toward A New Paradigm

DAVENANT ENGAGEMENTS
Enduring Divine Absence: The Challenge of Modern Atheism

OTHER PUBLICATIONS
Without Excuse: Scripture, Reason, and Presuppositional Apologetics
Being A Pastor: Pastoral Treatises of John Wycliffe
Serious Comedy: The Philosophical and Theological Significance of Tragic and Comic Writing in the Western Tradition
Ad Fontes: A Journal of Protestant Letters

ABOUT THE DAVENANT INSTITUTE

The Davenant Institute supports the renewal of Christian wisdom for the contemporary church. It seeks to sponsor historical scholarship at the intersection of the church and academy, build networks of friendship and collaboration within the Reformed and evangelical world, and equip the saints with time-tested resources for faithful public witness.

We are a nonprofit organization supported by your tax-deductible gifts. Learn more about us, and donate, at www.davenantinstitute.org.

Printed in Great Britain
by Amazon